Capitalism and Individualism in America

This book provides a concise and accessible history of the relationship between the individual and capitalism in the United States.

The text is devoted to tracking the historical development of important themes, while addressing key episodes in the progress of American capitalism within these, such as the Great Depression and New Deal. The book will introduce students to the key philosophical principles that have been the most influential in the history of free enterprise in the United States as well as exploring the ways in which these ideas have been popularly understood by Americans from the late eighteenth century to the present. Liberalism and Neoliberalism, entrepreneurialism, slavery and racial capitalism, and business and gender are all assessed.

The material in this volume is complemented by a set of primary source documents that bring the subject to life. It will be of interest to students of American history, business, and labor history.

Gavin Benke is Senior Lecturer in the CAS Writing Program at Boston University. He is also the author of *Risk and Ruin: Enron and the Culture of American Capitalism*.

Introduction to the Series

Series Editors
Clive Emsley and Gordon Martel

History is the narrative constructed by historians from traces left by the past. Historical enquiry is often driven by contemporary issues and, in consequence, historical narratives are constantly reconsidered, reconstructed and reshaped. The fact that different historians have different perspectives on issues means that there is often controversy and no universally agreed version of past events. *Seminar Studies* was designed to bridge the gap between current research and debate, and the broad, popular general surveys that often date rapidly.

The volumes in the series are written by historians who are not only familiar with the latest research and current debates concerning their topic, but who have themselves contributed to our understanding of the subject. The books are intended to provide the reader with a clear introduction to a major topic in history. They provide both a narrative of events and a critical analysis of contemporary interpretations. They include the kinds of tools generally omitted from specialist monographs: a chronology of events, a glossary of terms and brief biographies of 'who's who'. They also include bibliographical essays in order to guide students to the literature on various aspects of the subject. Students and teachers alike will find that the selection of documents will stimulate the discussion and offer insight into the raw materials used by historians in their attempt to understand the past.

Capitalism and Individualism in America

Gavin Benke

Routledge
Taylor & Francis Group
LONDON AND NEW YORK

Cover image: © North Wind Picture Archives /
Alamy Stock Photo

First published 2023
by Routledge
4 Park Square, Milton Park, Abingdon, Oxon OX14 4RN

and by Routledge
605 Third Avenue, New York, NY 10158

Routledge is an imprint of the Taylor & Francis Group, an informa business

British Library Cataloguing-in-Publication Data
A catalogue record for this book is available from the British Library

Library of Congress Cataloging-in-Publication Data
Names: Benke, Gavin, author.
Title: Capitalism and individualism in America / Gavin Benke.
Description: Milton Park, Abingdon, Oxon ; New York, NY : Routledge, 2023. | Includes bibliographical references and index.
Identifiers: LCCN 2022030520 (print) | LCCN 2022030521 (ebook) | ISBN 9780367547622 (hardback) | ISBN 9780367547608 (paperback) | ISBN 9781003090526 (ebook)
Subjects: LCSH: United States—Economic conditions. | Capitalism—United States. | Individualism—United States.
Classification: LCC HC110.C3 B45 2023 (print) | LCC HC110.C3 (ebook) | DDC 338.0973—dc23/eng/20220713
LC record available at https://lccn.loc.gov/2022030520
LC ebook record available at https://lccn.loc.gov/2022030521

ISBN: 978-0-367-54762-2 (hbk)
ISBN: 978-0-367-54760-8 (pbk)
ISBN: 978-1-003-09052-6 (ebk)

DOI: 10.4324/9781003090526

Typeset in Sabon
by Apex CoVantage, LLC

Contents

Figures

Chronology

1607:	English colonists establish the Jamestown colony in Virginia.
1619:	The first enslaved Africans arrive in North America.
1630:	English Puritans establish the Massachusetts Bay Colony.
c. 1689:	John Locke publishes *Two Treatise on Government*.
1776:	Adam Smith writes *The Wealth of Nations*.
July 4, 1776:	*The Declaration of Independence* is signed.
1791:	Alexander Hamilton issues *Report on the Subject of Manufactures*.
1793:	Eli Whitney invents the cotton gin.
1808:	The international slave trade comes to a close.
1815:	The Boston Associates forms, establishing textile mills across parts of New England.
1819:	In its ruling on *Dartmouth v. Woodward*, the U.S. Supreme Court declares that a corporation is an 'artificial person.'
1825:	The Erie Canal is completed.
1830:	The Indian Removal Act sets the stage for the violent dispossession of native American land and the continuation of settler colonialism.
1831–1832:	Alexis de Tocqueville visits the United States.
1832:	President Jackson vetoes a bill intended to recharter the Second Bank of the United States.
1837:	Economic panic.
1841:	The Preemption Act, 1841: Ralph Waldo Emerson publishes 'Self-Reliance.'
1857:	Economic panic.
1862:	The Homestead Act.
1863:	The Emancipation Proclamation.
1865:	The Thirteenth Amendment to the Constitution bans slavery in the United States.
1868:	Marshall Fields opens his store in downtown Chicago.
1877:	The Great Railroad Strike.
1882:	The Chinese Exclusion Act is signed into law.

1883: Frederick Winslow Taylor begins his time-motion studies to develop his ideas of scientific management.
1885: The Foran Act is signed into law.
1886: The Haymarket Riot.
1886: *Santa Clara v. Southern Pacific Railroad Company* cements corporate personhood in the law.
1890: The Sherman Antitrust Bill is signed into law.
1893: The World's Fair and Columbian Exposition is held in Chicago.
1893: Frederick Jackson Turner declares the frontier has closed during the Columbian Exposition.
1896: May 18: In the case of *Plessy v. Ferguson*, the U.S. Supreme Court declares segregation to be constitutional.
1899: May 30–31: Under the leadership of W.E.B. DuBois, Atlanta University's Fourth Conference for the Study of the Negro Problems focuses on issues facing Black businesses. DuBois publishes 'The Negro in Business' later in the year.
July: The Hampton Negro Conference specifically addresses issues of Black businesses.
1900: The National Negro Business League is established.
1906: Henry Ford develops the Model T.
1906: Theodore Roosevelt's administration invokes the Sherman Antitrust Act in a first step toward breaking up Standard Oil.
1911: Frederick Winslow Taylor publishes his *Principles of Scientific Management*.
1913: Ford introduces the continuous assembly line.
1914: Louis Brandeis publishes *Other People's Money*.
1917: Immigration Act.
1919: Marcus Garvey launches the Black Star Line.
1921: An enraged white mob attacks and destroys the Greenwood section of Tulsa, Oklahoma, also known as 'Black Wall Street.'
1924: General Motors introduces the annual model change, as well as the slogan 'a car for every purse and purpose.'
1933: National Industrial Recovery Act is signed into law.
1935: The Wagner Act is signed into law.
1936: Charlie Chaplin satirizes the effect of mechanized factory work on the individual in *Modern Times*.
The 'Sit-Down' Strike at a General Motors plant in Flint, Michigan, is a big win for organized labor.
1941: EO 8802.
1942: The Bracero Program begins.
1947: The Taft-Hartley Act establishes the 'right-to-work' principle that uses the rhetoric of individualism to curtail union power.

1947:	Mont Pelerin Society holds its first meeting in Switzerland.
1954:	Brownie Wise becomes the first woman on the cover of *Business Week*.
1958:	Ayn Rand publishes *Atlas Shrugged.*
1965:	Delano Grape Strike begins.
1969:	EO 11458 (OMBE).
1971:	Operation PUSH.
1973:	*Black Enterprise* begins publishing.
1973:	Real wages begin to decline.
1973:	OPEC oil embargo begins.
1980:	Milton Friedman's series, *Free to Choose*, begins airing on PBS.
1981:	President Ronald Reagan fires striking air traffic controllers, signaling a decline in union power.
1984:	January 22: Apple's ad for the Macintosh personal computer airs during the Super Bowl.
1987:	British prime minister Margaret Thatcher declares 'there is no society, only individuals.'
1996:	In his State of the Union address, President Bill Clinton declares the end of big government.
1999:	World Trade Organization protests in Seattle.
2011:	Occupy Wall Street.
2012:	Individual success becomes a key point of contention in the presidential election.

Who's Who

Alger, Horatio (1832–1899): Author of books for children that tell 'rags-to-riches' stories.

Brandeis, Louis (1856–1941): Progressive lawyer and Supreme Court Justice. Author of *Other People's Money.*

Carnegie, Andrew (1835–1919): Founder of Carnegie Steel.

Carnegie, Dale (1888–1955): Author of *How to Win Friends and Influence People* and proponent of positive thinking.

Carter, Jimmy (1924–): Thirty-ninth president of the United States.

Chavez, Cesar (1927–1993): Labor leader and cofounder of the National Farm Workers Association who organized and led strikes among agricultural workers in the western United States.

Clay, Henry (1777–1852): Politician from Virginia who served in both the House and the Senate.

Coolidge, Calvin (1872–1933): Thirtieth president of the United States.

Coxe, Tench (1755–1824): Businessman and Revolution-era politician from Pennsylvania.

Darwin, Charles (1809–1882): English scientist who developed the theory of evolution.

Debs, Eugene (1885–1926): Labor and union activist. President of the American Railway Union during the Pullman Strike in Illinois.

DuBois, W.E.B. (1868–1963): Sociologist, historian, public intellectual, and author of numerous books, including *The Philadelphia Negro* and *The Souls of Black Folk*.

Dreiser, Theodore (1871–1945): American author of books including *Sister Carrie*, a novel that was deeply critical of society during the Gilded Age.

Drucker, Peter (1909–2005): Management scholar and author of many books, including *Concept of the Corporation.*

Durant, William (1861–1947): Known as 'Billy' Durant, he was an industrialist who created General Motors by buying a number of different automobile companies. He was eventually forced from his position at the company because of mismanagement.

Emerson, Ralph Waldo (1803–1882): American transcendentalist philosopher and author of essays, including 'Self-Reliance.'

Ford, Gerald (1913–2006): Thirty-eighth president of the United States.

Ford, Henry (1863–1947): Founder of the Ford Motor Company who developed the continuous assembly line.

Franklin, Benjamin (1706–1790): Revolutionary-era politician, statesman, diplomat, and author.

Frick, Henry (1849–1919): Businessman and part of the leadership team at Carnegie Steel. He was also blamed for the Homestead Strike in 1892.

Friedman, Milton (1912–2006): American economist and proponent of free market politics.

Friedman, Thomas (1953–): *New York Times* columnist and author of books, including *The World Is Flat.*

Fuller, S.B. (1905–1988): Black businessman and founder of Fuller Products, a cosmetics company. Fuller's biographical narrative drew heavily on the idea of the self-made man.

Garvey, Marcus (1887–1940): Black nationalist and founder of the Black Star Line.

Gates, Bill (1955–): Cofounder of Microsoft Corp and philanthropist.

Gould, Jay (1836–1892): Notorious financier and business magnate.

Greenspan, Alan (1926–): Chairman of the U.S. Federal Reserve from 1987 to 2006.

Hamilton, Alexander (c. 1755–1804): First Secretary of the Treasury.

Handy, Henry Jamison (1886–1983): Founder of the Jam Handy Organization, which created numerous industrial films for corporate clients, including General Motors.

Hayek, Friedrich von (1899–1992): Austrian economist and author of *The Road to Serfdom.*

Hume, David (1711–1776): Scottish moral philosopher and intellectual influence on Adam Smith.

Jackson, Andrew (1767–1845): Seventh president of the United States.

Jefferson, Thomas (1743–1826): Primary author of the Declaration of Independence and third president of the United States.

Jobs, Steve (1955–2011): Cofounder of Apple Computers.

Johnson, John H. (1918–2005): Publisher whose titles included *Ebony* and *Jet* magazine.

Kendrix, Moss (1917–1989): Advertising and public relations executive who developed the first marketing campaign for Coca-Cola that featured Black Americans.

Keynes, John Maynard (1883–1946): English economist and proponent of countercyclical government spending.

Lawrence, Mary Wells (1928–): Advertising executive and cofounder of the advertising agency Wells Rich Greene.

Livermore, Jesse (1877–1940): Infamous stockbroker.

Locke, John (1632–1704): English philosopher who developed ideas associated with liberalism.

Lowell, Francis Cabot (1775–1817): New England businessman who established and operated textile mills in New England.

Luce, Henry (1898–1967): Publisher whose titles included *Time* and *Fortune* magazine.

Mellon, Andrew (1855–1937): Banker and treasury secretary throughout the 1920s.

Mises, Ludwig von (1881–1973): Austrian economist and founder of the Mont Pelerin Society.

Nader, Ralph (1934–): Lawyer and consumer rights activist.

Norris, Frank (1870–1902): American writer associated with naturalism and author of *The Octopus* and *The Pit*.

Obama, Barack (1961–): forty-fourth president of the United States.

Packard, Vance (1914–1996): Journalist and author of books, including *The Hidden Persuaders*, a critical account of the advertising industry and consumerism in the middle of the twentieth century.

Peters, Thomas (1942–): McKinsey consultant and coauthor of many management books, including the best-selling *In Search of Excellence*.

Pew, J. Howard (1882–1971): Free enterprise advocate and longtime president of the Sun Oil Company.

Rand, Ayn (1905–1982): Author and philosopher known for her unwavering defense of unregulated capitalism and unapologetic individualism. Her many books include *The Fountainhead* and *Atlas Shrugged.* She also developed her own philosophical system, Objectivism.

Randolph, A. Philip (1889–1979): Civil rights and labor leader. Randolph was also the founder and president of the Brotherhood of Sleeping Car Porters.

Read, Leonard (1898–1983): Founder and president of the Foundation for Economic Education.

Reagan, Ronald (1911–2004): Republican politician and fortieth president of the United States.

Riesman, David (1909–2002): Sociologist and lead author of *The Lonely Crowd.*

Rockefeller, John (1839–1937): Founder of Standard Oil.

Romney, Mitt (1947–): American businessman and conservative politician, who served as the governor of Massachusetts and senator from Utah. He was also the Republican nominee for president in 2012.

Roosevelt, Franklin Delano (1882–1945): Thirty-second president of the United States.

Roosevelt, Theodore (1858–1919): Twenty-sixth president of the United States.

Sandberg, Sheryl (1969–): Silicon Valley executive and author of *Lean In.*

Schumpeter, Joseph (1883–1950): Economist and author of *Capitalism, Socialism, and Democracy.*

Sloan, Jr. Alfred P. (1875–1966): President of the General Motors Corporation who developed the annual product change.

Smith, Adam (1723–1790): Scottish philosopher and author of *The Wealth of Nations.*

Spencer, Herbert (1820–1903): English philosopher who developed the idea of 'social Darwinism.'

Stryker, Roy (1893–1975): Director of the documentary photograph project undertaken as part of the Farm Security Administration.

Sumner, William Graham (1840–1910): American sociologist who advocated for social Darwinism and laissez-faire policies.

Tarbell, Ida (1857–1944): Muckraking journalist and author of *The History of the Standard Oil Company.*

Taylor, Frederick Winslow (1856–1915): Engineer who created scientific management.

Tocqueville, Alexis de (1805–1859): French scholar who wrote about politics, life, and history in his book *Democracy in America.*

Turner, Frederick Jackson (1861–1932): American historian.

Vanderbilt, Cornelius (1794–1877): Railroad tycoon.

Veblen, Thornstein (1857–1929): Economist and author of *The Theory of the Leisure Class.*

Volker, Paul (1927–2019): Chairman of the U.S. Federal Reserve from 1979 to 1987.

Walker, Madam CJ (1867–1919): The public name of businesswoman Sarah Breedlove who developed a line of beauty products for Black women.

Washington, Booker T. (1856–1915): Founder of the Tuskegee Institute.

Watson, Sr., Thomas J. (1874–1956): Founder of IBM.

Wilson, Sloan (1920–2003): Author of *The Man in the Gray Flannel Suit.*

Wise, Brownie (1913–1992): Businesswoman who developed and ran Tupperware's party sales model.

Whitney, Eli (1765–1825): Inventor of the cotton gin.

Whyte, William (1917–1999): Writer for *Fortune* magazine and author of *The Organization Man.*

Acknowledgments

Thank you to Gordon Martel for the invitation to write this book, as well as his words of counsel and encouragement along the way. At Routledge, Kimberley Smith and Emily Irvine have been incomparable in their guidance, assistance, and flexibility throughout this process.

Nobody writes in a vacuum, and this book would not have been possible without the input of colleagues, all of whom have been extraordinarily generous with their time. Specifically, I would like to thank Pamela Laird, Caitlin Rosenthal, Stephanie Kolberg, Renee Searfoss, Andrew Busch, and Irene Garza for their thoughtful and insightful feedback on the manuscript.

Finally, an additional thank you is due to Stephanie Kolberg, who has provided love, support, and encouragement while I worked on this project.

Introduction

This is a book about an idea and its consequences. For some, 'individualism' has long been recognized as one of the key organizing principles in American culture writ large. A commitment to and celebration of this value can be spotted in fields as various as policy-making and poetry. Perhaps the most lyrical expression can be found at the end of Mark Twain's masterpiece, *The Adventures of Huckleberry Finn*. At the end of that book, Huck tells the reader, 'I reckon I got to light out for the Territory ahead of the rest' (Twain, 1884: 362). The line captures the fundamental romance of American individualism. Huck is free in the most fundamental sense – unbound to anyone or anything. Yet this cultural commitment to individualism isn't limited to books like Twain's. In fact, the idea has informed how Americans have understood both business and capitalism. However, the connection between individualism and capitalism is anything but straightforward. Rather, the relationship between this idea and that system is enormously complex. For instance, the fictional Huck might have been master of himself, answering to no one. But in that novel, his companion, Jim, is a runaway slave fleeing the most brutal manifestation of nineteenth-century capitalism that is dependent on denying his own liberty. As the example of Huck and Jim suggests, any sense of American individualism is hopelessly complicated by the realities of capitalism's development.

Yet it is this very complexity that demands that the relationship between American capitalism and American individualism be interrogated. Ideas about individualism have played a role in a number of ways that capitalism operates, and the ways in which Americans have made sense of capitalism. What's more, capitalism's development has sometimes taken turns that have brutally suppressed the rights and ambitions of others (think again of Jim trapped in a wider economic system that includes his enslavement). Through it all, Americans have labored (often in vain) to make sense of these incongruities.

Untangling this relationship, though, is not an easy task. For starters, just agreeing on what capitalism is has proven to be difficult. As the historian Seth Rockman has remarked, in recent years, historians have variously

DOI: 10.4324/9781003090526-1

characterized capitalism as 'a force of liberation or destruction, as a top-down or bottom-up phenomenon, and as ideology or a structure' (Rockman, 2014: 440). Even relatively succinct descriptions, such as Jonathan Levy's statement that 'capitalism is an economy' that is ultimately focused on 'pecuniary gain' quickly, raise questions of the law, governance, production, labor, and ideology (Levy, 2021: xx). Some historians have even wondered if a set definition of capitalism is useful since its forms and processes are so multifaceted. For example, capitalism clearly involves market exchange. This was certainly a central aspect to capitalism for **Adam Smith**. Yet this description is far too simple. Market exchange predated capitalism, and there is often a certain amount of economic activity that takes place outside of such formal, legal market systems. In fact, some scholars have suggested that there can be – in specific times and places – a reciprocal relationship between such formal and informal capitalist economies.

Determining capitalism's boundaries can also be tricky. Some facets of capitalism that might be central to a market economy might be entirely missing from important different moments or spaces. American slave plantations, for instance, might seem to be a system that is far removed from a capitalist market, though this is hardly the case. Enslaved Black people were producing for the market, feeding the raw material for manufacturing, trade, and finance both in the United States and around the world. Historians now consider slavery to be integral to capitalism's development in the United States.

Just as importantly, the relationship between capitalism and geography is complex. On the one hand, capitalism is always a global process and phenomenon. This global aspect of capitalism has long been recognized by thinkers as early as Karl Marx. Some of the most fundamental aspects of a market system – such as trade – simply cannot be stopped by national political borders. Yet while capitalism clearly transcends national borders, it is not the same process in every place around the world. Different geographies have different cultures, businesses, governments, regulatory systems, and natural resources. Because of this variety, the way each individual experiences capitalism's processes can be very, very different. Likewise, the ways capitalism plays out in different geographies are all, ultimately, linked. This global, border-hopping quality means that the U.S. economy is tightly bound to a broader, worldwide system of buying and selling. North American companies have long done business abroad and relied on natural resources from other parts of the planet. Commodities produced in parts of the United States have been shipped to markets around the world. Even slaves in the American South who labored under the threat of torture and death picked cotton that was traded in faraway places like Liverpool, England.

Yet even if it is nearly impossible to separate capitalism's processes in one place from different parts of the world, capitalism is experienced differently in different parts of the world. Capitalism's experiences are intensely local. It can 're-rhythm' places, shaping local cultures and communities. These different geographic connections entail what the geographer Doreen Massey called **power geometries** (Massey, 1994). Massey used this term to describe how **globalization** was experienced by different people depending on their access to resources, money, time, and so on. Likewise, this idea of 'power geometries' offers a useful framework to consider capitalism and the individual in the United States. These power geometries are connected to factors (many of which are out of our control) such as economic power, social standing, what prejudices individuals face, and the infrastructure that people can access. Power geometries, in other words, play a big role in how individual people experience and navigate capitalism. Because of all these complexities and interconnections, some historians have conceived of capitalism as being like an ecosystem, with different participants and parts that all contribute to how people and institutions operate within this economic system.

In a somewhat similar vein, the economist **Joseph Schumpeter** evoked a sense of terrifying sublimity when he wrote about capitalism's 'perennial gale of creative destruction.' Yet Schumpeter also thought that on balance, capitalism was a benevolent force, arguing that the constant push and pull between profit and loss means that capitalism has been 'the propelling force of the rationalization of human behavior' (Schumpeter, 1942: 125). But this point is, to say the least, debatable. There is much about capitalism that defies this cool, logical ideal. Capitalism has always been bolstered by several different lines of political developments, philosophical schools of thought, and cultural currents.

Capitalism is a many-faceted phenomenon – by turns enchanting and repulsive. It encompasses both stories of personal triumph and reinvention that pepper popular celebrations and understandings of capitalism, as well as the grotesque inhumanity of an enslaved person being disfigured on a Southern plantation. Both realities are a part of capitalism's influence on American life and history.

Indeed, because capitalism is so complex and contradictory, it should come as no surprise that across all its different phases and guises, capitalism has had a number of different impacts on the ways in which Americans have understood themselves as individual citizens and in their relationship to the nation as a whole. In some ways, individualism occupies a contradictory space in the story of American capitalism. On the one hand, the lone, rugged individual – long a staple of American mythology – seems especially suited for a system based on competition in a market. To be sure, the individual thriving and triumphing against all odds in a capitalist system has appeared again and again in artifacts of American culture. Yet at the same time, the logic of capitalism – first and most fully articulated by Adam Smith in 1776 – seems to leave little room for the individual. To be sure,

Smith celebrated the idea of the worker who ingeniously invents a labor-saving device. Likewise, the work's early pages introduced the reader to the brewer, baker, and butcher – three individuals who discovered the task to which each was best suited and which would allow each to thrive in what Smith called a 'market society.' However, Smith was no individualist. Much of the early chapters in that book focus on the **division of labor**. Smith marveled at how quickly pins and nails could be produced when work was divided up thusly and people labored together. From capitalism's outset, then, the individual was caught in a trap – a perennially celebrated type, but always under the pressure of a system that demanded more and more efficiency at the cost of personal autonomy. This tension has defined American capitalism in a number of respects from the founding of the Republic to the present day.

A similar dynamic is at work when it comes to individualism. Because individual identity is never unified, any one person can experience capitalism's unfolding processes differently from moment to moment. For instance, someone might act as a consumer in the morning by going shopping before assuming their role as a worker in an office, factory, or farm for the next several hours. The particular character of capitalism's effects on an individual is also dependent on the intersections of one's race, class, citizenship, gender, sexual identification, and religious affiliation. In other words, 'the individual' is a distinctly unstable figure in both concept and practice.

Given the complex, interconnected nature of the topic, it is nearly impossible to tell this story in a straight line. The different processes and parts of capitalism zig and zag – sometimes in unexpected and counterintuitive ways. These different parts crisscross each other in each different historical circumstance, producing a range of different outcomes. In any one historical moment, there might be multiple and contradictory aspects of capitalism at play. Still, it is possible to outline some of the various contexts in which American capitalism and individualism have been in dialogue with one another. To that end, each chapter in this book focuses on one particular aspect of American life and history where the interplay between individualism and capitalism is observable. The first chapter traces this relationship as it has appeared in philosophical and political thought, with a specific emphasis on the Western liberal tradition. The second chapter explores how individualism has factored into legal and regulatory frameworks that have spurred and created American capitalism. The third chapter explores the ways in which individualism has played out inside business organizations that have, in general, become more and more complex and hierarchical over time. The fourth chapter explores the centrality of individualism in mainstream American culture, with a specific emphasis on how ideas of the self-made man have been central to popular representations of capitalism. The fifth and final chapter examines the tensions between individualism and the collective power of both workers and consumers.

Throughout these various contexts, it is clear that there is a lot at stake in ideas of individualism. It is an idea that immediately brings up questions of cultural legitimacy, agency, and power. Moreover, it is an idea that not all Americans have had equal claim to. For example, concepts such as rugged individualism and the self-made man are directly bound up with issues of race and gender in a number of ways. At times, steps to secure a sense of individualism have meant the direct subjugation or dispossession of entire groups of people. Similarly, American individualism is a widespread (though certainly not universal) cultural ideal that not everyone has had access to claiming. American capitalism has also developed in ways that are dependent on a sense of individualism. Ultimately, the interplay of individualism as a cultural ideal and capitalism as an economic system has proven to be a central force in American history.

1 Philosophies

In some accounts of capitalism's early development, the place of individual liberty is very complicated. Famously, the German thinker Max Weber posited a direct connection between Protestantism and capitalism. As he observed, the Puritans believed that if God provided someone who was preordained for salvation a 'chance to profit,' then that person 'must follow the call by taking advantage of the opportunity' (Weber, 1930: 162). In that way, 'the providential interpretation of profit-making justified the activities of the business man' (Weber, 1930: 163). At the same time, though, Puritans in the seventeenth century Massachusetts Bay Colony exercised 'the most absolutely unbearable form of ecclesiastical control of the individual which could possibly exist' (Weber, 1930: 37). In other words, the Puritans in New England did not extoll individualism as a value. However, the place of the individual and individual liberty in American capitalism eventually became a central feature of philosophical and political discourse. While, a precise definition of capitalism is hard to pin down, it is possible to trace some of the main streams of thinking that have influenced capitalism's development – especially capitalism's relationship to the individual – since its appearance. Some can be traced to distinct and formal philosophical systems. Other streams are derived from popular understandings of work, freedom, the economy, and government. Still other streams can be traced to the rhetoric that politicians have used to advance their own ideas.

Classical Liberalism and Political Economy

One of the earliest attempts to connect the individual to politics and economics can be viewed through the Western philosophical tradition of **liberalism**. To understand liberalism's basic tenets, there is no better place to start than with the seventeenth-century English philosopher **John Locke**. To be sure, the world that Locke inhabited was vastly different from the United States. He lived under an all-powerful English monarchy, but was aligned with his patron, the Earl of Shaftesbury, who directly challenged this official royal authority. During this time of enormous political risk,

DOI: 10.4324/9781003090526-2

Locke produced his *Second Treatise on Government*. In this text, Locke asserted that authority ultimately resided with God.

Removing the locus of power away from the English monarch, Locke wrote that human beings were born in a 'perfect state of freedom to order their actions, and dispose of their possessions and persons as they see fit' (Locke, 1690). Beyond the immediate political implications of such an assertion, Locke linked the concepts of property, work, and freedom. Lines in Locke's treatise, such as 'Every man has a property in his own person,' even went so far as to conflate individual personhood with property (Locke, 1690). Consequently, when somebody labored and produced something, they were infusing it with their own property. For Locke when men (he didn't really consider women) 'enter[ed] into society,' they forfeited 'equality, liberty, and executive power they had in the state of nature' and placed it 'into the hands of the society' (Locke, 1690). Such a sacrifice was made, though, in order to 'better to preserve himself, his liberty and property; (for no rational creature can be supposed to change his condition with an intention to be worse).' Significantly, Locke also asserted that men were inherently rational and could make rational choices. From the outset, then, such ideas as property rights became central to some of liberalism's big ideas. However, Locke's views of individual freedom only extended so far. In fact, Locke was a stockholder in the Royal African Company, which was busy trading slaves around the world. Locke would hardly be the last figure to offer up an expansive view of liberty while at the same time delineating who could and could not enjoy such freedom along the lines of race and gender. In fact, such exclusions have been a persistent feature that has accompanied the relationship between individualism and capitalism.

While Locke offered up an early articulation of the liberal thinking that emphasized individual rights, the Scottish philosopher Adam Smith did more than anyone to first articulate capitalism's functioning. Though Smith is now widely recognized as critical to the development of classical economics, during his own lifetime, he was really more of a philosopher and was deeply interested in questions of morality. These questions would eventually inform Smith's economic thinking and exert a lasting influence on the philosophical underpinnings of capitalism. Smith was deeply influenced by (and close friends with) the philosopher **David Hume**. Hume's own arguments about morality centered on ideas of 'sympathy.' For Hume, 'sympathy' was at the root of several important concepts, such as 'justice.' Yet Hume also believed that sympathy was, in the end, an irrational way to think, presenting something of a conundrum. It would be Smith who would help resolve the sympathy dilemma – how to foster an undeniably good, but ultimately irrational, quality in people.

In his work, *A Theory of Moral Sentiments*, Smith introduced his concept of 'self-love,' which informed some of his most famous ideas in *The Wealth of Nations*, which became his most influential work. As the title suggests,

Smith was primarily focused on the best way to build national economies, not individual fortunes. In fact, *The Wealth of Nations* is chiefly a critique of **mercantilism**, not a blueprint for capitalism. Still, the idea of 'self-love' permeates the entire book (and it is the reason subsequent individualists have been quick to invoke his name). This idea is present even when Smith is discussing key economic concepts like the division of labor. To illustrate this process, Smith asks his readers to imagine three different workers: a brewer, a butcher, and a baker. The labor of all three men (in Smith's world and time, that would be an easy assumption) was essential to keeping Scottish bellies full. But, Smith wrote, it was not from their 'benevolence' that 'we expect our dinner' (Doc. 1). Instead, when one bought bread or beer, both the buyer and the seller were acting out of self-love, or, to use a more modern term, self-interest.

This idea of individual actors, each working in his own interest and capitalizing on a particular strength, was the foundation of a market. For Smith, this market activity – buying and selling goods and services – was both an orderly and organic manner through which commercial activity took place. 'Every man thus lives by exchanging, or by some measure becomes a merchant,' Smith wrote (Smith, 1776). The implications for the philosopher were profound, and even structured overall society. Such widespread market activity meant that 'the society itself' would grow into a 'commercial society.' Miraculously, though, Smith argued that all of this self-interested work had the effect of organizing a vast range of activities. Indeed, the world and economy as Smith described it was one that proceeded (in the long run at least) with the orderly precision of a cuckoo clock. All of these ideas are central to understanding the famous (or infamous) idea of the 'invisible hand of the market' that Smith introduced in *The Wealth of Nations*.

In part, that phrase has had enormous staying power because it is a short and snappy line. However, it only appears once in the book. In this well-known passage, Smith writes that and individual merchant

> neither intends to promote the public interest, nor knows how much he is promoting it. By preferring the support of domestic to that of foreign industry, he intends only his own security; and by directing that industry in such a manner as its produce may be of the greatest value, he intends only his own gain, and he is in this, as in many other cases, led by an invisible hand to promote an end which was no part of his intention. Nor is it always the worse for the society that it was no part of it. By pursuing his own interest he frequently promotes that of the society more effectually than when he really intends to promote it.
>
> (Smith, 1776)

With this passage, Smith's ideas of a commercial society successfully reconciled the sympathy dilemma that had bothered Hume. The invisible hand of the market produced outcomes that were beneficial to everyone, even though the individual was really motivated by self-interest, or self-love.

While some tend to think of Adam Smith's invisible hand as offering the marketplace as a complete substitute for government involvement in the economy, in *The Wealth of Nations*, Smith clearly allowed a substantial role for government, particularly when it came to infrastructure. For instance, Smith argued, the state could step in and help with large, costly, and risky transportation projects, such as turnpikes, which private enterprises might not undertake.

Fittingly enough, *The Wealth of Nations* was published in 1776, the same year that England's colonies in North America declared independence. Significantly, the American Revolution was profoundly influenced by liberalism's focus on 'natural rights' and 'individual liberty' – even if those rights and that liberty were to be reserved almost exclusively for white men. In fact, some of the Declaration's most famous lines asserting that 'all Men are created equal' and are 'endowed by their Creator with certain unalienable Rights,' and that 'to Secure these Rights, Governments are instituted among Men, deriving their just Powers from the Consent of the Governed,' reveal a direct link to ideas first articulated by Locke nearly a century earlier. Over the course of the next 200 years, Americans of all sorts would blend the two ideas of market activity and personal liberty in a variety of ways.

The American Ideal of Self-Reliance

Locke and Smith, of course, were European philosophers. However, in the nineteenth century, one of the most prominent American philosophers articulated their own emphasis on individualism. In the middle of the nineteenth century, **Ralph Waldo Emerson** provided substantial intellectual heft to the idea of individual independence in his essay 'Self-Reliance,' which was published in 1841. In this essay, Emerson offered a distillation of some of the animating ideals of American individualism. For instance, he declared, 'Whoso would be a man must be a nonconformist.' Indeed, Emerson confessed that he was 'ashamed to think how easily we capitulate to badges and names, to large societies and dead institutions' (Doc. 6). The entire essay, in fact, was packed with such eminently quotable and pithy lines.

However, a close reading of this famous essay also reveals some of the anxieties that came with the era's changing economic landscape. In fact, 'Self-Reliance' is full of references to the potential fates of individuals who now inhabited a very different commercial world. Tellingly, in his essay,

Emerson drew on the idea of a **joint-stock company** to draw a contrast to his idea of a self-reliant individual, writing:

> These are the voices which we hear in solitude, but they grow faint and inaudible as we enter into the world. Society everywhere is in conspiracy against the manhood of every one of its members. Society is a joint-stock company in which the members agree for the better securing of his bread to each shareholder, to surrender liberty and culture of the eater. The virtue in most request is conformity. Self-reliance is its aversion. It loves not realities and creators, but names and customs.
> (Emerson, 1841)

The passage is notable in several respects. In it, Emerson registers a clear discomfort with larger forms of business enterprise, juxtaposing such organizations with a supposedly more natural state of one working for himself (again, Emerson was writing in an age that was decidedly male-centric). Though the joint-stock company here was simply meant to be a stand-in for a larger sense of stifling 'society,' no doubt the growing prominence of such companies provided the writer with this ready comparison. What is more, the passage here was an early articulation of the idea of a heroic individual pitted against a corporation. This theme would appear again and again much later.

Elsewhere, in the essay, Emerson critiqued what he saw as a destructive aspect of American culture that did not allow a rugged sense of self-reliance to take hold. 'If our young men miscarry in their first enterprises,' he lamented, 'they lose all heart. If the young merchant fails, men say he is ruined.' In a system in which credit played so large a part and in which bankruptcy was always a possibility, such a cultural disposition was problematic. In contrast to the young merchant ruined so fast, Emerson declared that 'a sturdy lad from New Hampshire or Vermont' was 'worth a hundred of these city dolls.'

Emerson's essay would prove to have enormous influence and staying power. People of all sorts would invoke this idea of self-reliance when commenting on contemporary matters of business and financial matters. To later generations who opposed the government involvement in a social safety net, 'Self-Reliance' provided a ready stock of quotations backed by the imprint of Emerson's own intellectual heft. For instance, he evinced a clear disdain for charity. Emerson was hardly alone in his thinking. Over the course of the nineteenth and twentieth centuries, other Americans developed similar ideas that conflated personal liberty and commercial activity.

In addition to Emerson, a number of different writers made the connection between commerce and the American character amid the market revolution in the years before the Civil War. In his sweeping assessment of American democracy, **Alexis de Tocqueville** emphasized both individualism

Figure 1.1 Alexis de Tocqueville, who wrote extensively about individualism after visiting the United States. Source: Beinecke Rare Book and Manuscript Library, Yale University.

as core American value and the role that business, commerce, and trade played in making the United States as distinct from Europe.

Famously, the French philosopher developed his ideas while visiting the United States in the 1830s, Tocqueville considered individualism to be a key trait in American culture and thought. In fact, the author dedicated a lengthy section of the second volume of *Democracy in America* to a consideration of this idea. For Tocqueville, 'Individualism' was

> a mature and calm feeling, which disposes each member of the community to sever himself from the mass of his fellow-creatures; and to draw apart with his family and his friends; so that, after he has thus formed a little circle of his own, he willingly leaves society at large to itself.

In this sense, individualism was a dangerous idea because it had the potential to weaken social bonds between people. Individualism, in other words, could be profoundly anti-social, keeping people apart from one another. The writer did, though, believe that Americans had developed ways to 'combat,' or at least mitigate, some of the negative effects of individualism. Indeed, as Dana Villa argues, Tocqueville saw individualism as a 'condition' to be 'overcome' (Villa, 2005: 681).

In addition to his observations about American individualism, Tocqueville also had a lot to say about capitalism. For Tocqueville, business and commerce were just as important to the American character. As he wrote:

> If the Americans never spend the money of the people in galas, it is not only because the imposition of taxes is under the control of the people, but because the people takes no delight in public rejoicings. If they repudiate all ornament from their architecture, and set no store on any but the more practical and homely advantages, it is not only because they live under democratic institutions, but because they are a commercial nation. The habits of private life are continued in public; and we ought carefully to distinguish that economy which depends upon their institutions from that which is the natural result of their manners and customs.
>
> (Doc. 4)

Throughout, Tocqueville posited a relationship between American democracy and business. For instance, he observed 'that the democratic institutions of the United States, joined to the physical constitution of the country, are the cause (not the direct, as is so often asserted, but the indirect cause) of the prodigious commercial activity of the inhabitants' (Tocqueville, 1835). In fact, the French writer was convinced that a preoccupation with business and commerce were central features of the American mind, influencing all other aspects of American life. He wrote, 'The passions which agitate the Americans most deeply are not their political but their commercial passions; or, to speak more correctly, they introduce the habits they contract in business into their political life' (Tocqueville, 1835). In an era in which commerce seemed to be defined by small firms and independent businessmen, such claims about self-made men or the connection between democracy and the individual were, in some respects, not huge intellectual leaps to make. However, capitalism was, if nothing else, a dynamic and constantly evolving system – and the nineteenth century ushered in some very dramatic changes with the rise of the large corporation and an increasingly industrial business landscape.

Free Labor Ideology

In the nineteenth century, these ideas could sometimes be found in the concept of 'free labor.' As more than one historian has noted, American slavery had an enormous influence over the ways in which white Americans understood the concept of freedom. While this was true from a political aspect in the eighteenth century, it was also true as capitalism took hold in the nineteenth century, profoundly changing the American economy. Without question, the presence of a growing slave system fueled a sectional crisis that would result in the Civil War. It was this tension that also produced the Republican Party, which was organized around what the historian Eric Foner described as a 'free labor ideology' (Foner, 1970: 58). This belief system offered a stark contrast to the enslaved labor in the South. Republicans believed that 'free labor' in Northern states had produced a better commercial system and, by extension, a better society. Interestingly, free labor ideology in some ways resembled Locke's ideas about the connection between property and labor. In any number of speeches during the 1850s, one can detect the traces of Locke's idealized vision of labor. What is more, 'free labor ideology' also promoted the idea of social mobility. Indeed, for these Americans, before the Civil War, the idea of 'labor' was big enough to include most types of work.

If these Republicans put a lot of stock in the dignity and value of labor, crucially, they also conceived of work's connection to freedom. In this context for these Americans, being economically independent and self-sufficient was enormously important. So important were these values, in fact, the Republicans held a special veneration for small **entrepreneurs** and producers. This vision, moreover, was inherently democratic. A nation composed of such small producers was bound to be a nation of 'middling' people. Such independent producers stood in sharp contrast to large businesses or anything that many have suggested as economic concentration. The idea of free labor, then, was a lens through which this group interpreted the era's events. This also included interpretations of the Panic of 1857. Republicans saw the plight of those who had been hurt by this panic (as economic downturns were then called) as a matter of individual responsibility. This would not be the last time that ideas of individualism would directly line up with political actions or stances.

As always, slavery and race continued to be a persistent (if sometimes unacknowledged) reference point. In the years before the Civil War, Foner argues that abolitionists promoted the idea of a 'free labor system' that was distinctly American (Foner, 1970). These abolitionists contrasted this concept with slavery, which, the implication went, was antithetical to the United States. For these antebellum Americans – primarily in Northern states – independent, working producers were distinctly American. 'Free labor' and 'free enterprise,' in other words, were moral – and not just economic – concepts. For abolitionists and other promoters, free labor was the type of work that produced American virtues and was crucial to American civilization.

This idea of free labor, besides providing one rhetorical contrast to slavery, is also, as we shall see, closely related to the perennial American ideals of the small, independent producer. Indeed, for these Americans, 'free labor' distinctly meant small artisans, and not big businesses.

As the historian Lawrence Glickman has demonstrated, this idea of free labor was closely related to the rhetoric of 'free enterprise' in the nineteenth century (Glickman, 2019). Though this phrase would take on a very specific meaning after 1900, before the Civil War, proponents of these ideas did not think of free enterprise as a lack of government involvement. Rather, government could support enterprise and commerce in a variety of ways, especially through building and maintaining infrastructure. In this regard, at least, free labor and enterprise advocates in the nineteenth century did not deviate too much from Adam Smith's ideas about the role of government. However, although abolitionists used the rhetoric of free labor as a contrast to slavery, the concept also bolstered connections among race, work, and citizenship. As the scholar Evelyn Nakano Glenn argues, in contrast to free labor that was racialized as white, 'other nonwhite racial groups were associated with unfree labor' in other parts of the country (Glenn, 2002: 68). Even after the Civil War, white workers equated contract labor with democracy and freedom in ways that would break down along lines of race and gender.

Nineteenth-century understandings of free labor, contract work, and the like reveal how central individualism was to notions of American political economy. Even as the economy became more complex and industrialized, the individual continued to hold sway as an organizing concept over the country's political and philosophical thought. The results could sometimes be exceedingly dark. For example, **William Graham Sumner** was one of the Gilded Age's most vocal believers in **social Darwinism**, and frequently connected such ideas to some of the era's more glaring inequalities. Sumner often put it bluntly: some men were simply better suited to great things, and it was only natural that such differences in ability should be reflected in sometimes wildly disparate piles of money. Sumner was hardly troubled by such ideas, and in fact wrote that 'the concentration of wealth is but one feature of a grand step in societal evolution' (Doc 10).

While such a statement might seem to be one more writer celebrating American individualism, in truth, the fate of the individual in Sumner's thinking was more complex when it came to this topic. The era's new, and massive, corporations meant that some individuals would have more power and more autonomy. For Sumner, fabulously wealthy men like **John Rockefeller** and **Andrew Carnegie** were clear signs of progress. But this progress would mean a loss of individual autonomy for many. As he wrote, 'the great scale on which all societal undertakings must be carried out' – meaning economic activity coordinated and managed by larger organizations – required 'the personal element in direction and control' (Doc. 10). As he stated flatly in his essay, 'The Concentration of Wealth: Its Economic Justification,' the 'competent management' of such organization meant 'far higher salaries to executive officers than to workers' (Doc. 10). As he put it in another essay, 'All organization implies restriction of liberty. The gain of power is won by narrowing individual range' (Sumner, 1963: 170). For Sumner, though, this was not a smooth process. Reflecting his own ideological grounding in evolutionary thinking, Sumner described the process of reaching such highly organized institutions as the product of a conflict and contest of wills. As he wrote, 'individuals and groups are forced against each other in a ceaseless war of interests, by their selfish and mutual efforts to fulfill their career on earth within the conditions set for them' (Sumner, 1963). While individualism was an active force in the world, it would not necessarily lead to independence and prosperity for everyone. Some might maintain their autonomy at higher levels inside a corporation – and they would then exercise that power over other individuals. Echoing the words of evolutionary biologists like **Charles Darwin,** Sumner was convinced that the Gilded Age's millionaires were 'a product of natural selection acting on the whole body of men to pick out those who can meet the requirement of certain work to be done' (Sumner, 1963). At the same time, though, Sumner thought that the net result would be good for everyone. As he put it, 'No man can acquire a million without helping a million men to increase their little fortunes all the way down through the social grades' (Sumner, 1963). However, Sumner and other advocates of this harsh sense of social Darwinism offered just one approach to this new world. Others believed that the state was needed to help preserve a sense of individualism.

Twentieth-Century Ideas of Free Enterprise

Views of American individualism under capitalism had remarkable staying power. Later in the twentieth century, a conservative, anti-government understanding of 'free enterprise' became an increasingly influential worldview. This concept of 'free enterprise' has, for all of its inconsistencies, proven to be remarkably durable. This political commitment to individualism, in part, explains the **red scares** that persisted throughout the twentieth century.

At different times during the twentieth century, the development of business and commercial activity seemed to some to threaten the connection between political liberalism and market activity. For conservative thinkers, it was the **New Deal** in particular that was most distressing. As we will see later in this book, the Roosevelt administration's response to the Great Depression took the form of numerous large-scale programs intended to stabilize the economy. Such measures included the National Recovery Act, which attempted to get businesses to hold the line on wages, as well as the **Wagner Act**, which provided a big boost to organized labor. For some, including business leaders and conservative politicians, New Deal programs and reforms represented nothing less than a total assault on the very foundations of the liberal tradition upon which the entire economy rested. To these conservatives, the Roosevelt administration and the New Deal amounted to a turn toward Marxism and socialism. It was, according to these men, the polar opposite of American individualism. Though the New Deal did represent a big shift in U.S. economic policy, the rhetorical response was hardly new. As the historian Lawrence Glickman argues, 'there was no time during which free enterprisers did not claim that their ideal was endangered' (Glickman, 2019: 128).

Despite this pushback from business, though, Roosevelt had little trouble winning the contest for public opinion. In addressing his critics directly, Roosevelt described them as 'economic royalists,' a phrase intended to suggest that bankers and other monied opponents of the New Deal stood outside American history and tradition. Roosevelt described the creation of a new economic dynasty concocted out of 'new uses of corporations, banks, and securities,' all of which had been 'undreamed of by the Fathers' (Doc. 12). This new American form of aristocracy left no room for the 'many thousands of small-businessmen and merchants who sought to make a worthy use of the **American System** of initiative and profit' (Doc. 12). The New Deal, in other words, was necessary to secure the future of American individualism.

In addition to the alarm the New Deal caused among conservative politicians and business owners, a group of European intellectuals were also looking at events around the world with worry. It wasn't just that governments such as the United States had taken extraordinary steps to try and manage an economy that seemed to be spinning badly out of control. The work of British economist **John Maynard Keynes** seemed to best explain what had happened and, more importantly, what role governments should take in order to prevent another collapse like the Depression. Keynes died before his brand of economics and policy implications became so influential, but for conservative intellectuals, his ideas were a cause for panic.

These market-oriented economists and other academics considered themselves as belonging to a longer intellectual tradition that included philosophers like Locke and Smith, and they regarded the regulatory states that seemed to be in ascendance everywhere in the world with alarm. Austrian economists like **Friedrich von Hayek** and **Ludwig von Mises** founded the **Mont Pelerin Society** to articulate and promote a renewed type of liberalism that they termed **neoliberalism**. In broad terms, these economists drew clear and irreversible links between free markets and individual liberty. The most famous example was *The Road to Serfdom*, published in 1944. In this book, Hayek argued that economic planning was a slippery slope that would eventually lead to the loss of political freedom. Not only were markets the best way to coordinate economic activity but they were also an essential component of liberalism's commitment to freedom (and individualism).

To be sure, some historians have subsequently questioned the sincerity of neoliberals' claims about individual liberty and democracy. Still, Hayek and others produced a compelling and coherent view of the world that would grow in influence over the course of the twentieth century. Significantly, this European philosophy perfectly complemented a conservative business backlash to the New Deal (and the newfound power of labor unions). Little wonder, then, that General Motors produced a short, illustrated edition of Hayek's book. The economist's ideas also circulated in the United States when *Reader's Digest* published an abridged version of the book. However, these ideas were not just coming down from a mountain across the Atlantic.

American business conservatives continued to promote their vision of free enterprise. In the 1940s, **Leonard Read** established the **Foundation for Economic Education**, just one of many organizations dedicated to free enterprise in the middle of the twentieth century. Other American business conservatives, such as **J. Howard Pew**, enthusiastically embraced the ideas of the Mont Pelerin Society and worked to promote them in the United States. Similarly, business executives at large corporations, such as General Electric, went to great lengths to promote these ideas. As a part of this effort, the company even hired **Ronald Reagan** (then an actor who had not yet launched his political career).

At times, such commitments to free enterprise mixed with religious belief. Pew, for example, was fiercely dedicated to both belief systems. Conservative evangelical leaders were just as wary as business conservatives were of government power. By the late 1970s, some conservative Christian organizations were also promoting ideas that were fundamentally neoliberal.

It was also during that decade that the University of Chicago's economics department became a huge proponent of market-oriented, neoliberal ideas. It was here that neoliberal economists like **Milton Friedman** developed their theories. Apart from his academic work, Friedman was also a public figure, never missing an opportunity to promote his ideas. Throughout his career, Friedman consistently touted a connection between free markets and individual political freedom. He even went so far as to proclaim, 'If you have a central direction you inevitably have coercion. The only way that has ever been discovered to have a lot of people cooperate together voluntarily is through the free market. And that's why it's so essential to preserving individual freedom.' (Friedman, n.d.)

In 1980, Friedman was given an even broader platform to promote his ideas: a television series, *Free to Choose*. In the series, Friedman introduced viewers to many of the basic principles of neoliberalism and even drew on a well-worn free enterprise example of using a pencil to demonstrate how a market efficiently coordinated individual economic activity. By then, of course, Friedman did not have to work too hard to push his ideas.

The Rise of Neoliberal Politics

Though free enterprise and neoliberal philosophy developed in the wake of the New Deal, such ideas largely remained on the margins when it came to political rhetoric and policy. However, this changed during the 1970s. In addition to publicly extolling free enterprise and other neoliberal ideas, Friedman also helped make Chicago-style neoliberalism an American export. Infamously, after Augusto Pinochet came to power in Chile following a military coup (which was supported by the CIA), a group of young Chilean economists who had been educated at the University of Chicago saw their moment. Not only did they advise Pinochet, a military dictator, on how to set up a market economy, the group, which came to be known as the Chicago Boys, even persuaded Milton Friedman himself to meet with Pinochet. On the face of it, of course, a supposedly fierce advocate for personal liberty should not have advised a military dictator, yet Friedman dismissed any criticisms. For some, the connection between Chicago-school neoliberalism and military violence around the world was a troubling and consistent pattern. In the aftermath of the 2003 Iraq War, for example, the U.S.-backed provisional government applied many of these same policies. Even decades later, Friedman insisted that his meeting with Pinochet fell in line with his persistent connection between markets and freedom. He thought that Pinochet's eventual downfall was due in part to the incompatibility between free markets and authoritarianism. Here, though, it is unclear if Friedman could claim vindication. Pinochet's rule lasted until 1990.

In the United States, though, neoliberalism was poised to move the center of American politics. Ronald Reagan soon won the presidency and began to institute a number of neoliberal reforms on a national level. Even though under **Jimmy Carter**, the country had been moving away from the New Deal state and the Keynesian consensus, Reagan's presidency represented a clear and big step forward in this process. Famously, in his first State of the

Union address in 1981, Reagan declared 'government is not the solution to our problems, it is our problem' (Reagan, 1981). Reagan worked to quickly undo the regulatory state that had existed for so long, extolling the 'magic of the marketplace' (Reagan, 1981).

Moreover, neoliberalism's assent was not confined to the United States. In England, Prime Minister Margaret Thatcher also instituted similar reforms. Thatcher, though not directly involved in U.S. domestic policy, provided perhaps the most iconic phrase of the era when she stated

> there's no such thing as society. There are individual men and women and there are families. And no government can do anything except through people, and people must look after themselves first. It is our duty to look after ourselves and then, also, to look after our neighbours.
> (Thatcher, 1987)

In short, the two politicians were a clear signal of a renewed emphasis on individualism.

Rhetoric aside, some of the president's early moves did much to advance neoliberalism at the start of the 1980s. In 1981, Reagan fired striking air traffic controllers. The move signaled a crushing blow to labor unions and indicated a new set of government priorities that were much more in line with the thinkers of the Mont Pelerin Society. This move was followed by a wider withdrawal of the government's providing services. At the local level, some scholars have called this process **rollback neoliberalism**, since the government was dropping support and services. In real terms, it meant that the safety net many relied on was greatly reduced. Reagan, to be sure, was a conservative politician, and such policies, as extreme as they seem in retrospect, were, to some extent, to be expected. However, Reagan's political stance was in many ways a sign of things to come – a signal that a certain worldview was now dominant.

Reagan's ascendancy was, in some ways, just the most visible manifestation of a new political philosophy becoming mainstream. In the decades before the 1980 election, for example, Latinx business owners in New York City began to assume a much more prominent role in local affairs. The success of these entrepreneurs fit nicely with a conservative approach to solving the urban crisis that cities (which were already racialized) across the country were experiencing. As Pedro Regalado has argued, even if these business owners had interests that diverged from New York's working-class Latinx residents, they held an enormous amount of symbolic power (along with their considerable economic and political influence) (Regaldo, 2021). During the 1980s, these Latino and Latina business owners held sway with the mayor's office.

Indeed, even when Democrats captured the White House again with Bill Clinton's election in 1992, it did not usher in a return to the New Deal or

Great Society politics that had characterized past Democratic administrations. Instead, Clinton adopted many of the ideas and conceits of Reagan-era neoliberalism, though he may have smoothed over some of the rougher edges and made such programs seem palatable to those Americans who considered Reagan and Thatcher to be too extreme. In fact, in many ways, neoliberalism became even more entrenched during Clinton's time in the White House. From an early point in his presidency, Clinton extolled 'American entrepreneurs' who were living 'the American Dream.' Even if he also insisted that the United States needed 'a government that can be a real partner in making this new economy work for all of our people' (Doc. 19). Clinton's thinking when it came to political economy was market-oriented. Famously, in his 1996 State of the Union Address, Clinton declared that 'the era of big government is over' (Doc. 19). Even though he followed this line by stating that Americans should not have to 'fend for themselves,' he also insisted that 'self-reliance' and 'teamwork' now had to coexist (Doc. 19). Neoliberalism, and its emphasis on individualism, was now basic common sense for many Americans.

The emergence of neoliberalism as a system could have impacts on other political struggles and movements as well. Toward the end of the 1990s, some civil rights leaders turned their attention toward expanding market participation for Black Americans. Most prominently, Jesse Jackson's Rainbow/PUSH Coalition started its 'Wall Street Project.' Calling the effort to help Black Americans become involved with Wall Street amid a historic bull market that had started in the 1980s, Jackson's plan involved getting a thousand churches to 'start investment and consumer clubs to teach their parishioners how to follow the trail on money in the stock market' (Qtd. in McCampbell, 1999). Jackson even went so far as calling such efforts the 'fourth stage of the civil rights struggle' (Qtd. in McCampbell, 1999).

In the twenty-first century, the idea of individualism was recast for the era of globalization. In particular, President George W. Bush began advancing his vision of the **ownership society**. Globalization, he argued, had resulted in a world economy that would be subject to a range of different disruptions. Americans could no longer count on lifelong employment from companies. Given the amount of dynamism and instability, Bush wanted Americans to own things to achieve a sense of economic independence and stability. He encouraged both home ownership and investment in the stock market. There was nothing particularly new about such ideas. Still, in packaging it all up as a part of the 'ownership society,' Bush was setting the individual against the backdrop of a global capitalism – and in this way, it was a profound affirmation of the idea of American individualism and that ideal's relationship to capitalism.

Yet the politics of the early twenty-first century also suggested that the neoliberal consensus and focus on atomized individualism instead of a broader society (that Thatcher had even suggested didn't exist) was losing its grip. For instance, rhetoric during the 2012 presidential election, issues of the relationship between individuals and society, took center stage. The Republican candidate **Mitt Romney** used an overall framework of 'makers versus takers' in his campaign. This rhetorical opposition of the two terms amounted to a celebration of individual success and a firm rejection of government interference in the market. Indeed, perhaps the lowest moment of his campaign came when a video leaked of him speaking before donors in a way that appeared to disparage people who depended on government. Romney declared that about 47 percent of all Americans did not pay taxes and felt 'entitled to health care, to food, to housing, to you-name-it' (Romney, 2012). The Republican candidate went on to say that he did not think he would ever 'convince them they should take personal responsibility and care for their lives' (Romney, 2012). The remarks were shot through with a neoliberal sensibility, though the context in which Romney said them – at a fundraising $50,000-a-plate dinner at a banker's home – only reinforced the sense of a system that was increasingly out of whack.

For his own part, President **Barack Obama** found himself defending comments when he expounded on the role of government in helping business and aiding personal economic success on the campaign trail. During an appearance in Virginia, Obama remarked: 'If you were successful, somebody along the line gave you some help.' He expanded on the point by saying, 'Somebody invested in roads and bridges. If you've got a business – you didn't build that. Somebody else made that happen.' The president further elaborated by saying, 'When we succeed, we succeed because of our individual initiative, but also because we do things together' (Doc. 20). President Obama was making the point that no one operates in a vacuum and that an individual's success needs to be considered in a larger context. In the midst of the election, though, such nuance was soon lost.

Though the 2012 election brought the relationship of American individualism and capitalism to the fore, political rhetoric in subsequent years suggested that the veneration of individual entrepreneurs might be waning. The surprisingly strong political fortunes of self-described 'democratic socialists' at the end of the Obama era suggested that neoliberalism was losing its luster for many Americans.

2 Systems

While individualism has been a persistent concept in political-economic thinking, real-world economics do not function along such neat lines. The individual might be a central focus of neoliberal political rhetoric, for instance, but each individual operates under much larger and overlapping commercial and political systems. Throughout the decades following independence from England, the nation's economy would be governed by different systems (both public and private) of regulation and production and commerce. These systems influenced individual autonomy and action in different ways. For example, some systems have constrained an individual's options based on race and gender. At times, questions of individualism were at the center of debate and policy-making. At other times, individualism appeared to fade as a top priority. Throughout these changes, though, the fates and fortunes of individuals have been, to a very large degree, dependent on and determined by these larger systems.

Early Debates about the American Economy

Many Americans faced dire economic conditions following the American Revolution. Economic disruption accompanied increased tensions between England and the colonies just before the Revolutionary War. After the war, Britain was hardly quick in reestablishing normal trade with its former colonies. New taxes and currency deprecation amid the need to pay for war debt meant that many Americans, while newly independent, faced a very uncertain economic landscape. There was a lot at stake.

Because of this, some of the first national debates over what systems would govern the individual's relationship to capitalism concerned the same group of men that had played significant roles in the formation of the Republic. Immediately after the Revolutionary War, the new nation faced a number of questions about political economy that quickly drew **Thomas Jefferson** and **Alexander Hamilton** into a protracted debate with one another. The two men had vastly different visions for the American economy and what the role of the individual would be in that economy. Moreover, both had

DOI: 10.4324/9781003090526-3

different ideas about how involved the government would be in this regard. Serving as the country's first Treasury secretary, Hamilton developed and advanced ideas about the shape of commerce and economics in the United States primarily by issuing a series of influential reports, beginning with 1790's *Report of the Public Credit* and *The Report on a National Bank*. In 1791, Hamilton also issued his *Report on the Subject of Manufactures*. In these documents, Hamilton argued for an American economic system that would include robust banking and manufacturing sectors. Even in these documents, though, Hamilton acknowledged the importance of individualism in a system that he imagined would be increasingly complex. For instance, in the *Report on the Subject of Manufactures*, he wrote:

> This is a much more powerful mean of augmenting the fund of national industry than may at first sight appear. It is a just observation, that minds of the strongest and most active powers for their proper objects fall below mediocrity and labour without effect, if confined to uncongenial pursuits. And it is thence to be inferred, that the results of human exertion may be immensely increased by diversifying its objects. When all the different kinds of industry obtain in a community, each individual can find his proper element, and can call into activity the whole vigour of his nature. And the community is benefitted by the services of its respective members, in the manner, in which each can serve it with most effect.
>
> (Hamilton, 1791)

In effect, manufacturing and industry would offer Americans the opportunity to flourish in a trade that best suited them. Manufacturing, in other words, could be good for individuals. Similarly, American industry would benefit from the 'genius of the people.'

At the same time, though, Hamilton's plans included a clear acceptance of wealth and inequality. To a degree, his plans depended on the reality of an upper class. Hamilton was convinced that the United States would not be able to grow (or recover from the burden of fighting the Revolutionary War) unless the wealth of the upper classes could be channeled into useful endeavors. Ultimately, he thought that the country would benefit when the rich invested their money into a range of productive activities, including manufacturing. Manufacturing was an important part of political economy for Hamilton, who considered it an issue of national security. Manufacturing capacity also meant that the United States would retain its ability to fight a war. In other words, manufacturing would bring a certain amount of independence from Europe.

The Treasury secretary also thought that a national bank was necessary. However, establishing such a bank was not necessarily a foregone conclusion. In fact, two future presidents, Thomas Jefferson and James Madison, were vehemently opposed to the idea. Because Hamilton's plan necessitated a wealthy class of investors and concentrated financial power in the form of a bank, Madison and Jefferson (along with others) believed Hamilton's vision ran contrary to the idea of 'republicanism.' Moreover, both Jefferson and Madison were wary of speculation, which some of Hamilton's ideas seemed to encourage. Hamilton was clearly aware of such criticisms. As the historian Michael O'Conner has pointed out, the bank report to the U.S. Congress was as much a philosophical defense of the very idea of a bank as much as anything else (O'Conner, 2014). Likewise, both Jefferson and Madison took a dim view of Hamilton's *Report on Manufactures*.

While Hamilton advocated for establishing big institutions and systems for addressing economic matters, Jefferson advanced a vastly different vision of what work in American life should be like. For politicians like Jefferson and Madison, independent farming was the ideal type of work for Americans. Working the land as **yeoman farmers** would help foster a desirable set of morals and independence.

As his *Notes on the State of Virginia* reveals, Jefferson regarded manufacturing as a threat to individualism. When he looked toward Europe and its manufacturing, Jefferson saw key differences between that continent and North America. Crucially, Europe simply did not have the same amount of land. Across Europe, the land was 'either cultivated, or locked up against the cultivator.' Because of this, he reasoned, Europeans had no choice but to manufacture things to 'support the surplus of their people.' America, though, enjoyed 'an immensity of land courting the industry of the husbandman.' Given this simple, but important difference, Jefferson argued that Americans should work the land. For Jefferson, this was more than a simple matter of one type of work over another. Manufacturing on a large scale was dangerous and would likely lead to a 'corruption of morals.' Without cultivating and living off of the land for oneself, he wrote, or to be involved in manufacturing ultimately meant a dependence on 'the casualties and caprice of customers.' Such 'dependence,' Jefferson warned, 'begets subservience and venality, suffocates the germs of virtue.' Jefferson ultimately wanted the 'workshops' to 'remain in Europe' (Doc. 2).

Madison echoed such ideas. For these two men, the independent farmer stood in stark contrast to men working in manufacturing, which ultimately meant working for someone else. It seemed incompatible with an emerging sense of American freedom. Manufacturing, in other words, entailed dependence – not just on one's employer but also on the market. As O'Conner points out, Madison, in particular, articulated such fears, reasoning that if a good went out of style, it would be devastating for market-oriented American producers (O'Conner, 2014). For these politicians, it was far preferable that Americans buy manufactured goods from Europe and maintain a degree of individual independence by working the land themselves.

Despite such opposition, the legislature voted to create a national bank. The foundations of an actual economic system had been established. However, the fears of concentrated financial power did not die with that vote. Indeed, worries and actions around banks would persist throughout subsequent decades. The debate between Hamilton and Jefferson over the nature of the economy would reverberate in subsequent years as early American lawmakers argued over the best ways to approach political economy.

In addition to questions about banking and manufacturing, international trade presented another challenge. Early on, American politicians adopted a tariff to protect and foster a domestic market. Indeed, such measures had been an open question as far back as the Constitutional Convention. **Tench Coxe**, for instance, had favored a tariff. However, questions about a tariff and how it might either help or hurt the American economy became especially salient in the early nineteenth century. The War of 1812 had been hard on American manufacturing businesses because the country had been flooded with cheap goods from England. Soon after the war, the United States faced an economic panic. To some, it seemed that the American economy could not be left unattended. **Henry Clay** soon emerged as an advocate for a new tariff (Baxter, 1995). This position, though, was not unanimous. By the time debate got underway, though, it was clear that different sections of the country had different economic interests. Manufacturers in some states wanted a degree of protection from the rough and tumble of international trade. Southern states, by contrast, worried over losing access to overseas markets. It was during this time that Clay (in 1820) articulated the American System, which advanced an active management of the American economy via a tariff. Above all, Clay's American System was in line with thinking that the United States' economy needed to be capable of functioning on its own, and not be reliant on trading partners across the ocean. Even if it was not consistently articulated in a clear manner, these early debates about the structure of American political economy had significant implications for the fortunes of individual Americans.

Significantly, these heated political debates early in the nation's founding unfolded alongside a well-established system that was rooted in unfreedom for large groups of people – slavery. (Some historians have gone so far as to argue that the presence of slavery in North America provided the rhetorical and conceptual framework for the American Revolution and articulations of American freedom). The slave system in North America complicated the connections between capitalism and individualism that philosophers established in their own work.

In many regards, slavery represents one of the first true economic systems in the United States. Though a superficial look at a slave plantation suggests the relic of an earlier system in the midst of a dynamic commercial modernity, it has become clear that American capitalism would not have developed in the same way without American slavery. The connection

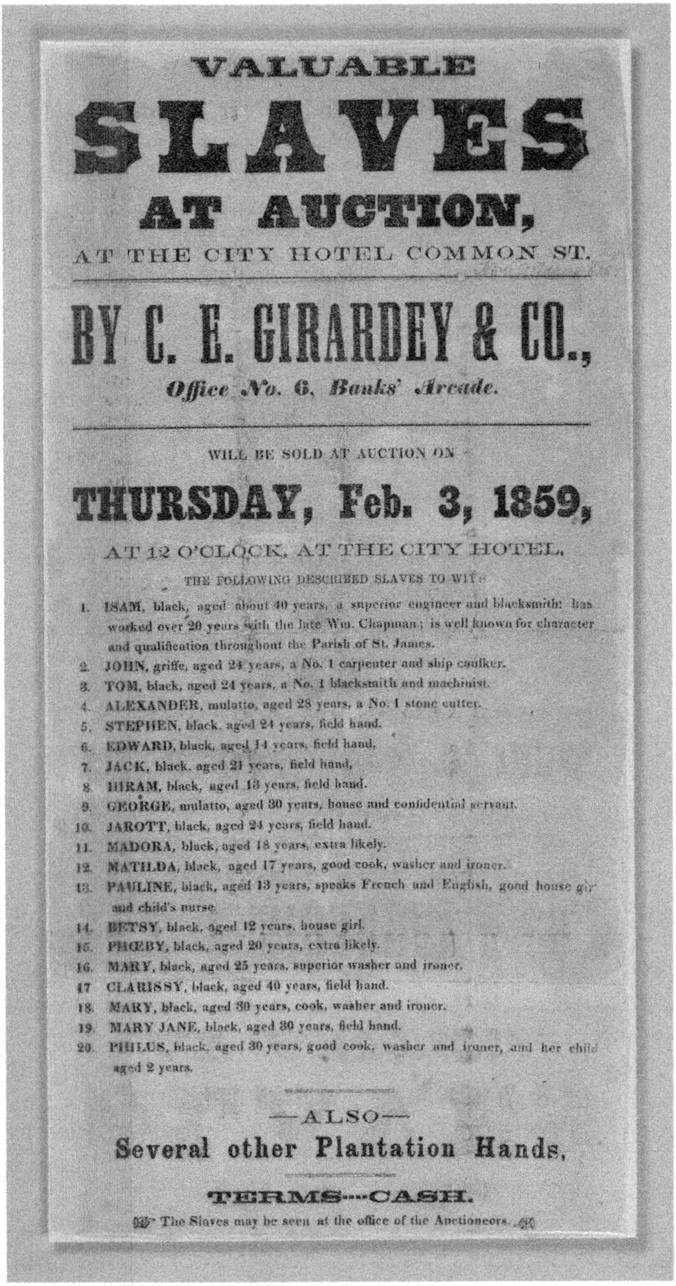

Figure 2.1 Broadside advertising 'Valuable Slaves at Auction' in New Orleans. The market logic and dynamics of the American slave system denied enslaved people's individual humanity. Source: National Museum of African American History and Culture, Smithsonian Institution.

between capitalism and slavery is one example of **racial capitalism**. To be more specific, the form of slavery in the United States was chattel slavery, which meant that slaves could be bought and sold, much like any other type of property. For instance, at a slave market, individual, personal qualities, and physical characteristics helped determined the price for a particular human being.

Consequently, slaveholders enjoyed property rights, one of the fundamental tenets of liberalism that philosophers like John Locke believed was central to ideas of individual liberty. Uncovering the capitalist impulses at work in the American slave system deeply complicates the neat philosophical line connecting capitalism and individualism. Slavery only functioned by depriving individual liberty for a whole group of people. As Daina Ramey Berry observes, 'Sales and transfers from one slaveholder to another marked moments in which a human being was treated as a commensurable commodity' (Berry, 2016: 153). The process by which Black people became slaves and commodities was aided and codified along the way by official policies and laws. In other words, and increasingly by design, individualism could be crushed by the slave system.

American slavery was tied to an emerging global trade in commodities like cotton and sugar. The price cotton could fetch in faraway places, such as Liverpool in England, influenced slavery's continued dominance and expansion into the American South. Such interconnected global markets that comprised the cotton economy directly shaped slavery in the United States. New technologies also contributed to the dominance of the cotton trade, and, by extension, slavery. Almost from the outset, slavery helped to propel capitalism's development – sometimes in surprising ways. For example, as it became clear that the slave system would take root primarily in the South, real estate and land speculation in the 1780s was one result. In the South, enslaved people became intertwined with the financial system. The historian Joshua Rothman observes, enslaved people were assets that owners borrowed against, bought on credit, and at times fueling speculative bubbles (Rothman, 2016).

In fact, because of slavery's centrality to nineteenth-century capitalism, it was a system that also intersected with that era's sense of individualism. Edward Baptist has revealed that in the early nineteenth century, some would-be entrepreneurs acquired land amid real estate speculation (Baptist, 2016). This entrepreneurial rush into the South was sometimes informally called 'Alabama fever.' However, the need to pay the interest on the loans that helped fuel such entrepreneurial dreams meant producing cotton, which was picked by enslaved people. In such instances, the emphasis on individualism collided with the need to subordinate others in the service of individual ambition. After the international slave trade ended in 1808, American slavery moved further south, becoming even further tied to cotton. The expansion of transportation networks, including steamboat travel, helped to stitch the geography of the United States together; it also enabled slavery's expansion.

Though the slave system was connected to a fundamentally global capitalism, that included the entirety of the United States, capitalism in the northern part of the country could superficially appear distinct. In the North, different systems, including an unruly and expanding market, began to take shape. American capitalism really developed in what is now known as the 'market revolution.' Beginning in the late eighteenth century and continuing into the early nineteenth century, significant improvements in infrastructure and transportation systems enabled market exchange across space and time. Engineering achievements like the Erie Canal, which was finished in 1825, had dramatic implications for the path that capitalism took. What this meant was that Americans could now produce for the market. The older master-apprentice system was doomed. As the historians Andrea Rees Davies and Brenda Frink have recounted, work increasingly moved outside of the home and wage labor began to rise (Davies and Frink, 2014).

The expanded transportation networks and the market revolution had vast consequences for the way that business was conducted in the United States. For the first time, something approaching a national market existed. What is more, the geography of capitalism shifted in profound ways. The distance and access to canals and the like could mean the difference between success and failure. Even if individual proprietors did not recognize it, the individual's fortune was now wrapped up in a larger capitalist system. Whole towns flourished or perished depending on their geographic relationships to these new avenues to the market.

As both the debates between Jefferson and Hamilton and the ways in which credit and speculation played an active role in the American slave system suggest, money and credit were questions that loomed large over the commercial life of the United States. In part, credit networks were a necessity because the United States was a 'cash-poor' society. There literally was not enough currency in the country to keep up with commercial activity. In some instances, particularly valuable crops could operate as currency. In colonial Maryland, for example, court records reveal that bushels of tobacco were used as currency. For many decades, business could often be conducted without currency, cash, or specie – the coins themselves – ever changing hands.

For many businessmen in the first half of the nineteenth century, commerce was connected in more ways than one with a sense of individualism. Yet during this time, a sense of self-employment and independence was, as ever, an important value. In the antebellum years, money itself rarely changed hands – credit did. Personal credit, in other words, became an important factor in facilitating business. As Edward Balleisen has demonstrated, to be an entrepreneur during this period was to become part of a deeply interconnected world of other small businesspeople. The men who lived in this world had to address the constant possibility of bankruptcy (Balleisen, 2001). Moreover, accounts of debt and credit for a range of different things were not immediately settled. Consequently, merchants who took part in the market revolution were pulled into open-ended networks where personal reputation and business activity overlapped and informed one another.

For instance, in order for a person to get credit, they might need an **endorsement**, essentially having someone vouch for the borrower. The inner workings of this credit system presented, in some ways, a clear threat to the long-held and still strong sense of independence and individualism in the United States. Rather than the entirely self-reliant yeoman farmer or republican artisan, a merchant or owner of a small business in the early nineteenth century was part of an increasingly interconnected system. In real ways, being a part of the credit economy meant losing some of that much cherished individualism. Even beyond the critical importance of personal reputation, these small merchants were now susceptible to events far beyond their control. Changes in market conditions could quickly spell ruin for antebellum entrepreneurs. The Panic of 1837 demonstrated this condition in a dramatic fashion. In these years leading up to the panic, British manufacturers' appetite for cotton translated to easy credit for Americans engaged in the cotton trade (which was, of course, ultimately bound up with slavery).

As some historians have pointed out, the declining economy in Great Britain led to tightening credit in the United States. For merchants and small businesses, particularly on the east coast, this meant failure and bankruptcy. During the economic expansion of the market revolution, the barriers to entry for new businesspeople, merchants, and so on were relatively small. For someone with an optimistic disposition, the air must have seemed full of promise. Consequently, a number of inexperienced and unprepared would-be merchants rushed into the marketplace only to meet with financial ruin (Balleisen, 2001). As ever, such new economic realities also had direct implications for Americans' sense of identity. To fall into bankruptcy as a result of business misfortune was not just a financial matter. In cultural terms, the proprietor's sense of manhood and masculinity might also be a casualty (Balleisen, 2001).

There were, of course, many reasons for the 1837 panic, and **Andrew Jackson**'s fight with Nicholas Biddle and the Second Bank of the United States was surely one. Jackson became president in 1828 in no small part by fashioning a populist political image for himself, and Biddle's Bank (as it was sometimes called) was an easy political target. Though Jackson has become best known for waging war on native Americans, he was also thoroughly hostile to the concentrated power that the bank represented. The bank itself was not wholly public, nor wholly private, but rather rested in a middle ground between the two realms. In his struggle against the bank, Jackson drew on a populist rhetoric of equality as opposed to the bank's leaders, who had been granted 'exclusive favors' from the government and were using their positions to enrich themselves. It was an opportunity that ordinary men did not have. The president's message resonated with some Americans, particularly in the way the bank seemed to represent an unjust monopoly (Levy, 2021: 112). In 1832, Jackson went so far as to veto a bill that would have rechartered the bank. Four years later, the bank was gone, its charter finished. The whole struggle, which became known as the **Bank War**, paved the way for a much more unstable banking system and contributed to the panic. Both the Bank War and the market revolution suggest that American individualism would now exist in an increasingly complex political-economic system. However, Jackson also extended earlier visions of American individualism.

Jackson's time in office was also significant in which his administration advanced frontier individualism to its bloodiest conclusion. In some respects, Jackson's vision of political economy was similar to Jefferson's vision of individual yeoman farmers, which was hardly innocent. Realizing a nation of settlers working the land would require dealing, somehow, with the native Americans already occupying much of the land. To be sure, conflict and violence had been prominent features in the relationship between North America's indigenous people and European colonists since first contact. However, the connection between the government's support for individual economic activity and dispossession of indigenous land was systemic in the nineteenth century. It was Andrew Jackson who accelerated this process. Though the American government did buy land from Indians in the first half of the century, the government also took this land by force. Laws such as the Indian Removal Act (1830) and the Preemption Act (1841) worked to open up more land for white settlers.

Growing Complexity from the Mid-Nineteenth Century to the Progressive Era

Since the market revolution, the nation had begun a process of becoming interdependent as large-scale public works projects like the Erie Canal helped improve transportation. It was a process that was increased dramatically by the emergence and growth of railroads and, with them, corporations. When railroads first appeared in the nineteenth century, they represented a dramatic change in American capitalism that would have profound implications for notions of individualism. Over the course of the century, American commerce got quicker and far more wide reaching as railroad lines and networks unfurled across the country.

Commodities trading was one way railroad networks transformed older forms of commerce. In what is now regarded as a classic study, William

Cronon explained how Chicago became a central hub for trading all sorts of commodities, such as wheat and grain (Cronon, 1991). Before railroads, a small, independent farmer might sell grain to a merchant, who would ship that commodity to its final destination. With railroads, that same farmer would use the rails to transport grain from farms across the American hinterlands in bushels. Once in Chicago, the grain would be put into grain elevators. By 1856, a few years after the Crimean War changed the global grain market, the Chicago Board of Trade (itself a relatively new institution) established a set of categories for different types of grain. The products of American farms had now been thoroughly commodified. From that point on, grain would be part of an increasingly sophisticated trading system that included buying and selling futures contracts. The appearance of the telegraph also helped the development of the market. The independent, yeoman farmer that had been so central to early iterations of American individualism was linked to an increasingly complex and impersonal system of commerce. Yet the profound change to trading was not the only transformation that railroads and other large corporations ushered in.

The 1860s was a tumultuous time in the United States. The Civil War represented the culmination of a sectional crisis that had been building over the course of the entire century. To be sure, the central issue at stake, slavery, also involved questions of capitalism and economics. What is more, during these years, a number of developments transformed the contours of American individualism and its connection to capitalism. First, and most obviously, the Emancipation Proclamation in 1863 represented a significant step toward ending chattel slavery in the United States. The Thirteenth Amendment to the Constitution in 1865 officially ended slavery (aside from the forced labor of prisoners). Although exploitation and subjugation along racial lines remained a central problem in national life, Black Americans could no longer be considered properly in the precise way that they had been before the Civil War. In addition to the struggle over slavery and the Civil War, the federal government passed a number of measures intended to expand the nation itself with an emphasis on the western part of the continent. In the midst of the war, Lincoln signed a number of different laws, including the Homestead Act in 1862.

The law itself opened up the western part of North America to settlers, in effect giving Americans parcels of federal land for a very modest application fee. The government, in other words, was subsidizing and incentivizing individualism, hoping that the land would be more productive. Yet this did not come without violence. Indeed, this push into the west, a process known as settler colonialism, represented further pressure on indigenous Americans. In sum, a profound reordering of American individualism was underway.

Large commercial and economic operations were not wholly new when the age of railroads arrived in the United States. In fact, early English

Figure 2.2 Homestead Act Stamp, 1962. The Homestead Act encouraged colonial-settler activity in the western United States by mobilizing and encouraging individualism. Source: Bureau of Engraving and Printing Smithsonian National Postal Museum.

colonies in North America, in Virginia and Massachusetts, were chartered as joint-stock companies (Waterhouse, 2017). Still, the corporate form was new enough that it posed a number of important conceptual and legal challenges to nineteenth-century Americans. Corporations themselves had to be chartered by states. At first, such charters tended to be granted only to corporations that might engage in some activity that would be considered beneficial to the public good. Gradually, though, this thinking began to shift. In 1837, Connecticut began to allow for general incorporation. From there, other states also began to allow for general incorporation. These new forms of business organization led to new legal questions which ultimately ended up in the Supreme Court.

The nineteenth century was also a time in which Americans struggled to make sense of the new corporations. For a good part of the century, the legal thinking around corporations was ambiguous and the nature of corporations changed dramatically. Supreme Court cases like the *Bank of the United States v. Deveaux* in 1809 and *Dartmouth College v. Woodward* in 1819 conceived of corporations as 'artificial' beings. Thinking about corporations in this way allowed the corporation to 'act as a single individual' (Trustees of Dartmouth Coll. v. Woodward, 1819). Additionally, the move away from joint-stock corporate charters that were intended to fill some specific need, and toward general incorporation laws, expanded the activities now open to corporations. Finally, in the 1886 Supreme Court case, *Santa Clara v. Southern Pacific Railroad Company*, corporations began to enjoy the same rights that people had under the Fourteenth Amendment.

By the latter half of the century, it was clear that corporations – and the men who controlled them – had a tremendous amount of power. During these years, these corporations would challenge older ideas, including those that connected free labor with individual freedom. This dynamic was most visible along the country's expanding rail network. Labor on the railroads was also deeply problematic. To be sure, it was hard work, and the threat of bodily injury was very high. Moreover, the racial and ethnic tensions that characterized much of the Gilded Age (and beyond) extended to railroad construction. In the American West, railroad companies often relied on Chinese immigrants to help build the lines. The employment arrangements were often very unfair and exploitative. Railroad companies would work with businesses that supplied contract laborers – but this arrangement was hardly a free exchange. The companies that found the labor deducted various charges before they paid the workers themselves (White, 2011). (These same companies followed a similar process with Japanese workers.) In these cases, Chinese workers would have to pay back the travel costs with interest.

Without question, these Chinese workers faced appalling exploitation at the hands of the railroad companies. Companies often withheld some of their meager wages to pay for various and dubious 'fees.' As the historian Richard White and others have noted, the notion of being able to contract one's labor out was a fundamental way in which antebellum white laborers conceived of themselves as being 'free' (White, 2011). Indeed, white railroad workers viewed Chinese labor with an ugly mix of deep-seated racism and economic anxiety during the economic depression of the 1870s. These Chinese immigrants soon found themselves in a bind. White workers began to see contract work as distinctly nonwhite and, therefore, inferior. These tensions around such labor practices in the western United States culminated in overtly racist policy prescriptions.

Specifically, they informed the Chinese Exclusion Act of 1882 and the Foran Act of 1885, both of which targeted immigrant labor. In this moment of labor tension and racism, we can clearly see how the processes of capitalism intersected with politics – just one of the reasons that it makes sense to think of the United States as having a 'political economy' and not just 'the American economy.'

Yet such overtly racist laws were not the only ways in which a sense of individualism – and the rules that governed individualism – shifted during these years. In all, American political economy changed dramatically over the course of the nineteenth century. In particular, risk became a new concept that emerged that, as the historian Jonathan Levy argues, linked older ideas of 'freedom, self-ownership, and the personal assumption of risk' (Levy, 2012: 9). Levy goes on to suggest that new ideas about risk (a concept that spanned a range of fields, such as finance, insurance, and the law) was the product of 'a new individualism and a new corporate financial system' in the nineteenth century (Levy, 2012: 13).

However, such further entrenchment of individualism during these years was not the only development. This period also gave rise to the first regulatory agencies in the country. The first of these was the Massachusetts Railroad Commission, which was created in 1869 with Charles Francis Adams, Jr., in the leadership role. This impulse for systemic fixes to American capitalism was heightened during the Gilded Age, when monopoly power seemed to be an ever-present threat. In fact, these men worked to develop monopolies and other business practices that would crush competition. This emphasis on stifling competition was a core argument among **Progressive Era** reformers at the turn of the century.

At points during the Progressive Era, the idea of individualism could be used to draw a contrast to big business and even form the basis for trust-busting. President **Theodore Roosevelt**, for instance, had gone to great lengths to cultivate a public image of manly individualism (despite his far-from-humble background). Roosevelt himself had been born to wealth and privilege but through books such as *The Strenuous Life* as well as his exploits with the Rough Riders, Roosevelt appeared to be the very essence of American masculine individualism. This persona would serve him well when he entered political life. Though he would eventually become associated with progressivism, Roosevelt was not an obvious candidate for this role. In many ways, progressivism seemed at odds with individual action and freedom. Still, Roosevelt's concern over large industrial combinations was in line with progressive concerns.

When he was president, Roosevelt became known for 'trust-busting.' In the early years of the twentieth century, Roosevelt took measures to prevent illegal or potentially harmful corporate combinations. These actions led to a famous exchange between the president and J.P. Morgan. When Roosevelt's administration invoked the Sherman Act in an effort to stop a merger between two railroads in 1902, Morgan reportedly suggested that the Administration 'send your man to my man' to 'fix it up' (Rego, 2008: 105). Roosevelt was apparently appalled by the suggestion that the two were equals. The federal government, he reasoned, should rightfully have more power and authority than any one business or businessman. In subsequent years during his presidency, Roosevelt and his administration moved to stop a price-fixing scheme hatched by the 'beef trust.' Most famously, in 1906, his administration invoked the Sherman Antitrust Act to break up Standard Oil, though it would not be until 1911 before the dissolution was complete.

Roosevelt was just the most prominent example of how Progressive Era reformers made the case for trust-busting (and generally reigning in big business) in part by drawing on the rhetoric of individualism and invoking long-cherished American ideals such as artisan producers. Roosevelt's image as a trustbuster and the use of the Sherman Act to topple Gilded Age behemoths like Standard Oil were the most visible examples of Progressive Era economic regulation. It was during these years that Congress established the Department of Commerce (after the president publicly called for it). Likewise, the Hepburn Act gave the Interstate Commerce Commission the ability to set railroad shipping rates. In broad terms, Roosevelt's economic agenda became known as the 'Square Deal.' The political scientist Paul Rego argues that when he invoked the phrase in political speeches, Roosevelt was trying to articulate his regulatory interventions and trust-busting as actions that would secure American individualism (Rego, 2008).

Roosevelt was not alone in his attempts to balance checking corporate power with an emphasis on individualism in the Progressive Era. When **muckrakers** like the journalist **Ida Tarbell** took on monopolies like Standard Oil, the outrage could sometimes mix with a sense of admiration that was rooted in American ideals of individualism. In her series of articles that eventually became the book *The History of the Standard Oil Company*, Tarbell charted John Rockefeller's rise and ultimate domination of the oil business before explaining how his practices had helped to quash competition and ultimately corrupt the political process. However, before reaching some of these conclusions, in some of Tarbell's earlier articles, she described Rockefeller in ways that clearly drew on popular understandings of individualism, despite Rockefeller's own declaration that the era of American individualism had passed. In Cleveland, where the oil business was growing, Tarbell wrote that Rockefeller 'was but twenty-three years old when he first went into the oil business, but he had already got his feet firmly on the business ladder, and had got them there by his own efforts' (Tarbell, 1904). In a passage where Rockefeller speaks for himself, he remembers an episode from his boyhood when he experienced the 'pleasure' in working for a neighbor 'digging potatoes.' Although he was only a young teenager, John Rockefeller labored 'from morning until night.' In addition to his work ethic, though, Rockefeller was also smart with this money. As he recalled, 'as I was saving these little sums I soon learned that I could get as much interest for fifty dollars loaned at seven per cent' as he could 'digging potatoes for 100 days' (Tarbell, 1904). In a phrase that reveals how race and slavery cast a long shadow over the American mind, the young Rockefeller decided 'to let the money be my slave and not make myself a slave to money' (Tarbell, 1904).

In another installation, however, Tarbell explained the ways in which Rockefeller's business practices ultimately ran contrary to American values of individual initiative. As his power grew, she explained, he became the enemy of 'the producers and independent refiners of the Oil Regions' (Tarbell, 1904). These men, she wrote, 'believed in independent effort – every man for himself and fair play for all' (Tarbell, 1904). These independent spirits, Tarbell explained, 'wanted competition' and 'loved open fight.' Indeed, 'it had become the moral code of the region' (Tarbell, 1904). In this telling, it was Rockefeller's business practices and deals with railroad companies to secure **preferential shipping rates** that were undoing the more noble, independent form of business. In one of her more colorful passages, Tarbell explained that Rockefeller's ability to command better shipping rates for himself and his company enraged his competitors. She wrote, 'Every particle of independent manhood in these men whose very life was independent action had been outraged' (Tarbell, 1904). To be sure, Tarbell's argument in *The History of the Standard Oil Company* was grounded in the era's political economy. Her work dealt with questions around monopoly power, preferential shipping rates, and an unsavory connection between government and business. All of these were questions that both Gilded Age and Progressive Era Americans struggled with. However, that Tarbell both established Rockefeller as a self-made man and his villainy in contrast to purer notions of individualism and competition is a testament to the cultural power behind such ideas.

Other Progressive Era reformers, such as **Louis Brandeis**, invoked the idea of the individual in making their case for business reform. In the late nineteenth and early twentieth centuries, some Progressive Era Americans drew on American ideals of individualism – the individual producer and small businessmen – to make the case for business reform. When Louis Brandeis wrote *Other People's Money* in 1914 to warn Americans about the **Money Trust**, he described concentrated wealth as antithetical to American democracy and a threat to small businessmen that went to the very core of their identity as men. In words that echoed some of the ideas behind **artisan republicanism** that had permeated the nation much earlier, Brandeis wrote, 'Vast fortunes like those of the Astors' were 'inconsistent with democracy' (Brandeis, 1914). Ultimately, though, Brandeis was concerned with the ways in which what he termed 'dynamic' wealth used people's money against them. 'The fetters which bind the people are forged from the people's own gold,' he ominously declared (Brandeis, 1914). Indeed, for Brandeis, the overall danger that the Money Trust posed was the ways in which it exerted control at multiple levels of the economy. In his telling, during the wave of consolidations in the late nineteenth century and the workings of J.P. Morgan and others, 'railroads, public service corporations, and industrial concerns were brought into complete subjection' (Brandeis, 1914). Even more worrisome, the threat of subjection and control threatened to unman a nation of independent producers – a tradition (or at least a national myth) that ran as far back as the nineteenth century. Notably, Brandeis warned that 'far more serious even than the suppression of competition is the suppression of industrial liberty, indeed of manhood itself' (Brandeis, 1914). In this line, Brandeis tapped into the long-standing belief that working as an independent producer was crucial to economic and political independence, as well as a man's core sense of self. In fact, Brandeis's argument for using the Sherman Antitrust Act to break up these large businesses was intimately connected to this existential threat to American manhood. These 'money lords' had the ability to deny crucial access to capital. What is more, the power of the monied interests also meant that independent businessmen could not really challenge them effectively. 'He who openly opposes the great interests,' he commented, 'will often be found to lack that quality of "safe and sane"-nee which is the basis of financial credit' (Brandeis, 1914). The threat of having access to this capital was significant enough that few would dare to stand up to Morgan. While Brandeis did write that 'here and there you will find a hero, – red-blooded and courageous, – loving manhood more than wealth, place or security, – who dared to fight for independence and won,' yet he also concluded the United States 'cannot be content with conditions that fit only the hero, the martyr or the slave.' For Brandeis, then, the anticompetitive nature of the money trust was 'undemocratic' and substituted 'the pull of privilege for the push of manhood' (Brandeis, 1914). It is important to keep in mind that in writing such lines Brandeis was deliberately trying to convince a broader public about the necessity of using the Sherman Act in an area of the economy that remained abstract (it still is to this day). It is significant that in making his rhetorical choices, he referenced ideas about the independent businessman and manhood. His choices, in other words, hint at the pervasiveness and staying power that these ideas continued to have in American life.

Even if Americans widely bought into the belief in the individual making his way, in reality, there was an entire institutional edifice helping him the whole way. For instance, the 1905 Supreme Court case *Lochner v. New York* eliminated laws that governed how many hours one could work. The ruling stated that a worker and an employer had the right to enter into a contract with one another. In fact, such a freedom to enter into a contract was, according to the ruling, 'part of the liberty of the individual' which was protected by the Constitution. The ruling was overturned in the late 1930s. Still, the original Lochner ruling provides evidence of a powerful connection between capitalism and the individual in the United States.

The new slate of laws and regulations introduced during the Gilded Age and Progressive Era did not exclusively focus on reining in big business. The rules and systems governing the ways in which Black Americans participated in economic activity also changed. Almost immediately after emancipation, formerly enslaved people were subject to disenfranchisement on a number of different fronts. Much like slavery was a system that deprived Black Americans of freedom, rights, and citizenship, widespread racist practices and **Jim Crow laws** comprised another unfair system that hampered individual economic aspirations for Black Americans. In the slave-holding states, Black Americans were suddenly no longer property.

Navigating economic matters would now be very different. However, this new status arrived with its own problems.

In the former slave states, many Black Americans in the South found themselves working as sharecroppers. This system was a form of debt peonage. These sharecroppers would work the land, providing the landlord with crops for profit. Though sharecroppers were allowed to farm a bit for themselves, they were also caught in a cycle of debt that was nearly impossible to escape. Other Black Americans found employment as domestic workers.

Still others struck out on their own as individuals working for themselves. However, the legacy of slavery had thrown a number of significant barriers in the way. Former slaves did not have access to capital, and white supremacist attacks – both violent and legislative – systematically rolled back much of the early Reconstruction period. These impediments directly shaped the direction that these early Black entrepreneurs took. Working as barbers and in catering were two early paths. Indeed, well into the twentieth century, local barbershops would remain an iconic image of the small Black business.

Even with emancipation, these Black businesses were shut out of a full market. Indeed, one of the legacies of ***Plessy v. Ferguson***, the 1896 Supreme Court ruling that formalized segregation, was that Black businesses developed markets that served Black Americans. After the Civil War, then, Black entrepreneurs found themselves in a unique situation. With Jim Crow and the Supreme Court ruling in place, they did not face direct competition from white businesses. Rather, Black businesses were serving Black customers. However, as Juliet Walker points out, Black businesses did not enjoy the same access to capital that white businesses did (Walker, 2003). During these years, Black-owned banks and insurance companies emerged to provide access to the sorts of financial services that were being denied to Black Americans. In fact, Maggie Lena Walker became the first woman to start a bank in the United States, the Saint Luke Penny Savings Bank, in Virginia.

Walker, though, was in some ways the exception to the rule. Women, regardless of race, faced numerous barriers to fully participating in economic life. The ideology of **separate spheres** proved enormously difficult to shake. This belief structured policy and practice around women in the workforce. In fact, there had always been a degree of discomfort with women working outside the home. In the twentieth century, public policy could be shot through with a tension between offering women the opportunity to operate as individual economic actors and the desire to provide a frankly paternalistic 'protection' against the world of work. For example, the 1908 Supreme Court case, *Muller v. Oregon*, affirmed that state's law which imposed a maximum on how many hours a woman could work. The decision did not impact the working hours for a man. The logic behind such a decision (and other state laws like Oregon's) centered on the idea of protecting women. In fact, the Supreme Court case that eventually ended the Lochner era in U.S. law was based on a 1932 law in Washington State, 'Minimum Wages for Women.' As the name suggests, the law established a minimum wage for women (and children) in an effort to protect their morality and health. As such laws (and the logic behind them) indicate, claims on 'individualism' were highly gendered and reserved for white, Protestant men.

Systems of Capitalism in the Modern Era

In the first years of the twentieth century, the American economy continued to grow in size and complexity. Consequently, the twentieth century brought even more need for developing systems to help manage capitalism. Economic and commercial coordination during World War I highlighted this reality. During these years, the future president Herbert Hoover was serving as Secretary of Commerce. In this capacity, Hoover worked on rationalizing and coordinating business activity toward the larger goal of the war effort. After 1918, when the war ended, Hoover continued to lead the Commerce Department in this fashion. In some ways, Hoover was attempting to create systems of business that were not so dependent on the actions of specific individuals. Rather, Brian Balogh suggests that Hoover used the Commerce Department to establish an associational state (Balogh, 2015). Through both the department and **trade associations**, economic activity was intended to be orderly and cooperative. It was during these early years of the twentieth century that organizations such as the **U.S. Chamber of Commerce** and **the National Association of Manufacturers** first appeared. These choreographed actions resulted in aspects of commercial life that are still recognizable today, such as industry standards. However, such coordinated economic activity did not mean the same thing as government regulation. Trade associations like the American Petroleum Institute actively (and effectively) argued against industry regulation. What is more, the men in charge of government after World War I believed that prosperity and progress would ultimately come from the private sector.

Despite the growing complexity of American capitalism, the 1920s also represented a period of institutional retreat. In addition to Hoover's work at the Commerce Department, **Calvin Coolidge** sought to restore the 'passive presidency,' and his Treasury secretary, **Andrew Mellon**, also advocated a hands-off approach to the economy. Even if Hoover emphasized the coordinated efforts of large organizations, the 1920s seemed to be a time when individual fortunes could be made. Likewise, Coolidge offered what amounted to updated iterations of Adam Smith's invisible hand. Coolidge might have been ultimately concerned with a general sense of prosperity, but it was something achieved through the aggregate of individual action.

Mellon was opposed to the impetus behind the Sixteenth Amendment to the Constitution, which established federal taxes. In fact, Mellon used his position to lower the tax rate throughout the 1920s. During this time when an emphasis on business and prosperity seemed to reign supreme, the stock market began to assume a more prominent role in American commercial life.

Yet for all of the prosperity that seemed to characterize the 1920s, the decade ended with a shock to the system. With the onset of the Great Depression and 1929 stock market crash, to be a lone individual was to face a frighteningly uncertain future. If some Americans had celebrated the success of individual investors throughout the boom times of the 1920s, the reversal of fortune for some was shockingly swift. On October 24th, which would become known as 'Black Thursday,' millions of shares traded hands amid panic selling. The pattern of losses continued throughout the next week. The drop in stock prices might have been bad enough for some, but to make matters worse, a lot of those stocks had been purchased on margin or with 'call money.' In effect, Americans had borrowed in order to buy. To be sure, there were plenty of Americans who did not own stocks, and the crash was not the primary cause of the Depression, but the event portended a much broader crisis to come.

Consequently, American government was forced to reassert its management of these larger systems. Although the country had experienced financial panics in the past, the magnitude of the Depression was staggering. Banks and other businesses were failing at an alarming rate. Throughout the first few years of the 1930s, the unemployment rate shot up, hitting over 25 percent in 1933. Hoover, who was elected president in 1928, seemed temperamentally unsuited to the moment. During his time as Commerce secretary, Hoover had encouraged business coordination. However, amid a growing economic crisis, such an approach was inadequate. Infamously, Hoover insisted that the economy would turn around before too long even as 'Hoovervilles' – Depression-era homeless encampments – cropped up around the country. Although Hoover's administration eventually created the Reconstruction Finance Corporation, it would be his successor, **Franklin Delano Roosevelt**, who would redirect government resources toward economic recovery.

Because the problems of the Great Depression were vast, the responses – from all quarters of American life – were equally large. In responding to the challenge, Roosevelt redefined the relations between the American public and the federal government in ways that could sometimes seem very personal.

In some ways, the sense of individualism that seemed to define American cultural ideals moved into the background during the 1930s. During the Great Depression, many Americans wanted stability above all else. As cultural historians have argued, Americans wanted to 'belong' and 'fit in' during these anxious years (Recken, 1993). Such anxiety borne of economic turbulence contributed to the success of **Dale Carnegie**'s 1936 book, *How to Win Friends and Influence People*. In this book, Carnegie seemed to turn away from values and ideas that had been central to American individualism, such as hard work and financial thriftiness. Instead, Carnegie's book was about being liked and having self-confidence. In other words, it was a modern attempt to tackle the economic challenges of a modern era; and there was not much room for earlier ideas of rugged individualism. Roosevelt's administration and the New Deal similarly offered a slate of new projects and programs that in some ways seemed to deemphasize the sort of individualism that Hoover had extolled before the crash.

For instance, New Deal projects such as the Civilian Conservation Corps created job opportunities and job training programs for many American men. In some ways, the CCC seemed to operate in a military fashion. This was not some rugged individual striking out on his own – it was about being a part of a much larger whole. Other New Deal programs, such as the National Recovery Act (which attempted to get businesses to hold the line on prices and wages), also inserted the federal government into economic life. When a business owner placed a blue eagle poster in the window (signaling a business's participation in the program), it revealed how complex economic life had become.

Simultaneously, though, individual Americans began to feel the presence of the government more directly than they had in the past. Lizabeth Cohen has likened it to Roosevelt becoming the very face of the government for many Americans (Cohen, 1990). Roosevelt himself had been sure to cultivate a paternal and approachable image. Famously, the president instituted regular radio addresses known as 'fireside chats.' The effect of New Deal programs was significant in the way they seemed to change understandings of the American Dream for the working class. Now, this ideal was connected to federal action in many respects.

With programs like the Tennessee Valley Authority and Rural Electrification Authority, the New Deal also helped in providing electricity to parts of the country far beyond city centers. In this way, the yeoman farmer living out Jefferson's dream of American independence could now operate within a more modern economy. The Home Owners Loan Corporation was another New Deal initiative that helped many Americans save their homes through generous mortgage terms. Other New Deal-era laws similarly tied the individual to the state in clear ways. Most notably, the Social Security Act introduced a safety net for many American workers that included insurance for both unemployment and old age. However, the shifting relationship between the individual and the state had vastly different implications based on one's race or gender. Critically, Social Security was directly linked to work in ways that excluded many Black Americans and women from enjoying these new benefits. Neither women's work, such as domestic labor, nor the work that was primarily performed by Black Americans qualified for Social Security. Likewise, the Home Owners Loan

Corporation established a rating system for neighborhoods around the country. This rating system resulted in **redlining**, a practice that gave a neighborhood a bad rating if it was predominantly Black or if the white inhabitants were from undesirable parts of Europe. The consequences of redlining would be far-reaching, impacting neighborhood growth and the ability for Black Americans to accumulate generational wealth.

Yet amid all of this transformation, the New Deal still traded on ideals of American individualism. This was particularly the case with the Farm Security Administration's photographers, who documented the plight of agricultural workers in the southwest whose lives had been upended by the **Dust Bowl. Roy Stryker** sent photographers out through the parched landscape, tasked with producing images that would illuminate the experiences of the Dust Bowl. In response, the photographers produced a number of images depicting Americans that had fallen on hard times. Notably, many of the most iconic images from this project focused on single subjects, depicting Americans as bruised, but dignified, individuals. The New Deal may have been an era defined by big solutions to big problems and public works projects, such as the gargantuan Hoover Dam, but the works of photographers like Dorthea Lange offer a testament to how ideas of American individualism persisted through such massive change.

Beyond programs meant to stabilize the economy amid the Great Depression, during World War II, the federal government took other measures to keep the economy moving. Even before the United States entered the conflict, the Roosevelt administration redirected the nation's industrial capacity toward producing for the war effort. Of course, the U.S. had taken similar steps during the First World War, but the New Deal and Great Depression meant that the context in which war production took place was quite different. Through new government entities such as the War Production Board and Defense Plant Corporation, government became intimately involved in steering economic activity.

Much like the New Deal before it, the war effort immediately called up questions about American capitalism, citizenship, and identity. Business leaders regarded such developments as further evidence of government overreach. Some business owners resented and resisted further government intrusions into their operations. The most dramatic instances of this tension between employers and the administration took the form of manufacturing plant seizures. Yet these business leaders also used the war as an opportunity to promote the ideals of free enterprise. Organizations such as the National Association of Manufacturers and **the Chamber of Commerce** were particularly active in this push, producing radio spots and publications extolling free enterprise. The historian Mark Wilson argues that notions of individualism factored heavily in this public relations campaign (Wilson, 2016). Fascism, as it turned out, provided a foil that allowed American business interests to conflate free people with free enterprise. The implication, of course, was that American individualism was best secured through a brand of capitalism that largely left businesses to their own devices.

Most prominently, business advocates and leaders attached a Fifth Freedom of free enterprise to the **Four freedoms** that Roosevelt articulated to the public as a rationale for U.S. involvement in the war. In some regards, the public relations push was successful. In a sharp contrast to the Depression years, the enlistment of private corporations in the war effort helped businesses and businesspeople depict themselves as important elements in the fight against the Axis powers. In this way, even amid the massive coordination across business and government to mobilize industrial capacity to prepare for war, understandings of individualism and its relationship to American capitalism's evolution still shaped public debate.

The war ushered in other changes, too. Economic issues are always also political issues, and this connection is often present in the struggle for racial equality in the United States. Indeed, civil rights strategies often involved economic matters. In fact, because the United States had waged war against overtly racist adversaries, in the 1940s, prominent Black Americans saw a rhetorical and political opening to pursue greater equality across a range of issues, including matters of money, jobs, and business. One example of this was A. **Philip Randolph**'s threat of a March on Washington to protest segregation in the growing defense industry. Amid World War II, President Roosevelt was eager to avoid such a public relations problem and, in exchange for canceling the march, signed **Executive Order 8802**, ushering in anti-discrimination employment rules for defense contractors.

In some instances, the government's response to economic issues during the war intersected with citizenship and identity in complex ways. Notably, the U.S. government relied on laborers from Mexico to make up for the shortages in agriculture as male U.S. citizens left jobs to fight in Europe and the Pacific. In some ways, this was not a new arrangement. For years, agricultural operations in the southwest had relied on laborers who migrated back and forth across the border on a seasonal basis. Still, since 1917, with the passage of the Immigration Act, such patterns and practices existed in a legal gray zone. Because that law imposed fees on authorized immigrants, workers informally moving across the border were crucial to the agricultural labor supply in the United States. The war exacerbated this need. Consequently, in 1942, the United States and Mexico entered into an agreement called the Bracero Program, which allowed for Mexican laborers, or braceros, to work as contract workers on farms in the United States. To be sure, the program was controversial. Prominent figures in the U.S. labor movement were vocal critics, suspecting that the program would depress wages for American farm workers. Likewise, the braceros who arrived often faced both racial hostility and deplorable living conditions. Despite these problems, though, the Bracero Program outlived the war and was renewed repeatedly until 1964. However, this arrangement highlighted vexing questions about how work and American identity were connected. How individuals have labored has long been central to cultural ideas of what it means to be an American. This labor strategy decoupled work with citizenship for Mexican immigrants on farms in the American southwest.

The Bracero Program and all its contradictions are just one example of the systematic exclusion that permeated the economy, and how government institutions continued to be a focus of political struggle. All of the changes and developments that both the New Deal and the war effort brought meant that American capitalism would look different after Allied victory in 1945, and understandings of individualism would change, too.

Postwar Systems

If the 1930s represented a peak of twentieth-century economic instability, and World War II represented political turmoil, in the postwar era, beginning in 1945, the United States entered what seemed to be a period of relative stability. This is not to say that American capitalism had been purged of conflict. In fact, a strike wave immediately following the war offered a testament to a newly empowered labor movement. Nonetheless, much of the postwar era seemed to represent a move beyond the Depression. It was also an era in which the wild economic disparities that seemed to have defined the U.S. economy after industrialization appeared to have abated. As recent economic analysis has shown, the wealth gap was much smaller than in the past. What is more, the experience of the Depression and war had led to a new common sense when it came to government involvement in the economy. In fact, the British economist John Maynard Keynes provided the prevailing logic for managing the economy. Across the globe, and through institutions such as the **International Monetary Fund** and the **World Bank**, governments committed to full employment policies. **Henry Luce** also provided a sense of U.S. global responsibility in his essay 'The American Century.' It was an age of big systems and solutions, much like the New Deal era. The postwar era, in other words, had big implications for the further development of individualism.

In some ways, though, older ideas of American individualism still had enormous political power. Just as organizations such as the Chamber of Commerce and National Association of Manufacturers worked throughout the war to rehabilitate the image of big corporations and shouted that the New Deal was tantamount to an attack on capitalism itself, business-allied politicians after the war set their sights on rolling back some of the gains that unions had made. In fact, though the Wagner Act offered a big boost to labor, in 1947, the **Taft-Hartley Act** undid some of the most important gains. Most significantly, Taft-Hartley established **'right-to-work' laws** which cut at the financial power that unions had. Moreover, the very name of these laws rhetorically linked gutting union power to ideas of individualism. One did not have to be a part of a collective in order to engage in economic activity. Though labor unions had more power than they had in the past, Taft-Hartley and right-to-work laws set the stage for a gradual erosion of organized labor.

Taft-Hartley had created a patchwork of different environments for labor power in the United States. In fact, throughout the postwar era, companies began to move some operations to right-to-work states, where labor unions had less power. This movement offers just one example of how postwar prosperity as well as American economic might was never quite as stable as it may have seemed to some.

Still, compared to previous years, the United States in the middle of the twentieth century was more equitable than it had been in the past. In his monumental study of income and inequality, Thomas Piketty noted that after the conclusion of World War II, 'the United States was in fact a more egalitarian society' than countries in Europe (Piketty, 2014: 294). However, this sense of economic equality did not extend to Americans who were not white.

Despite such clear evidence of exclusion, some observers drew lines connecting socioeconomic mobility and American culture. The link between American capitalism and what it meant to be an American was visible again. For instance, in a classic sociological study that he began in 1950, David Potter argued that the nation's 'economic abundance' was tightly linked to the 'American character' (though such terms were full of assumptions about that American – white, male, heterosexual, and probably a Protestant). It was a dream (not a reality) of a classless society.

Yet it was a dream that could end in a rude awakening for Americans. The pervasive sense of individual upward mobility meant that class distinctions were not nearly as pronounced as they were in other parts of the world, particularly Europe. According to Potter, an American sense of 'equality' meant 'the universal opportunity to move through a scale which traversed many levels' (Potter, 1954: 91). This sensibility, he noted, 'breeds great expectations' (Potter, 1954: 99). However, Potter clearly saw this as somewhat of a 'myth' in the twentieth century (even if he did not question its validity in earlier periods of American history). The economic and social systems of the mid-twentieth century had become too complex to support such simple aspirations. Americans could no longer change their lot in life by striking out for the frontier. Indeed, the abundance that Americans enjoyed meant that even if one was down on their luck, they could find renewal just beyond the horizon – remaking themselves on the frontier or in a city.

When this reality ran up against the deeply held belief that an individual was in command of their own destiny, the results could be rough. Americans were, Potter wrote, 'less able to psychologically adjust' to a lack of mobility. As a result, Americans would either 'lose confidence in themselves or rebel' (Potter, 1954: 101). Notably, in this analysis, the individual bore the brunt of a much wider problem. 'By presenting an unattainable ideal as if it were a reality,' he warned, 'the mobility drive has created damaging psychological tensions' (Potter, 1954: 102). Still, Potter was sure to note that the class differences that existed in the United States were not the same as those in Europe. In fact, such a sense of upward mobility might have even worked as a way to prevent the sort of revolutions and uprisings one could see elsewhere in the world. Indeed, in Potter's telling, literally moving from one place to another in America's vast geography was the primary means by which one could move up in life.

Neoliberal Systems

However, the sense of prosperity that some – though certainly not all – Americans felt did not last forever. By the late 1960s, as factories and businesses left cities such as Detroit, blue-collar workers faced an unemployment crisis that directly fed into what was more broadly termed the urban crisis. As is so often the case in American life, it would be Black workers who faced the initial brunt of these changes. When such good-paying middle-class jobs left cities in states like Michigan, there was nothing left to replace them. The situation would continue to worsen over the next decade. Making such connections between civil rights goals and expanding economic opportunity continued throughout this period. A range of civil rights groups expressed a number of different visions of Black participation in the economy. Some called for more white-owned businesses to support Black enterprises. Even in the early 1970s, Jesse Jackson's Rainbow/PUSH Coalition worked for gains in Black employment and called on white businesses to provide more contracts to Black-owned businesses. The loss of these jobs and the social problems that accompanied this economic transformation was hardly the only shock that hit the American economy.

By the early 1970s, **inflation** was also getting out of control. Prices began to move upward, changing the daily experience of many American households. The **oil embargo** in 1973 and 1974 made matters far worse. A dollar simply did not go as far as it once had. To make matters worse, the economy did not seem to be growing. This pernicious combination of rising prices amid an otherwise flaccid economy became known as **stagflation**. In sum, the early 1970s represented a dramatic reversal of fortune for the nation. It was also the first glimmering of an economic transformation that would undo the New Deal and postwar emphasis on managing the economy.

At first, though, the Nixon administration tried to manage the unfolding crisis with its **New Economic Policy**. With this plan, the Nixon administration attempted to stabilize the economy with wage and price controls. At the same time, the administration stopped linking the U.S. dollar to the price of gold, a decision that would, in time, contribute to the growth of the financial services sector. When the political scandal of Watergate put an early end to Nixon's presidency, the country was hardly in better economic shape. His successors, **Gerald Ford** and Jimmy Carter, both confronted the same problems, though their approach was far different than Nixon's New Economic Policy.

Both presidents set about deregulating part of the American economy. In Carter's case, **deregulation** proceeded along the lines of forcing competition and breaking what consumer advocates like **Ralph Nader** saw as **regulatory capture**. Actions like deregulating the airline industry were moves that bore a striking resemblance to Progressive Era reforms and actions against large companies in the name of smaller business and competition. Carter also tackled inflation with the chairman of the Federal Reserve, **Paul Volker**, who pushed interest rates up, essentially causing a recession that finally broke the decade's inflation crisis (though not without a personal cost to many who lost jobs).

One of the ways in which some sought to rehabilitate the public opinion of business (and, by extension, capitalism) was to focus on business education in the United States. At the collegiate level, especially in Southern states, business school classes focusing on the 'entrepreneur' began to emerge. These classes offered a systemic focus on the individual, even though much of the twentieth century had been defined by businesses that were getting bigger and bigger. As the historian Bethany Moreton argues, the students who took these classes were most likely destined to end up as rank-and-file employees in larger corporations (Moreton, 2008). However, the curricula that they encountered in undergraduate classes emphasized a spirit of individuality. It was, in that sense, a perfect education for the rise of neoliberalism, which emphasized the individual as well.

Though deregulation of the economy was already underway when Ronald Reagan assumed the presidency, once in office, Reagan extended both deregulation and an emphasis on entrepreneurialism. Beyond defense spending (in which the new administration spared no expense), Reagan's approach to economic management and business regulation reflected the neoliberal, market-oriented thinking that gained traction throughout the 1970s. This turn toward neoliberal policy-making was not limited to the Republican Party. Some **Atari Democrats** representing states that had a stake in new high-tech industries advocated for a new approach to the economy that represented a clear departure from an earlier emphasis on unions. Individual economic actors now occupied a central place in U.S. political economy.

The 1980s would also prove to be a time when the stock market took off and Wall Street seemed to represent the center of business life. Fittingly, this type of economic activity emphasized individual success, not the larger, coordinated moves that typified the middle of the twentieth century. At least some popular accounts suggested that middle-class Americans had suddenly turned to the stock market. In 1987, a story in *Time* magazine championed the 'millions of individual Americans who are making a private killing in the wild bull market of the 1980s' (Koepp, 1987: 14). Simultaneously, though, the rise of finance also overshadowed another economic change – the decline of manufacturing in the United States. Wall Street in the 1980s may have created large individual fortunes, but the often-celebrated American middle-class life began to slip. In fact, the wage compression that had been a key aspect of postwar prosperity began to widen. Foreign competition had been building over the previous decades, placing pressures on U.S. manufacturers that they had not really felt in previous decades. Japanese companies in particular seemed to be the future of industry.

When Bill Clinton signed **NAFTA** into law in 1993, it offered a definitive symbol of manufacturing's disappearance. As NAFTA suggests, though Clinton's election meant that a Democrat had returned to the White House for the remainder of the 1990s, the new president did not fundamentally alter the neoliberal approach to the economy. Throughout the course of the 1990s, Clinton signed a number of bills into law that continued the march of deregulation and faith in markets that had started in the 1970s. Ultimately, the most consequential act of deregulation would prove to be the **Graham-Leach-Bliley Act**, which regulated the financial services industry and undid some of the protections that had been put in place as a part of the New Deal.

Issues of individualism were also at play in the 2008 financial crisis in more ways than one. First, the crisis was fueled in large part by a drive toward home ownership. This long-held value also translated into policy, both in George W. Bush's ownership society and in directives to Fannie Mae and Freddie Mac. Given that home prices were continuing to rise in the early twenty-first century, conditions were ripe for fraud. Unscrupulous mortgage companies and other institutions offered Subprime mortgages to Americans at a remarkably fast clip. The business practices were dubious at best and criminal at worst. Over the course of a number of years, more and more Americans were brought into a web of risk that was amplified as investment banks and other financial institutions spread that risk around the world by using a number of complicated financial products. The stage was set for disaster. Once the introductory rates on many of these original mortgages changed and homeowners began to default on their loans, a global economic crisis ensued.

The failure seemed to strike at the heart of the American Dream. Many Americans lost their homes or postponed retirement as huge amounts of personal wealth disappeared. Banks themselves teetered on the precipice of collapse, and after some heated arguments and failed votes, Congress passed a massive bailout package for financial institutions in an effort to forestall a complete economic collapse. Many Americans, though, were angered by what they saw as the federal government abandoning individuals and families in a time of need in order to help wealthy banks and bad actors. As would become clear in subsequent years, the crisis – and the government's response – deeply wounded the perceived relationship between politicians and ordinary Americans. In other ways, though, post-crisis actions, such as the creation of the Consumer Financial Protection Bureau, represented new ways in which systems of regulation were designed to directly impact the fortunes of individuals in the United States.

The systems of both commerce and regulation in the United States have hardly been static. Rather, they have evolved and shifted in response to a range of different factors and developments. Moreover, these systems have not always been the product of consensus but have grown out of sometimes furious debate. Throughout, the role of the individual and individualism has moved in and out of focus. At the same time, however, it has been clear that the degree of agency and the options individuals have are in large part shaped by these very systems.

3 Organizations

Though philosophies, ideologies, policies, and systems have all played a consequential role in capitalism's development, many Americans most directly experience American capitalism in their lives through their experiences with specific organizations. As the course of American history moved on, the size and complexity of these organizations grew. Along with this growth, the impact on the individual would change, often in conjunction with specific parts of a person's identity. Indeed, the organizations that increasingly defined American capitalism would have big implications for individualism and associated values such as freedom and independence.

While there have long been large-scale commercial enterprises that engaged in trade across entire oceans – such as the slave trade – a fair amount of commercial activity in the early Republic was conducted on a small scale. Businesses relied in part on a network of 'factors,' or merchants, who helped broker deals between merchants and other commercial concerns. Such arrangements could bear directly on one's identity.

Ideas of manhood and independence were in flux after the Revolution. Even before American independence, concepts of masculinity were tied to notions of economic and business acumen, and in the years after the American Revolution, an ideal of artisan republicanism became dominant, celebrating the small, independent producer. The apprentice system was also a fixture in the early Republic. With such arrangements, an apprentice would live with the master craftsman's family, working in the home.

There was a lot at stake in shoring up the myth of individualism. Working for wages could even be a reason for suspicion. Likewise, Jeanne Boydston points out that working for someone else did not necessarily comport with a new sense of independence (Boydston, 1996). Was a man really a man if his livelihood rested on another man paying for his labor? However, the reality of economic life and success during these years was more complicated and interconnected than the lone artisan laboring away. In fact, both husband and wife had to work to keep a household afloat. Indeed, this arrangement holds true today for a range of situations, including small farms and businesses.

DOI: 10.4324/9781003090526-4

Rather than the lone figure of the self-made man, during the mid-1700s, 'competency' became a term that described a household's successful balancing act of operating in the market while also maintaining some aspects of self-sufficiency. Under such terms, economic success was not simply a matter of entering the commercial world but of maximizing home resources. Many women worked in the house but produced goods for the market. In some cases, households literally employed women from outside the family with wages to help manage the work needed to run the home. In fact, women could sometimes enjoy a degree of flexibility when it came to the market and work. Masculinity may have been precarious in light of a changing economy, but women did not face these sorts of challenges. 'Women's work,' in other words, could mean many different things.

Though 'Republican motherhood' became one of the signal ideals of the era, in colonial North America and after the American Revolution, women participated in economic activities in a number of ways. In cities, women could participate in a more commercial market, working in a variety of trades. Eventually, as gender categories and roles began to solidify, women's presence in the market and commercial world was less and less welcome. The rise of 'separate spheres' as an idea clearly demarcated the home as the appropriate space for women. As some historians have argued, elite women who did not rely on the market for their livelihood also pressed in this direction. But the ideal of separate spheres remained out of reach for many women. For instance, working-class and rural women might 'take in' work to complete at home. Women have always performed labor that has been instrumental to capitalism's functioning in the United States. However, much of this labor has gone unrecognized, unmeasured, and, most importantly, unpaid. In fact, as the historian Eli Cook has argued, the language and instruments of measuring the economy could obscure women's work (Cook, 2020). Women's labor was deliberately left out of official accounting. As Cook points out, even the word 'priceless' – which was used throughout the 1830s and 1840s – suggested that certain activities should not be measured in economic terms. The word reflected a belief that certain realms of activity needed to be protected from the crassness of the market – one of the core tenets of the ideology of separate spheres. However, the word 'priceless,' as well as the belief system that it involved, served to 'bracket off certain pockets of life from the cash nexus' (Cook, 2020: 33). In fact, Cook points out that as white men in the nineteenth century developed quantitative methods of measuring the economy, they were not creating objective instruments but were instead 'universalizing specific class interests' (Cook, 2020: 33). Identifying women's work in this way is just one example of how popular understandings of individualism and capitalism are infused with gendered logic.

In general, business during these years was often conducted by smaller firms where, importantly, the operator and owner of the business were one and the same. Some historians have called this period the era of the **entrepreneurial firm**. These firms were run by their owners and could often be small in size. As always, though, the small sense of scale can be deceptive. Though business might have appeared to take place on such an intimate level and felt local and personal because of these factors and entrepreneurial firms, these people and transactions were connected to a wider, global capitalist system that was always present. Gradually, though, some businesses became larger, particularly over the course of the nineteenth century. As they did, the fates of individuals would change along with these developments and would be highly dependent on one's race, class, and gender.

In contrast to individual merchants and entrepreneurial firms, slave plantations in the cotton-producing states operated on a much larger scale. One of cotton capitalism's key developments was **Eli Whitney**'s cotton gin, which he devised in 1793. The cotton gin facilitated the fast removal of cotton seeds, turbo-charging production and leading to the dramatic expansion of the American slave system. Additionally, over the course of the nineteenth century in the years before the Civil War, the trade in slaves became increasingly dominated by professionals. Slavery also became increasingly 'rationalized' and systemic. By the nineteenth century, cotton was big business and the vast majority of it came from large-scale plantations in the Southern states. Just before the start of the Civil War, over 80 percent of cotton came from plantations that were over 100 acres in size. As Sven Beckert notes, these large plantations also accounted for over 90 percent of the slaves in the United States (Beckert, 2014: 110). To be sure, these were violent places, dependent on the brutal denial of individual freedom for Black Americans.

Overseers punished and disciplined enslaved people with brute force. In fact, the historian Ed Baptist has argued that some of the 'innovations' that plantation capitalists developed were essentially more brutal forms of torture and terror to keep the enslaved people disciplined and efficient (Baptist, 2016: 93). Significantly, the efficiency and productivity of slave plantations steadily increased throughout the nineteenth century. The economists Alan Olmstead and Paul Rhode argue that new varieties of cotton were largely responsible for this increased efficiency (Olmstead and Rhode, 2008). Yet the ways in which this productive, efficient, and profitable system was achieved were in part the result of devising ever new ways to get enslaved people to work harder, including developing new forms of violence and new weapons, including different types of whips, and ways of organizing work on the plantations themselves. Sven Beckert argues, 'The all encompassing control of workers – a core characteristic of capitalism – experienced its first great success on the cotton plantations of the American South' (Beckert, 2014: 115).

As recent historical scholarship has shown, slavery as a system was wholly infused with capitalist logic. Crucially, slavery's capitalist drive also had the effect of denying enslaved people's humanity. Slavery was a violent and brutal system, but that violence was also 'rational' and calculated. Slave plantations also used accounting systems that were more sophisticated than the methods businesses used in the more industrialized North. Owners and overseers on Southern plantations used these modern methods of measurement to extract as much value as possible from enslaved people (Rosenthal, 2016). Overseers could use this information to figure out just how productive an enslaved person could be – and to figure out when they might be deliberately slowing things down. This measurement and surveillance were used to set picking paces and quotas. Here, however, the men who ran these slave plantations kept the enterprise running by relying on torture that could even be precisely connected to missed production targets. As accounting practices developed alongside large-scale plantations, enslaved people were referred to and categorized as 'hands, rhetorically dismantling any acknowledgment of individual humanity.' The highest category of a slave was called a 'prime field hand.' From there, less-productive slaves were talked about in 'fractions of a hand.'

Moreover, the cotton that was produced on these slave plantations served both global markets and domestic manufacturing enterprises in Northern states, like Massachusetts. Textile manufacturing was an important part of New England's economy in the early decades of the nineteenth century. Beginning in about 1815, a number of merchants in the region formed the Boston Associates to operate the mills. However, the mills in this part of North America were meant to offer a big contrast to England. As factories amid that country's Industrial Revolution roared to life, they revealed a gruesome scene. English factories were notoriously dark, hot, loud, and unsafe. **Francis Cabot Lowell**, one of the Boston Associates, set up his mills along the Merrimack River and tried to present the mills in a pastoral setting – nestled in an otherwise natural environment. Despite the idyllic setting and the close association that the mills had to New England, they were also part of a global capitalist system. In fact, Francis Cabot Lowell set out to produce cheap clothing for slaves in the American South (perhaps even the same slaves who picked the cotton in the first place). Enslaved people even began to refer to any rough cotton cloth as 'Lowell.' In this way, Lowell and his mill were able to supplant Indian cloth (Beckert, 2014).

In addition to their connection to a global economy and slavery, the New England textile mills were also notable for the young women who came from the surrounding countryside to live and work there. As the historian Sven Beckert observes, the use of women as labor meant that the families in the area could – at least for a time – remain on the land (Beckert, 2014). Indeed, for many, factory work did not necessarily represent a new opportunity as much as it signaled the disappearance of more familiar patterns of work and life.

However, the Lowell Mills were more than just a factory. Francis Cabot Lowell believed his mills could fulfill a much loftier role: helping to instill 'republican values.' In addition to a strict work schedule at the looms, the young women of Lowell also worked on improving themselves. The work schedule at the mills was intensive. The women typically worked six days out of the week. The workday itself was twelve hours – and, in what was a new experience for them – bells rang at specific times to start and end the work day. The time away from the loom (on Sundays) was devoted to improvement. The women attended lectures, read, and even produced periodicals such as *The Lowell Offering*, writing poems and essays. This pedagogical, moral aspect to mill life made recruiting easier. However, along with the educational opportunities that were available to the mill girls, their labor and, more generally, their daily schedules were tightly controlled by the operators.

Though women had been involved in textile production before these mills appeared, the nature of the work was very different. In addition to bells that rang at different times to regulate the rhythm of the day, the looms and other machines meant that the space was loud and hot. The pace of work – of spinning and weaving – was also faster. Moreover, the women found that they labored under a form of capitalism that did not allow for too much freedom. As the historian John Kasson notes, the women could find themselves 'blacklisted' for any number of infractions and unable to find work elsewhere (Kasson, 1976). What is more, the women were never meant to spend their entire working lives in the mills. Rather, the Lowell Mills employed the women for a few years before they went on to a different stage in life (presumably marriage). This method of employment also prevented the women from organizing in any real way. Still, the mill girls were hardly passive in the face of such labor conditions. By the mid-1840s, the women in the mills formed the Lowell Female Labor Reform Association. However, in what has become a perennial capitalist strategy, the men with the money simply shifted production abroad – to Spain, in this case. The totalizing aspect of the Lowell mill was one way in which nineteenth-century experiments with business organization threatened to overtake the sense of individualism that had long been a part of some Americans' thinking.

The Rise of the Corporation in the Latter Nineteenth Century

As the nineteenth century wore on, the growing scale of business organizations presented further challenges to a sense of American individualism. A lot of organization and coordination was required to operate new enterprises, such as railroads. In effect, the internal workings of railroad companies had to become standardized and orderly, with systems of reporting up a hierarchy. This arrangement was, to put it mildly, a long way from the sort of individualism that continued to be a part of an imagined American identity and – more to the point – masculinity. The appearance of these large-scale corporations profoundly changed the ways in which white men experienced work. While Jefferson's yeoman farmer represented a small, independent producerist ethos that became an enduring mythos of American life and culture, large-scale corporations presented a serious challenge to this understanding. White men quickly filled the ranks of these new business firms. As the **managerial revolution** (as the historian Alfred Chandler memorably termed it) took shape, this new professional class experienced a distinct lack of autonomy (Chandler, 1977). Without question, these new arrangements offered lessons in efficiency and the ability for companies to continue to grow, but they also created the need to remake understandings of American individualism.

In part to deal with the anxieties of this new working life, the new class of office workers developed romantic notions about other types of American life. Some retreated to health spas, where they exercised on strange contraptions called Zander machines. The devices (and there were many different types) were meant to mimic the sort of physical activity one might experience outdoors. A new and mysterious ailment – **neurasthenia** – also appeared. The symptoms were maddeningly vague. The office workers who were diagnosed with neurasthenia might have felt fatigued, but the cause was generally thought to be brought on by the hectic, disorienting pace of modern life. The treatment, much like the Zander machines, was to get away from urban life and reconnect with nature. In other words, neurasthenia and Zander machines were cultural responses to the changes to working life that these large corporations introduced.

In other ways, these large-scale corporations seemed to represent a distinct threat to ideas of individuality and independence. As these corporations developed into monopolies, it became harder and harder for independent businesses to compete. The **economies of scale** and organizational strategies such as **horizontal integration** and **vertical integration** put independent businesses at a distinct disadvantage. The juxtaposition of work that increasingly took place inside corporations and what seemed to be the disappearing and dwindling fate of individual economic pursuits produced a range of different responses.

The world of working-class industrial culture ran along similar lines, though the stakes were even higher. In the nineteenth century, labor – in both its practices and who got to practice it – was intimately connected to ideas of what it meant to be white. As we have seen, the idea of the individual producer was a central conceit of American democratic ideology. Beginning with Jefferson's ideal of the yeoman farmer, the idea of 'freedom' presupposed that a man (since those in power couldn't conceive of a woman in these terms) worked for himself. The appearance of wage labor in the nineteenth century, though, presented a significant challenge to such notions. Increasingly, as the labor force included immigrants from different parts of Europe, the idea of labor, whiteness, and freedom became mixed up with one another. In fact, during these years, ideas of who was white and who was not could be very, very narrow. For instance, David Roediger has demonstrated how Irish and German immigrants had to fight to establish themselves as 'white' by emphasizing their own difference from Black Americans (Roediger, 1991). These anxieties around racial status and the long-standing ideal of personal liberty permeated working-class culture in the nineteenth century. In fact, the rapidly changing idea of individualism and work during the nineteenth century also provided Southern states the means through which they would defend the slave system. In the decades leading up to the Civil War, the South's defenders repeatedly tried to draw a contrast between slavery and wage in labor in the North.

In sum, the size and scale of these new businesses, such as Carnegie Steel and Standard Oil, were incomprehensible for many Americans, and it quickly raised fears that – for many – went right to the root of the American character. Political cartoons railing against the evils of big business often represented the corporations themselves as monstrous or royal (or sometimes both) pitted against the small producer. One such cartoon was titled 'The Tournament of Today' and depicted a medieval joust between railroad monopolies and a small, pitiful worker.

Figure 3.1 The Tournament of Today - a set-to between labor and monopoly, Graetz, F. 1883. This political cartoon reveals the conflicted nature of individualism in the Gilded Age. The individualistic Robber Barons appear as spectators rooting for the demise of the beleaguered farmer – himself a far cry from Thomas Jefferson's idealized yeoman farmer.

This was hardly a fair fight – and that was the point. The knight representing the railroad had thick armor that at certain points morphed into parts of a railroad train. Wheels replaced the horse's legs, and, just to make sure the viewer did not miss the point, the illustration included the word 'monopoly' on the side. Rather than a dashing hero, the knight was in the process of thrusting the jousting javelin into the unprotected breast of his opponent, who was riding a malnourished nag and was armed with nothing but a hammer. The laborer himself seemed exhausted. The uneven fight was also reflected in the different audience members. Behind the railroad knight, a few of the more famous Robber Barons, including **Vanderbilt** and **Jay Gould**, watched behind lavishly draped stands, while a huddled mass of ordinary folk watched as the bare-footed laborer on the tired old horse waited for what seemed like certain death. This political cartoon, typical of the time, neatly illustrates the threat to individualism that Gilded Age corporations seemed to present. The idea of an equal playing field did not seem to exist anymore. The laborer in the joust seemed to exemplify the loss of autonomy and vigor that would come from honest and free labor. Significantly, the man was fighting a corporate body – not another man. The inclusion of words like 'monopoly' and 'subsidized press' suggested that a whole range of institutions, from the government to newspapers, were lining up against ordinary Americans.

The cartoon also hints at some of the other ways in which the relationship to individualism amid capitalism's rapid development was more complex. The clearly recognizable Robber Barons in the illustration reveal that even as corporations grew into big bureaucracies employing thousands, they were so new and unfamiliar that popular representations of the Gilded Age economy still centered on specific personalities. In many ways, Peter Knight suggests, the Gilded Age represented a particularly fraught and contradictory understanding of the fate of the individual in an era in which the world of work and business was morphing into increasingly complex and hierarchical systems (Knight, 2016).

In addition to the managerial revolution that transformed working life in the offices, a similar rationalizing and mechanized approach to physical labor was also an aspect of the Gilded Age. Division of labor, of course, had been a featured value of capitalism even before Smith's *Wealth of Nations*. However, in the Gilded Age, such logics could extend all the way to individual bodily movements. **Frederick Winslow Taylor** produced the most coherent and systematic concept of this rationalizing impulse with his so-called 'scientific management.' Taylor himself was an engineer by training and approached factory work with this mindset. In 1883, Taylor began his stopwatch time study of laborers while working for a steel works in Pennsylvania. It was through this process that he was able to develop a **piecework** system of managing and monitoring worker productivity and efficiency. Aided by his stopwatch, Taylor studied the movements of workers in order to determine 'the exact series or elementary operations or motions.' From there, Taylor would excise 'all unnecessary movements,' preserving only the 'quickest and best movements.' The very movements of workers, in other words, should be standardized. In order to capitalize and promote his ideas, Taylor created the Manufacturing Investment Company in the 1880s. Taylor and scientific management provide a particularly extreme example of an increasing impulse toward organized, deindividualized work in which men (and they were, during these years, all men) were but mere parts of a larger whole. Taylor published his ideas in 1911 in the book *The Principles of Scientific Management*. For the owners and executives of industrial corporations, scientific management had an obvious appeal. In practice, though, things did not run as smoothly as Taylor would have hoped.

Black Business in the Early Twentieth Century

While the rise of big business and ideas like scientific management presented new challenges to ideas of individualism, Black businesses faced a different set of obstacles. Shut out from many of the formal avenues through which the American economy functioned during the era of Jim Crow, some Black businesses and business leaders attempted to forge a separate economy. Vicki Bogan and William Darity Jr. have documented how some of these Black businesses also had to develop strategies around being denied access to retail stores (Bogan and Darity, 2008). Despite such challenges, though, it was clear to some Black leaders that business would play some sort of role in racial uplift. As many scholars have argued, two of the era's most prominent Black leaders, **W.E.B. DuBois** and **Booker T. Washington**, were very interested in the role that Black businesses could play in pushing for racial equality after the Civil War. Working toward such ends, DuBois organized a conference titled 'The Negro in Business' in 1899. Washington established the National Negro Business League at the start of the twentieth century two years later.

Throughout the early twentieth century, both DuBois and Washington drew attention to Black business and spoke publicly about the issue. As at least one scholar has observed, Washington was such a towering figure when it came to notions of Black business that his vision dominated such discussions. However, the business historian Shennette Garrett-Scott has tracked how debates about Black businesses became far more varied after Washington's death in 1915 (Garrett-Scott, 2009).

One particular injustice that Black businesses faced was the precarity of their wealth. Capital and businesses could literally be destroyed in outbreaks of racial terror, as was the case in Tula's Greenwood neighborhood in 1921. The historian Juliet Walker writes that through atrocities like the Tulsa Massacre, individual Black success stories were literally erased from the map (Walker, 2003). In addition to these spectacular outbursts of violence, the practice of **whitecapping** –forcing Black businesspeople to leave a specific town – represented another way in which white supremacists targeted Black businesses. Perhaps most systemically, though, white banks and lenders simply denied Black business owners access to working capital and lines of credit. Some of the most basic instruments of business, in other words, were out of reach for Black Americans. Consequently, as Juliet Walker argues, Black businessmen such as Herman Perry have been omitted from the longer narrative of American individualism and business success (Walker, 2003).

Such overt racial hostility and violence was not the only challenge that Black entrepreneurs faced. At other times, particularly outside of the South, non-Black-owned businesses (usually with greater access to capital) operated in Black neighborhoods, competing directly with Black businesses. Despite these challenges, there was a lot at stake in the success of individual Black businesspeople. The Great Migration, which began in the early part of the twentieth century and accelerated with World War I, fundamentally reshaped the relationship between Black Americans and capitalism. After leaving Southern states, many recent transplants to Northern cities with industry meant that Black workers had better-paying jobs and spent their money at Black-owned businesses. What is more, with Black Americans in northern cities concentrated in specific neighborhoods, like Harlem in New York, the connection between Black businesses and consumers could be strong. Much as both DuBois and Washington had done earlier, many leaders and organizations linked the fate of Black businesses to a broader effort for racial uplift. During the 1920s, though, such thinking veered away from Washington's original vision. Rather, as Garrett-Scott suggests, some initiatives focused on an economic vision that complemented wider Black nationalism (Garrett-Scott, 2009).

Washington's view of using business as an avenue to a broader racial equality ran alongside more overtly Black nationalist efforts. Most famously, **Marcus Garvey** founded the Universal Negro Improvement Association and the Black Star Steamship Line. This specific business was intended to help Black people achieve economic independence apart from a broader and overtly racist society. By the time Black Star Line was announced in 1919, Garvey had become, in some respects, a religious figure, but this was a business endeavor. Not only would the business provide jobs for Black workers, it would also offer luxury travel accommodations for Black passengers who were denied such services on white ocean liners. The business would also offer shipping services. Garvey hoped the venture would build economic independence across the African diaspora (Hancock, 2018). However, Black Star Line ultimately proved to be unsuccessful. Negotiating capitalism's evolution along with both systemic racism and outright racial hostility continued to present a challenge to Black Americans throughout the twentieth century.

Similarly, Native Americans also had to adapt to the era's dramatic changes. Scholars such as Brian Hosmer have argued that a number of nations in different parts of the continent were able to adjust alongside capitalism's growth (Hosmer, 1999). In some cases, these changes included incorporating the values of individualism. For instance, in the late nineteenth century, commercial logging among the Menominees in Wisconsin fostered the growth of an entrepreneurial class with 'individualistic values concerning economic behavior' (Hosmer, 1999: 61). Hosmer describes a 'complex interplay between cultural and economic change' that included both 'evolving concepts' but was 'still rooted in certain fundamental values' (Hosmer, 1999: 222).

The Corporation in the Modern Era

In many ways, the conflicts of the Gilded Age and early twentieth century reflect a genuine ambiguity about the larger role that the corporation was playing in American life. Undoubtedly, though, the businesses themselves were getting bigger and bigger. Perhaps the most iconic business in this regard was the Ford Motor Company. **Henry Ford** devised a production system for his Model T that was so large in scale and so successful that the term **Fordism** became an easy way to describe production methods for the first half of the twentieth century. In order to produce the Model T, Ford looked back to the principle of division of labor. When he placed that assembly line on a moving conveyor belt in 1913, the resulting **continuous assembly line** was indeed revolutionary.

Producing his company's signature Model T became more efficient and faster. As the car slowly rolled along the conveyor belt, each employee could focus on one aspect of putting the car together. The new approach to car manufacturing proved to be wildly successful. Just five years after introducing this production method, more than half of the cars in the United States were Fords. From there, Ford moved production to his River Rouge plant in Dearborn, Michigan. It was a massive operation, employing over 80,000 men during the 1920s.

Yet, Fordism could complicate notions of individualism. The Model T itself offered wide access to the automobile, which would, over the course of the century, come to symbolize an individualistic sense of freedom in the popular imagination. Moreover, Ford instituted a five-dollar-a-day wage, which was very generous, in 1914. However, the continuous assembly line threatened the autonomy of the company's workers. Most of the company's workers were recent arrivals from Europe, which frustrated efforts at unionization because of issues such as language barriers. Ford also attempted to control the personal lives of his employees through Ford's 'Sociological Department' that investigated the employees' personal lives. Ford's dominance of the automobile industry, though, was relatively short-lived.

By 1928, General Motors, Ford's direct competitor, was the biggest company in the world. In part, **Alfred Sloan**'s organization of different car brands under the umbrella of a single company produced more consumer options, and his approach to production, especially the **annual model change**, was as revolutionary as Ford's approach. However efficient the continuous assembly line might have been, though, it also seemed to provide a central metaphor for this new era of American business. The Gilded Age may have introduced the nation to the first truly big businesses, but companies like Ford and General Motors heralded an unprecedented scope of commercial enterprise. This modern era also had direct implications for the individual who had to operate inside such massive institutions. In some instances, this new business world seemed to demand the subordination of individualism.

For example, in 1927, IBM even published a songbook of hymns dedicated to the company and its founder, **Thomas Watson**. The company offered an expanded edition a decade later. Like much about the ways in which corporations tried to locate a place for individualism amid an increasingly complex organization, some of the songs focused directly on Watson, celebrating the executive as an example of individual entrepreneurialism. Watson was, one song declared, the 'head and soul' of the 'splendid IBM.' The company had 'grown and broadened with his vision' (MacLardy, 1937). Such lines, as corny as they may seem in retrospect, fell squarely in line with a much older sense that a great visionary and entrepreneur was at the helm of a large institution. Indeed, the IBM Songbook can be viewed as a particularly laughable attempt at **charismatic capitalism**. At the same time, however, other lines in '*To Thos. J. Watson, President, I.B.M. Our Inspiration*' were antithetical to older notions of American individualism. Lyrics such as 'We will follow and serve with you forever' reflected the need for corporations like IBM to constrain ideas of individualism, at least enough so that work could get done. Other songs were even more deliberate in the double movement of extolling the supposed individual brilliance of Watson while working to create a culture of homogeneity and obedience at the company. In one song (to be sung to the well-known melody of 'Happy Days are Here Again,') a chorus of IBM men would sing 'All loyal T. J. Watson men,/ Love our noble President' (MacLardy, 1937). The lyrics described leadership as particularly brilliant and inspiring. In contrast to Watson's singular abilities, the singers declared that they would do 'whate'er he desires.' These were hardly bold declarations of American individualism.

Corporate capitalism in the century's first decades also posed a threat to small, independent business owners. Such was the case with the rise of chain stores in the early years of the twentieth century. Chain stores like A&P offered very clear benefits to consumers in the same way that a big store like Wal-Mart would offer today. The effects on local merchants, though, were devastating. The economies of scale offered by these chains opened up the sort of price competition that posed a grave threat to smaller merchants, who began warning of a **chain store menace**. Some of these warnings about the chain store menace were also coming from groups like the Ku Klux Klan. They were, in effect, a blend of racism and anti-modernism, reflecting the era's anxieties and prejudices amid a rapidly changing business landscape.

Likewise, attitudes toward gender and work also reflected the era's tensions. As workplaces became more hierarchal, organized, and complex, women increasingly entered these spaces, but under strictly predefined conditions that echoed earlier ideas of gender and work. Even the geography of large offices was notably segregated by gender. Still, the number of women working in clerical positions in big companies continued to grow. By the end of the 1920s, women performed the majority of clerical work in the United States. Such numbers, though, did not mean that women had suddenly made inroads or cracked a glass ceiling. Most of these jobs were intended expressly for unmarried women and employers assumed that these women would exit the company after their weddings. In fact, even at the twentieth century's halfway point, some businesses would not hire married women.

Famously, World War II meant a change in the composition of the workforce. Women began to work jobs that had formerly been cut off and clearly defined as male spheres. War production demands and men entering the military created a space for women to take up industrial jobs. This development was celebrated in works like Norman Rockwell paintings. His iconic image of 'Rosie the Riveter' offers yet another example of the tension between individualism and capitalism. Working with older American tropes, Rockwell focused on a single, heroic woman instead of the assembly line where Rosie and her fellow workers worked. However, such cultural representations did not document the Black women who also entered such jobs. Moreover, the arrangement was short-lived. After the war the idea (though not the reality) of separate spheres only seemed to tighten, which had clear and direct implications for working life.

The Individual in the Midcentury Corporation

After World War II, the U.S. economy had recovered from the 1930s and seemed poised for an era of growing prosperity. The expanding size of corporations continued apace. The postwar corporation also raised questions about autonomy and individualism. One of the most prominent thinkers in this regard was the management theorist **Peter Drucker,** who conducted a study of General Motors. Drucker's theories about the modern economy were rooted in the horrors of World War II. Drucker himself was Austrian and had witnessed Hitler's rise in Europe. Though he was hardly the only one puzzling through how Nazism had taken hold in Germany, Drucker's interpretation rested on a larger critique of modern economic development. In his analysis, both industrial capitalism and the various permutations of socialist and communist economic systems were overly 'mechanistic,' leading to a widespread existential crisis. For individuals who existed in modern, industrial societies, their existence had become 'irrational and senseless' (Gilman, 2006: 112–113).

In his book *The Future of Industrial Man*, which he wrote as fascism was on the rise in Europe, Drucker contemplated the fate of the individual amid a society that was so mechanistic that individual meaning was lost. 'For the individual without function and status,' he wrote, 'society is irrational, incalculable, and shapeless' (Drucker, 1942: 28). Combating such a catastrophic loss of meaning presented a clear challenge to Europe in the 1930s. By contrast, though, Drucker thought American culture's emphasis on the individual had produced a much more desirable state of affairs. Drucker declared that 'in the society of the American frontier with its complete fluidity, the individual had just as much definite social status and function' as the most elite member of other societies with rigid caste systems (Drucker, 1942: 30). In fact, Drucker went so far as to assert that 'no society ever succeeded as perfectly in integrating its members in a functional relationship between individual and group as the frontier of Jackson, Henry Clay or Lincoln' (Drucker, 1942: 30). Even when contemplating the discontents of twentieth-century industrial society across the world, the myth of American individualism and all of its tropes continued to exert a powerful influence.

The stakes of preserving a sense of individuality amid twentieth-century modernity could not have been higher. Drucker was convinced that Nazism had stepped in to provide a sense of meaning for individuals that had been lost with the arrival of industrialism. To be sure, Drucker was not advocating for a preindustrial mode of life or an embrace of fascism. Rather, he believed that corporations needed to be reformed so that they could help provide a sense of meaning and purpose for individuals (Gilman, 2006). In these earlier works, Drucker was writing in a European context. He had the decline of religious institutions in mind, and not, say, the closing of the frontier. Still, his ideas prefigured later critiques about the corporation in the United States. They also informed some of his own writing about capitalism when he arrived in the United States. It was in the 1940s that Drucker intensely studied General Motors, eventually resulting in his book, *The Concept of the Corporation*. In some ways, Drucker's prescription for what General Motors was supposed to do was also a critique of older styles of American management. Informed by his diagnosis of what had happened in Germany, Drucker offered U.S. managers a path that was very different from Taylor's ideas of scientific management and Ford's continuous assembly line. In all, Drucker thought that workers inside corporations needed far more autonomy.

Ultimately, Drucker regarded corporations as 'social institutions,' serving a purpose beyond simply organizing economic activity. Yet Drucker also believed that Americans would evaluate such social institutions based on how those institutions furthered a goal that was 'beyond society' (Drucker, 1946: 130). To be more specific, that goal was individualism. This larger cultural value had vast implications for the corporation. He wrote, 'The very means which strengthen the corporation and which render it more efficient must also promise to bring about substantial realization of the basic beliefs and basic promises of our society' (Drucker, 1946: 134). Drucker also saw this emphasis on the individual (and, more to the point, a unique individual) as the basis of 'middle-class society.' For Drucker, the core of this middle-class society was that each person could have 'a life in which he has status and function as an individual' (Drucker, 1946: 138). In some ways, these values also translated into a hostility to any sense of a society determined by class distinctions. Moreover, these ideas also had clear implications for work inside the corporation. Because the 'social function' of a corporation was 'as important as its economic function,' the needs of the individual had to be addressed (Drucker, 1946: 140). Indeed, Drucker argued that 'individual dignity and fulfillment in an industrial society' could 'only be given in and through work' (Drucker, 1946: 140–141). Yet this also presented a paradox since 'like every other institution which co-ordinates human efforts to a social end, the corporation must be organized on hierarchical lines' (Drucker, 1946: 141). The solution to this contradiction was that large corporations had to 'offer equal opportunities for advancement' (Drucker, 1946: 141).

Drucker's ideas and conclusions about the corporation as the dominant social institution in a profoundly individualistic society highlight some of the paradoxes and core tensions around capitalism in the middle of the twentieth century. No doubt large corporations and their ability to organize economic activity played a significant role in providing postwar stability for many (though certainly not all) Americans. Yet the same concerns over bigness that worried Thomas Jefferson did not end after the war.

Although the midcentury corporation and business system seemed to represent stability (for those privileged enough to climb the ladder), they also set off a quiet panic among some intellectuals. The critiques that emerged during these years focused by and large on the fate of the individual in these organizations. The *Fortune* editor **William Whyte**, for instance, offered his critique in *The Organization Man*. In it, Whyte worried about the potentially corrosive effect of midcentury life and work in large organizations. American midcentury life, dominated by large corporations, had produced a middle class of men (and, to be sure, Whyte was imagining white, heterosexual men) who had 'left home, spiritually as well as physically, to take the vows of organization life' (Whyte, 1956: 3). Yet the very hierarchical structure of these corporations meant that very few of these 'organization men' would rise to the top. The vast majority of them were 'destined to live poised in a middle area,' as it was this group of middling men who comprised the 'dominant members' of midcentury American society (Whyte, 1956: 3). What ultimately concerned Whyte was a new 'ideology' that seemed to be emerging from this group.

For Whyte, the prevalence of large, midcentury organizations – the corporation chief among them – meant a number of challenges for individuals. Indeed, Whyte had individualism in mind when he wrote the book. Not seeking a wholesale rejection of the organization society, Whyte was concerned with securing 'individualism *within* organization life' (Whyte, 1956: 12). Whyte was also interested in how 'subtle' the challenge to individualism was. According to Whyte, midcentury life for organization men was comfortable and secure. Unlike threats to individualism in the Gilded Age, the 'trapping' in the 1950s was 'mundane' (Whyte, 1956: 13). In some ways, the organization and the individual were pitted against one another. Whyte argued, 'Organization people have concluded that the trouble is that the professional tends to be career-oriented rather than company-oriented' (Whyte, 1956: 446). The solution, from the corporation's perspective, was a program of indoctrination by rewarding the individual with 'company status' and turning the individual into a 'company man.' The implications of creating these company men were vast and the effects corrosive. Everywhere Whyte looked, he saw a society that was increasingly defined by this organizational life and ethos. Indeed, the effects of the organization even spread across the postwar suburban landscape, which the organization man had remade 'in his image.' Indeed, that same sort of conformity that corporations had instilled in their employees now informed community decisions. Whyte warned that in the suburbs, it was often an organization man who 'organizes the committees, runs the schools, selects the ministers, fights the developers, makes the speeches and sets the styles' (Whyte, 1956: 295). Here, though, Whyte may have been ignoring the wife's contribution to such matters.

In effect, what Whyte wanted to do with *The Organization Man* was redefine what American individualism could be in a world in which cooperation and coordination was a necessity. Toward the end of his book, Whyte declared it 'futile to speak of individualism as if unrestrained self-interest will somehow produce the greater good' (Whyte, 1956: 443). Calling upon what he termed 'human relations,' to find more 'living room for the individual' inside the organization, Whyte reexamined some of the basic forms of corporation organization that had been in place since the Gilded Age. In particular, he argued for more autonomy and moving away from an assembly-line approach to work. Rather, allowing corporate men to solve problems creatively was preferable. Ultimately, though, Whyte argued that the individual had to 'fight' the organization, even if Whyte harbored no sense of nostalgia for the sort of Darwinian self-interest that had corrupted ideas of individualism.

Likewise, the lawyer and social science professor **David Riesman**'s book *The Lonely Crowd* called attention to what was happening to individuals' interior lives amid all of this prosperity. For Riesman (and his co-authors, Nathan Glazer and Reuel Denney) modern life had produced other-directed personalities at the expense of an inner-directed character. Notably, the inner-directed character was bound up with a sense of individualism.

Such anxieties, though, were the products of what was otherwise seen as prosperous and stable times. For many, the trade-off seemed worth it (if it they regarded it as a trade-off at all). Perhaps no figure best represented the buttoned-down world of midcentury corporate life than management consultants. Virtually everything about this line of work represented conformity and at least the superficial obliteration of individualism. The dress code for consultants was self-consciously conservative. The suits and – most importantly, hats – were all ways of telegraphing sober-minded business analysis. The work itself also emphasized conformity and standardization. Consultants essentially standardized operations and approaches to businesses when their services were called on. In other words, midcentury management consultants were not products of an era dedicated to rugged individualism. Rather, such men offered clients walking manifestations of the era's emphasis on stability.

However, by the end of the twentieth century, working life would indeed be very, very unstable. Ironically, though, over the course of subsequent decades, these consulting firms would recommend flexible approaches to human resources. In other words, as the historian Louis Hyman has documented, management consultants helped end the midcentury's supposed trade-off between individual expression and the stability of a large-scale corporation (Hyman, 2018). A number of different consulting agencies saw that this emphasis on stability boxed in the corporation in a lot of different ways. Eventually, the language of 'flexibility' gradually took over. Companies might be staffed with independent contractors who could be 'let go' at any moment, depending on the company's needs. Proponents of big business celebrated the gradual disappearance of steady work.

It is also important to note that both the privilege and ennui of postwar corporate life were by and large reserved for middle- and upper-class white heterosexual men. Large, midcentury corporations offered fewer paths to advancement for Black white-collar workers. Some of these obstacles, of course, were deliberate. Others, though, were much more subtle. For example, the historian Pamela Laird argues that a white male executive was likely to select a younger white male executive as his protégé (Laird, 2005). Despite such barriers, some Black entrepreneurs found success amid postwar prosperity and consumer culture. Most prominently, **John H. Johnson** founded his publishing empire, which would eventually include magazines like *Ebony* and *Jet*, in 1942. However, the individual success that men like Johnson enjoyed did not mean an equal playing field. Just as it had been in the past, the individual success in the marketplace that became the stuff of American mythology was much harder for Black entrepreneurs to achieve. There were still many, many doors that remained closed to them.

Women in the Midcentury Corporation

For women and people of color, work was never truly stable. For years, the word 'temp' evoked the image of a young woman answering the phone at a larger company. In the 1950s, services like Kelly Girls helped supply companies with such workers. As Louis Hyman notes, the justification for such obviously exploitative work arrangements relied on the belief that these women enjoyed stability in other parts of their lives. In these imagined lives, temps were either biding their time until marriage or earning some extra money while their husbands were the real breadwinners.

When women did make inroads into corporate life, they did so in ways that, at least initially, did not directly challenge prevailing assumptions about gender. Most prominently, women were able to work in sales for gendered products, such as cosmetics or housewares. One of the most notable examples in this regard was **Brownie Wise**, who pioneered party sales for Tupperware plastic food containers. Wise built a sales force of suburban housewives who would host parties for other women in the neighborhood where the saleswomen would demonstrate how the plastic containers worked. This approach to selling strategically used gender norms and roles, blurring the line between domestic and commercial space, as well as social and economic connections. The party sales also took advantage of postwar capitalism's spatial arrangements. With the suburbs growing rapidly after World War II, Wise had found a captive audience for Tupperware. However, this was not a cynical sales strategy. The company offered a real opportunity for women to earn money and build something of a career. The sales meetings in Florida were often extravaganzas that could sometimes resemble festivals. Wise had clearly found a successful sales strategy. In 1954, she was featured on the cover of *BusinessWeek*, the first woman to be given that honor.

However, Wise's story is instructive because it reveals the ways in which gendered ideas about specific products and the need to sell them to women created opportunities – even if those opportunities were, in many ways, heavily circumscribed. Women might have been the backbone of Tupperware's sales force, but apart from Wise, the company's management team – and true power structure – was entirely male. Ultimately, things did not end well for Wise, who left the company with very little after a falling out with Tupperware's founder. Similarly, during these years, limitations on career advancement led other women, and Black men, to leave corporations to start their own companies.

Gender and the large, midcentury corporation complicated and structured ideas of individualism in other ways, too. Well into the twentieth century, the idea of separate spheres persisted and was sometimes codified in very concrete terms. For instance, the idea of a **family wage** further reinforced the idea that men should be the ones participating in the workforce. As some have pointed out, even the postwar ideal of the husband climbing a corporate ladder was not, in reality, the triumph of a single individual striving in the marketplace. The postwar family was a distinct and powerful norm. In such instances, it was assumed that there was a wife waiting at home for the male executive. As some historians have pointed out, as a man climbed the management ladder in the 1950s, his wife might also sit down for an interview with the company. In these instances, Andrea Davies and Brenda Frink argue, company representatives were assessing the wife's suitability for social events and how complementary the male employee's home life was to his work (Davies and Frink, 2014). The widespread cultural celebration of the nuclear family after the war also portended changes in the way women entered the workforce. Because women were marrying younger, the jobs that single women had filled before the war might now be filled by older women who were also married.

Even if official channels of employment inside corporations were supposedly open to women and Black Americans, the reality could be far more complicated. Alongside official corporate policies, a number of informal practices worked to advance the careers of some while frustrating others. For instance, the white men who joined Rotary Clubs were given access to additional networking opportunities that were closed off to others. Likewise, fixed stereotypes of women – and the language used to describe specific women – could also have an outsized influence on how women faired in the corporate world. Laird notes that less formal means of gatekeeping hindered women's advancement in the workplace. One study in the 1940s reflected many of the sexist assumptions about women in the workforce – that women lacked the drive or vision needed to succeed in a corporate environment. Even as women made strides of all sorts with the feminist movement, these informal, pervasive attitudes still presented problems. Laird observes that women might be labeled as too 'aggressive' should they exhibit any ambition, while also being labeled as 'just a woman' if they did not appear ambitious (Laird, 2005: 261).

For example, the advertising executive **Mary Wells** eventually started her own advertising firm after it became clear that she had hit some sort of glass ceiling. However, though Wells found success by offering her services to companies that wanted to market specifically to women, Wells had to adopt her business persona to join the old-boys club. In this way, Wells forged a business persona that was at once an embrace and rejection of feminine identity.

However, Wells still occupied a privileged and powerful position. For other women, challenges inside the corporation persisted. As feminism and the women's movement in the 1970s sought to address a range of ways that women's lives were negatively impacted, some focused squarely on economic and career issues. However, tackling such issues inside large corporations did not proceed in a uniform fashion. As some in the women's movement pushed to remove barriers to career paths inside the corporation, the plight of women in these other positions suffered. Eventually, as Allison Elias has documented, advice literature encouraged a separation between these older positions for women in business and such newer career goals (Elias, 2015). By the late 1970s, for instance, some publications emphasized individual perseverance in navigating this male-dominated world instead of offering a systemic critique. In other words, women needed to play the game and not challenge the rules. Such advice publications, including the magazine *Working Woman*, offered a path to women who already enjoyed a host of advantages, including more education. However, this brand of corporate feminism that focused on individual achievement and success once again proved the lasting effects of the cultural connection between capitalism and individualism. Likewise, affirmative action measures had sometimes paradoxical implications for women in the workforce. While college-educated white women now faced reduced (but certainly not absent) barriers to corporate jobs, the color of clerical work began to change. As Elias has shown, the number of Black women working in positions that were dismissed as 'dead-end jobs' grew throughout the 1960s and 1970s (Elias, 2018). White collar work was becoming more of a mix between male and female, but this was not the case lower down the wage and salary ladder. Blue-collar jobs that had long been viewed as the province of rugged men remained doggedly male.

Postindustrialism

The emerging service economy, though, was another matter. Without question, the large-scale corporation and the gray-suited men who diligently climbed its ranks offered symbols of stability in the postwar United States. However, this sense of stability teetered at the end of the 1960s. As the industrial economy of the middle part of the century began to give way to more abstract forms of work, new job categories began to appear. At the lower end of the income scale, service work often replaced factory jobs that were otherwise disappearing. When, for example, Wal-Mart began to open stores in the sunbelt, it was often women who went to work not in managerial positions, but on the shop floor. Many of these new jobs – in what we could broadly term the postindustrial economy – did not have the same security and relatively high salaries that came with midcentury industrial work. These new jobs might be part-time, or 'flexible.' In addition to being paid less, these jobs did not include benefits or the security of employment. This type of work could also fall along gender lines – as was the case of Wal-Mart. As the historian Bethany Moreton has argued, 'middle-age mothers' were the 'backbone of the new workplace' (Moreton, 2009: 51). Still, the specter of separate spheres still lingered. Even in the twentieth century, the idea of a family wage clearly suggested that a man should be family's breadwinner.

Significantly, the women who came to work at Wal-Mart in the 1970s and 1980s were entering the official, measured workforce at a time when the 'family wage' was slipping away for many. The part-time, casual work that these women performed for Wal-Mart helped contribute to family incomes that now relied on multiple sources and jobs. Moreton argues that as these women came to work at Wal-Mart, they brought with them broader cultural constructs of which they were a part – redefining the meaning of their work as Christian service to a family (Moreton, 2009). Wal-Mart, in this case, represented a big shift in the way that capitalism functioned. Yet these developments were bolstered by such older cultural ideals and identities. Wal-Mart's rise in the 1970s was not the only shift in the way corporations operated. The end of the 1970s and 1980s revealed a general souring in feelings about the giant, midcentury corporation. The critiques came from various places and from a range of different ideological dispositions, but many of these critiques also had clear connections to a general sense of individualism.

Beginning in the late 1960s, some in the business world worried about the fate of capitalism. Specifically, younger Americans – the very sort who should have graduated college and moved right into corporate ranks – seemed poised to reject corporate life en masse. In the 1960s, the anti-war movement along with the **New Left**'s call for reforming a 'sick society' indicated that the corporation's place in the postwar order was not entirely secure. Large-scale corporations seemed to be the very sorts of organizations in need of reform. Significantly, a loss of individual freedom and meaning were among the reasons that some younger Americans were wary of large businesses. In fact, by the late 1960s, corporations began to worry that such organizations would have to address a growing frustration with the life of a man in a gray suit. By the late 1960s and early 1970s, some business leaders acknowledged that the next generation of corporate executives would demand more 'meaningful' work and more workplace autonomy. Things were changing. Such turmoil offered the first signs of a more general disconnect with American corporations and the ways in which they stifled individual fulfillment. Some in the business community perceived what one infamous memo characterized as an 'attack on business.'

Others, though, determined that corporate life had to change and meet such young people in the middle. This group of thinkers was convinced that working life had to be made meaningful. Some believed that management systems had become too hierarchical, leading to a lack of personal autonomy that many would simply not stand for. By the early 1980s, the sustained critique of supposedly suffocating bureaucracies began to appear in the corporate world itself. Ironically, one of the most prominent calls would come from two McKinsey consultants, Tom Peters and David Waterman, who co-wrote the 1982 book *In Search of Excellence*. One of the book's primary conclusions was that workers needed to have more flexibility and autonomy to experiment. In other words, the two consultants were calling for a little bit of individualism inside the corporation. The economies of scale that had helped create corporate giants in any number of industries were now a burden. The organized, top-down hierarchies that first appeared with the nineteenth century's managerial revolution did not seem suited to a moment that needed employees to be free to quickly respond to changes. To be sure, such assessments were rooted more in the long-standing cultural mythologies of individualism than actual reality. Still, these analyses led to a renewed emphasis on individualism at the end of the twentieth century.

The about face from management consultants regarding the supremacy of the large midcentury corporation was reflected in other aspects of American business. On Wall Street in particular, hostile takeovers and leveraged buyouts in the 1980s (at the hands of corporate raiders) threatened the autonomy and power of these big companies. Such takeovers were indeed controversial, producing clear winners and losers. The employees of an unlucky business that was unable to fend off such an attack braced for pay cuts and layoffs. Yet as destructive as it could be, the action on Wall Street was profoundly individualistic in how it was depicted in the news. For the first time in years, America had genuine business celebrities. Many, to be sure, quickly assumed the mantle of 'villain' in the public eye. The 'Junk Bond King' Michael Milken was perhaps the most infamous example from the 1980s.

The tables seemed to have turned against large corporations. Of course, no one truly acts alone. But at least in the media's telling, individual actors were conquering entire **multinational corporations** in high stakes struggles in the financial markets. Through it all, Wall Street's investment bankers insisted that they were imposing a much needed discipline on these old companies. Wall Street in the age of Reagan signaled the decline of large corporations as symbolic of American capitalism's virtues.

But championing individualism did not necessarily mean egalitarianism. For instance, one classic study of Wall Street culture in the late 1990s reveals that the ideas of who is the 'smartest' often contain unspoken assumptions that the 'smart' person is white and male. Even though Wall Street was infused with the rhetoric of meritocracy and the triumph of the individual, the old barriers that both women and people of color faced in large, midcentury corporations persisted in the world of finance. People who did not fit this unspoken ideal of a 'smart' person found themselves working a 'back office' job. These jobs were less prestigious and less compensated. They were also less secure. The people who worked in these jobs were less likely to get promoted or to keep their jobs. Additionally, the rhetoric of individualism can sometimes have negative personal effects. For instance, on Wall Street, and other highly compensated jobs in the postindustrial economy, some have speculated that it has led workers to accept a high degree of stress and instability in their work lives.

From all angles, pundits, consultants, entrepreneurs, activists, and financiers assaulted the large-scale corporation as a relic of an institution standing in the way of real progress. In the years that followed, smaller, more nimble businesses that provided their employees with more freedom to think with new ideas became what many in the business world considered to be the future.

Throughout the 1990s, such antipathy toward large, bureaucratic corporations could be found inside the companies themselves. The business press filled with terms like the 'intrapreneur' which attempted to reconcile the long-cherished figure of the individual entrepreneur in the overall context of larger organizations that, for the most part, where not really going to go away. For instance, before the Texas-based energy company, Enron, became known for a notorious accounting scandal, business writers and others lauded the company's leadership for giving employees much more free rein in starting new businesses and acting independently inside the company. The company's employee magazine even published feature stories about employees with daredevil hobbies outside of work. Likewise, the company's television advertising campaign touted the 'nonconformist' who always asked 'why?' Enron may have employed tens of thousands of workers, but, at least in the company's telling, each one of them had a fierce independent streak.

Such ideas gained traction in the 1980s and 1990s, fueled, at least in part, by the rise of Silicon Valley. During the 1960s and 1970s, Silicon Valley had existed in a weird mix of high technology and an affinity for the counterculture. **Steve Jobs** in particular was one devotee of both, and this was reflected in the ethos and culture at Apple. Likewise, as the Internet began to transform many different aspects of American life, some business observers were convinced that the era of the large-scale corporation had come to a close. Though Silicon Valley's emergence as an economic powerhouse was initially connected to the defense establishment, it increasingly became connected with the personal computer – a handy symbol for an updated sense of American individualism.

Over the final decades of the century, the culture of individualism in Silicon Valley became pervasive in a number of different respects. CEOs became celebrities and the public images of companies such as Apple and Microsoft (and, later, Facebook) were dependent on the popularity and biography of their founders. Similarly, Silicon Valley workers tended to be far less loyal to specific businesses than had the white-collar workers William Whyte had worried about decades earlier. Job-hopping in Silicon Valley was common, and some have argued that such individualistic behavior contributed to the region's success as ideas and skills traveled along with workers from one company to the next. However, Silicon Valley also reflected many of the same problems and barriers that had long existed in American working life. Indeed, the tech industry's liberatory patterns of work that excited so many remained out of reach for many more.

Even as late as the 1990s, the racial and ethnic employment patterns were very clear. They were, with some exceptions, white. Labor in the United States has always deeply been bound up with race and gender. Gender – and gender exclusion – was also at play in the development of Silicon Valley. For years, high-tech industry, Margaret O'Mara has written, developed in a way that was overwhelmingly dominated by engineers and coders who were white and male (O'Mara, 2019). Well into the twenty-first century, the informal networking that had presented career obstacles for both women and Black workers was very much a part of Silicon Valley culture, in which employment was often tied to informal networking and referrals. In other words, despite the rhetorical and cultural celebration of scrappy, persistent individual entrepreneurs in the late twentieth and early twenty-first centuries, a review of the facts suggests a different (or at least more complex) state of affairs.

Companies like Apple may have retained an image as a company that stayed true to its now-mythic origins in a garage, but it was also a multinational corporation whose products were made by subcontractors on the other side of the world. In many ways, Apple represented a larger operation than firms from earlier decades. Likewise, as much as Wall Street raiders, business journalists, and others insisted that the business world had become more of a meritocracy, open to people who had hit very different brick walls in the middle of the twentieth century, the persistent lack of diversity and representation across a range of industries suggested that individual identity had a lot to do with business success.

However, at least some pundits clung to the idea that individualism was alive and well in the age of globalization. Though giant, multinational corporations often seemed faceless and poised to swallow up the individual figure altogether, some popular accounts of globalization celebrated the ways in which this newer economy appeared to empower individuals around the world. The author and *New York Times* columnist **Thomas Friedman** was perhaps the most vocal and enthusiastic chronicler of globalization. Yet one of the reasons Friedman championed global capitalism was because he believed that it had empowered individuals around the world.

Ultimately, the growth of large work organizations and businesses presented a distinct dilemma for American individualists. From the outset, large corporations seemed antithetical to ideals of the lone individual. In fact, there was something about the concentrated power of such businesses that seemed un-American. Yet at the same time, such organizations fueled economic growth and urban development, connecting geographic regions, and providing a flood of consumer goods. More importantly, large businesses provided stable jobs for many American workers. Yet this stability involved a trade-off, requiring employees working inside these corporations to sacrifice a degree of autonomy. What is more, identity markers, such as race and gender, shut out some Americans from working inside these organizations. Finally, over the course of the twentieth century, the job stability that these corporations may have represented began to loosen as political and economic currents shifted.

4 Mythologies

American capitalism has been supported by various philosophical and political traditions, systems of governance, and different types of organizations. However, capitalism, just like any economic system, needs the consent of people in order to function. In this regard, cultural narratives about individualism have been crucial to capitalism's functioning. American culture, just like any culture, is stuffed with durable, persistent ideas and stories that circulate across long periods of time, sometimes appearing under different guises. These mythologies are enormously consequential, helping to shape belief systems, actions, and understandings of events. In the case of the United States, ideas of individualism have held a central place in these cultural myths and stories. These mythologies are not stable, and there are many different variations, but they have helped cement what might otherwise be a tenuous connection between capitalism and the individual.

American political discourse has long been infused with such narratives. For instance, Thomas Jefferson's vision of an economy comprised of independent farmers was an early manifestation of these cultural mythologies. Even if economic reality ultimately reflected Alexander Hamilton's plans, Jefferson's more romantic vision has never really disappeared. In fact, it is just one example of this broader cultural myth.

Defining the American Character

More than anyone else, it was **Benjamin Franklin** who most fully developed enduring ideas about how an individual should proceed in the commercial world. Just as importantly, subsequent voices called on Franklin in order to give American capitalism its most enduring and durable character: the self-made man. As the historian Pam Laird notes, the idea of the self-made man was not always connected to the idea of business success (Laird, 2005). Rather, the ideal originated with an earlier Calvinist emphasis on improving oneself and serving the community. In the United States, Benjamin Franklin popularized the idea with works such as the

DOI: 10.4324/9781003090526-5

'Way to Wealth.' Franklin was, among other things, a prolific writer and crafted a compelling public image as someone who, through tremendous hard work, had pulled himself out of adverse conditions and had evolved into a man of stature and importance. Crucially, though, he did not offer the same sort of rags-to-riches story that would become so familiar to Americans. To be sure, Franklin did draw attention to economic matters, but in discussing traits such as thriftiness, Franklin's writing was couched in explicitly moral terms.

In addition to the self-fashioning in his autobiography, Franklin also promoted the ideas of individual virtue in a fundamentally commercial nation using a character he created named 'Richard Saunders,' better known as 'Poor Richard.' The character first appeared in Franklin's 1733 book, *Poor Richard's Almanack*, but perhaps the most direct statements about individual virtue and economic matters appeared in the 1758 edition of the almanac, *Poor Richard Improved*. In the preface to that book, Franklin wrote under the character 'Father Abraham,' who Franklin claimed was a 'plain clean old man, with white locks' (Doc. 3). In a fictitious homily now known as 'The Way to Wealth,' Father Abraham provides a host of little aphorisms that have become very famous. While many of these little sayings would become familiar to American school children, they established a clear link between individual virtue and financial security. Franklin (as Father Abraham supposedly quoting Richard Saunders) also injected a great deal of morality into his writing. For instance, he wrote that though some might complain about government taxes, people were 'taxed twice as much by our idleness, three times as much by our pride, and four times as much by our folly' (Doc. 3). A little later on in the sermon, Father Abraham (again channeling Richard) makes the direct connection to work, declaring: 'he that hath a trade hath an estate.' In fact, the reasoning went, 'at the workingman's house hunger looks in, but dares not enter.' All of these pithy sayings offered up popular understandings about the place of individual responsibility in an inherently just economic world. It is, of course, significant that one of the founders packaged these ideas in a format that became the stuff of American lore. Indeed, according to Franklin (again, using the character Poor Richard as his vessel) thrift and industry were critical not just to economic security but also to the very concept of freedom.

Yet certain realities that cut against such an idealized world were present in Poor Richard's advice. First, Franklin's use of the words 'slave' and 'chain' were no doubt influenced by the very real presence of enslaved Africans in the North American colonies. Indeed, slavery would serve as a dark reference point for American ideas about individual freedom and its connection to work. Moreover, for many Americans, Poor Richard's advice about credit and debt was impossible to follow. Still, for all the ways in which Franklin's writing may have deviated from the reality experienced by many Americans, these would be powerful ideas and foundational mythologies that would prove to have enormous consequences for centuries.

After the American Revolution, Franklin continued to promote an idealized vision of the United States. As always, he was sure to place ideas of work and individualism at the center of this vision. In 1784, writing for a European audience, Franklin published the pamphlet *Advice to Such as Would Remove to America*. While ostensibly written to dispel any misunderstandings Europeans thinking of emigrating might have had about the new country, it was also something of an advertisement for the United States, and the presentation of some of the most enduring mythologies about the American character. Crucially, Franklin portrayed Americans as a people occupying a great and noble middle. As he claimed, 'though there are in that country few people so miserable as the poor of Europe, there are also very few that in Europe would be called rich; it is rather a general happy mediocrity that prevails' (Franklin, 1784). In the absence of such extremes that defined the Old World, through working the land and cultivating a sense of personal industry (of the sort he had extolled through the character Poor Richard), Franklin claimed that a culture of practical usefulness had taken root in the United States.

In contrast to a status-conscious Europe, Franklin wrote that in America, 'people do not inquire concerning a stranger, what is he? but, what can he do?' (Franklin, 1784) This difference was crucial to social mobility. According to Franklin, if an American man had 'any useful art, he is welcome.' In an appeal to Europeans considering making the journey, Franklin wrote there was 'room enough for them all,' and that Americans would not be 'jealous.' Rather, the United States had 'laws to protect them sufficiently, so that they have no need for patronage of great men; and every one will enjoy securely the profits of his industry.' The land itself, according to Franklin, promised success. Invoking the idea of the frontier, Franklin told readers that land was 'cheap,' and that 'vast forests' were 'still void of inhabitants, and not likely to be occupied in an age to come, insomuch that the property of an hundred acres of fertile soil full of wood may be obtained never the frontiers.' Of course, this idealized sense of economic opportunity in America ignored the presence of native Americans. The lands that Franklin described were hardly 'devoid of inhabitants.' Still, Franklin presented an appealing picture of individual opportunity in America, declaring that 'hearty young laboring men, who understand the husbandry of corn and cattle,' could 'easily establish themselves.' Invoking, once again, the idea of the self-made man, Franklin claimed:

> Tolerably good workmen in any of those mechanic arts are sure to find employ, and to be well paid for their work, there being no restraints preventing strangers from exercising any art they understand, nor any permission necessary. If they are poor, they begin first as servants or

> journeymen; and if they are sober industrious, and frugal, they soon become masters, establish themselves in business.

Repeatedly, Franklin's pamphlet emphasized the connections between individual freedom and work. Just like his other works, though, the presence of enslaved people tugged at this idyllic image. Franklin even claimed that (white) Americans were 'pleased with the observation of a Negro,' that white Americans forced Black people, horses, and ox (along with everything else except for the lazy hog) work (Franklin, 1784).

There is no denying Franklin's overall importance to the course of American history and his role during the Revolutionary era. However, there was also a certain amount of self-mythologizing at work in his celebrated autobiography. The historian Pamela Laird has noted that Benjamin Franklin did not rise up from abject poverty. Franklin came from a Boston family of artisans and his father enjoyed a favorable reputation in that city. Still, Franklin did leave an apparently unpleasant apprenticeship under his brother and decamped to Philadelphia, beginning a long connection between the man and the city. Even there, Laird notes, Franklin benefited from quickly entering into networks of the city's elite. Significantly, Laird notes that as a white, Protestant man, Franklin resembled the people in the rarefied circles he wished to enter (Laird, 2005).

Still, even if Franklin's personal success was enabled by connections and circumstances that others might not have access to, he – along with subsequent storytellers – also established a durable mythology about American success. The 'rags-to-riches' story and 'self-making' that he presented in his autobiography and *Poor Richard's Almanack* provided later generations of Americans with a template for telling stories (both about themselves and others) to explain and dramatize the promise of a nation where a person would not be limited by the circumstances of birth. It was up to the individual to stake out a claim in a country full of possibilities. It was, to be sure, an optimistic vision of American individualism and would seem to be perfectly suited for the capitalist system that would soon take hold. The 'rags-to-riches' story is one of a handful of narratives that has continued to circulate in mainstream American culture, providing an enduring connection between capitalism and individualism. Franklin, though, was destined to become a symbolic figure in the United States, perpetually interpreted and misinterpreted long after his own time.

Self-Made Men and Social Darwinism in the Gilded Age

Benjamin Franklin may have popularized and updated the idea of the self-made man, but this mythology proliferated in the second half of the nineteenth century. Almost from the outset, the rise of big business posed a challenge to American individualism that, in many ways, has never really been resolved. In the late nineteenth century, the idea of the yeoman farmer or the lone producer seemed to be real peril. Large corporations of all sorts could easily put small producers out of business. Railroads posed what was perhaps the biggest threat in this regard. Through setting preferential rates for long hauls, benefits passed to large corporations. The spatial complexities endemic to capitalism still played a profound role in this new threat to the yeoman farmer. Just as transportation networks facilitated the market revolution earlier in the century, where a railroad appeared could drastically alter the fortunes of independent merchants. Small producers and farmers – as well as observers – complained about the unfair favors and treatment that large companies seemed to get. Not only did railroad companies offer preferential shipping rates to large companies seeking to transport goods, but the government itself could also provide measures that gave railroads business advantages.

With the rise of big corporations in the second half of the 1800s, long-standing cultural ideals about self-reliance and independence came crashing into new economic realities. Indeed, what were Americans to make of these very large corporations, as well as the stock market that grew alongside them? To be sure, notions of individualism did not fade during this era. The documents that Gilded Age Americans left behind reveal how the idea of individual agency persisted even in the face of large institutions. In some ways, a sense of American individualism became even more entrenched.

The first era of the large corporation was really the era of the first famous businessmen. John Rockefeller, Cornelius Vanderbilt, Andrew Carnegie and J.P. Morgan all became household names. These men would draw on American ideas of individualism to justify the vast fortunes they have amassed. Indeed, the myth of the self-made man provided a way to make the era's ideas of social Darwinism culturally palatable. Some of the savviest of these new industrialists actually worked on their public image. Andrew Carnegie was especially adept at connecting his own biography to American ideas of the self-made man.

Carnegie's public image and pronouncements had deep ties to nineteenth-century ideals about personal character and hard work. To hear Carnegie tell it (and he did tell it many times over), success in business was largely owing to desirable personal traits. For instance, in an address to a group of young men hoping to enter the world of business, the steel tycoon's advice included abstaining from liquor. The basic contours of Carnegie's conception, though, largely tracked with his own public image as a self-made man. To be successful, he advised, young men needed to start at the bottom of the ladder and work their way up. 'Many of the leading businessmen in Pittsburg,' he claimed, 'were introduced to the broom, and spent the first hours of their business lives sweeping out the office' (Carnegie, 1885). Though such a start at a business would be humble, that young man with the broom should hardly be satisfied. 'I would not give a fig," he declared, 'for the young man who does not already see himself the partner or the head of an important firm' (Carnegie, 1885). Likewise, Carnegie also gave a lot of weight to the idea of going above and beyond what was being asked. Finally, he told his listeners that they should never be content with their stations in life. Young men in business should always be thinking about how to climb that next rung in their career ladder. This sort of rhetoric may indeed have been inspiring to some – and it very clearly picked up on the ideals of individual hard work and fortitude that had long been a part of the American mythology. Carnegie was, however, in very real ways, also presenting an ideal vision of the worker in this new world defined by large corporations. When Carnegie advised these young men that 'the rising man must do something exceptional,' he was drawing on that longer tradition of individualism and the self-made man that formed the bedrock of his own persona. However, he immediately followed this advice by saying that low-level employees, like messenger boys, could 'lay the seed of promotion by going beyond the letter of his instructions.' Doing so, Carnegie explained, meant that an employee would be well-regarded by his employer. 'Your foot,' he declared, 'is upon the ladder; the amount of climbing done depends entirely upon yourself' (Carnegie, 1885). To be sure, such sentiments could be inspiring to hungry young men – and they tapped into that longer sense of individualism. Yet at the same time, Carnegie was describing the behavior of an ideal employee in a larger organization. The idea of individualism was alive and well, but by the late nineteenth century, Carnegie and others had to adapt it to a new world of commerce that was dominated by these large corporations.

The transformation of the economy was also reflected in the stories that Americans told themselves about the world of business and the self-made man. The most famous and enduring example of such storytelling could be found in the works of **Horatio Alger**. Alger was a children's author, and many of the novels he published in the 1860s promoted the ideas of the self-made man. Often, these stories would feature young boys in a city setting that make their way up in the world through hard work, responsible money management, and drive.

Alger's stories, in other words, all fit the classic narrative of American self-making that one could see as far back as Ben Franklin. In one of his better-known children's novels, *Ragged Dick*, the titular character begins as a streetwise shoe-shine boy who befriends a wealthier boy and guides him around the city. Along the way, Dick climbs up the socioeconomic ladder. Because they were written for children, Alger's novels were pedagogical in nature – meant to instruct his young readers about the world and instill in them proper habits. To be sure, this made the writing a little direct and obvious. For instance, in introducing the title character, Alger states that though Dick (like everyone else) had his flaws, he 'was frank and

Figure 4.1 Ben the Luggage Boy, 1867. The Gilded Age fiction of Horatio Alger promoted the idea of the self-made man to the author's young readers.

straight-forward, manly and self-reliant.' Because of these essential qualities, Alger hoped that even though Dick 'was only a bootblack,' readers would 'find something in him to imitate' (Alger, 1868).

Throughout the book, Dick meets a number of people who give him advice about making his way in the world and learning about the world of business. For instance, Dick's friend's uncle, who is also a banker, tells Dick, 'I hope, my lad, you will prosper and rise in the world. You know in this free country poverty in early life is no bar to a man's advancement' (Doc. 8). These lines offer a direct and distilled expression of American individualism amid a rapidly evolving capitalism. These sentiments informed the entirety of the novel. Significantly, though, none of Alger's protagonists became fabulously wealthy. Instead, through their hard work, they secured positions in the wide middle strata of American life. What is more, because Alger sought to impart an unambiguous message to his young readership, the path that Dick took and his experiences in no way clashed with such statements about individualism and self-made men. In some ways a contrast to ideas such as social Darwinism, the world as it appeared in Alger's stories was fundamentally benevolent. Throughout the twentieth century, conservative voices did not hesitate to invoke the children's author when opposing unwanted business regulations.

Without a doubt, Carnegie, Alger, and others offered up a powerful story about the promise of the United States. Carnegie was even able to cast himself as an underdog immigrant. However, what such storytellers did not usually say outright was that the heroes of these stories were almost always white and Protestant. Despite this very thinly cloaked racial division, the story of the self-made man had immense appeal for many.

However, these Agler-esque tales and public biographies like Carnegie's were not the only stories about the Gilded Age. Even if the Robber Baron rhetoric of social Darwinism rested on the assumption of individualism, American writers during the Gilded Age by and large sought to tell a different story. During these years, **naturalism** as a literary movement came to the fore. The idea behind this sensibility was a dark view of the world – one that was amoral and without an inherent justice. Forces could overwhelm and crush people despite their own efforts. In some ways, this line of thinking was of apiece with the social Darwinism that monopolists used to justify their own wealth. However, naturalist writers were more attuned to the ways in which lone individuals simply did not stand a chance among broader forces in the world. The term 'naturalism,' though, can be misleading. Significantly, many of these novels were not set in the natural world but rather centered on different aspects of the emerging economy. **Frank Norris**'s 1901 novel, *The Octopus*, depicted the ways in which railroads were destroying a more pastoral way of life. Likewise, his novel from 1903, *The Pit*, explored similar themes in the world of commodities trading. Still, even if naturalist fiction like Norris's novels were offering powerful rejoinders to the inequities and perils of the Gilded Age, they did not circulate nearly as widely as the myth of the 'self-made man.'

Criticism of these new business leaders also reflected an emphasis on individualism. As the historian Peter Knight demonstrates, political cartoons conflated well-known industrialists and stock operators with the larger, more abstract processes they commanded (Knight, 2016). These images often depicted people like Jay Gould or Cornelius Vanderbilt as stand-ins for these new, impersonal institutions. Such illustrations suggested a profound unease with shifting power relations in the 1870s and 1880s. Rather than celebrating the rise of men like Gould, such political cartoons sometimes trafficked in ugly racial stereotypes. In fact, the pointed ears on illustrations of Jay Gould are evidence of how such critiques and fears could be laced with antisemitism. During these years, the term 'robber barons' emerged as a way to characterize ruthless business tycoons. The phrase stuck, making it difficult to separate our collective memory of the late nineteenth century from these famous individuals.

Fearing the Frontier's End

For adherents of an American culture that was based on the idea of individualism, the steady rise of larger institutions was cause for either alarm or mourning. By far, the most famous example of this sensibility was the historian **Frederick Jackson Turner**'s 'frontier thesis.' In this public address, Turner argued, 'Up to our own day American history has been in a large degree the history of the colonization of the Great West. The existence of an area of free land, its continuous recession, and the advance of American settlement westward,' he reasoned, 'explain American development.' For Turner, the frontier was the 'meeting point between savagery and civilization,' where the American character was forged. This process for Turner made Americans through individual struggle. Contrasting an effete European sensibility with what he viewed as the savagery of native Americans, Turner saw the frontier as a place where a white man, alone and without institutional support, had to adopt Indian ways. The frontier was, for Turner, 'the line of most rapid and effective Americanization.' Adopting native American garb and practices such as 'planting Indian corn' and 'fitting [himself] into the Indian clearings and follow[ing] Indian trails,' Europe's influence would vanish, leaving behind an American sense of individualism. In fact, Turner declared that the frontier was 'productive of individualism' which in turn 'promoted democracy.' Turner, though, famously concluded that the frontier was now closed, and with it, 'the first period of American history' (Turner, 1893). The remark must have been all the more poignant given that he uttered those words at the 1893 **Columbian Exposition** in Chicago, surrounded by all of the age's industrial marvels.

Clearly, large and complex institutions seemed to be overtaking the purifying violence that characterized Turner's imagined frontier. Indeed, the age of the small merchant of the plucky individual seemed to be over. Never mind that this had always been, to some extent, a myth. In fact, one of the most iconic symbols of American individualism, the cowboy, was in some ways directly tied to much larger industrial processes. Cowboys might have run the Chisholm Trail cattle drive that began in Texas – figures on their horses covering an undeveloped, roughly beautiful American landscape, building fires at night and riding again in the morning. Yet those cowboys were ultimately driving that cattle to trains that would transport the cows to Chicago and its industrial meat processing plants. Yet Turner was, in many ways, wrong. That mystic commitment to individualism persisted well into the twentieth century even as the institutions themselves got bigger and more complex.

The Self-Made Man in the Twentieth Century

If the Gilded Age was shaped in part by romantic ideas of the self-made man, the situation was more complicated for Black Americans. Still, the mythology around the self-made man could sometimes be useful as Black Americans began to navigate business life after the Civil War. In this regard, Booker T. Washington proved to be the best example. Though Washington's early experiences were far different from Carnegie and other Gilded Age-era business magnates, he repeatedly drew on similar rhetoric.

In his autobiography, *Up From Slavery*, Washington presented himself in the mold of the self-made man. He himself read Carnegie's *Gospel of Wealth*. Moreover, Washington cultivated relationships with many of these Gilded Age tycoons. In fact, both Andrew Carnegie and John Rockefeller gave money to the Tuskegee Institute. Through these relationships and Washington's work, both the retail magnate John Wannamaker and Julius Rosenwald (the man behind the Sears mail-order business) gave speeches to the National Negro Business League.

Much like Carnegie and others, Washington's economic and business thinking emphasized industry and practical knowledge. However, as at least one historian has noted, Washington differed from these Robber Barons in one crucial respect. Washington did not advocate a 'survival of the fittest' philosophy. Rather, Washington believed that Black business success was the best path to improving the station of Black Americans and chip away at Jim Crow. Rather than pursuing political power, Washington argued that Black businesspeople could make themselves indispensable members of American society. In an 1895 speech, Washington argued that 'no race that has anything to contribute to the markets of the world is long in any degree ostracized' (Washington, 1895). In other words, even if Washington drew on the rhetoric and ideas of late nineteenth-century individualism, he directed it toward community uplift. However, these ideas were dependent

Figure 4.2 Booker T. Washington drew on the mythology of the self-made man in crafting his own autobiography. Source: Harris & Ewing Collection, Library of Congress.

on overcoming the reality of two different economies and markets that had emerged in the Jim Crow era.

Washington picked up on the rhetoric and popular ideals of the self-made man in other ways as well. His book, *The Negro in Business* (which included help from other, uncredited writers), was filled primarily with glowing features of specific Black businesspeople. Much like Carnegie and others of the era, Washington's account drew a straight line between personal morality and business success.

Washington was hardly the only public figure to draw on ideas of the self-made man during these years. In the early twentieth century, the president of the National Association of Manufacturers used the idea of the self-made man in order to argue that successful businessmen deserved the respect and support of the whole country. As both of these examples suggest, the mythology of the self-made man continued to have wide political applications. What's more, the story continued to appear in a number of different guises.

For example, during the twentieth century, the connection between individualism and the stock market continued to grow. Indeed, a sense of **contrarian thinking** was widely admired in this era. Finance became an area of commercial activity where tales of individual smarts and initiative easily translated into business success. Such tales quickly made up a certain mythology that took root in high finance. One of the earliest examples of this came in the form of the book *Reminiscences of a Stock Operator*. The book was written in the first person by the journalist Edwin Lefevre. However, the real subject of the book was the stock operator **Jesse Livermore**. Published in 1923, the book's narrator takes readers through the world of investing and playing the stock market on Wall Street. Throughout, the narrator relates to the reader many of his thoughts about this line of work. What is immediately striking is how individualistic the narrator's thinking is.

What is more, the book opens in a fashion that closely models the rags-to-riches story that would be familiar to readers of Horatio Alger's novels. As the narrator puts it: 'I went to work when I was just out of grammar school. I got a job as quotation-board boy in a stock-brokerage office' (Lefevre, 1923). From the outset, the young man, much like Carnegie and others before him, presents himself as diligent and preoccupied with work. There was, though, a key difference. After all, Carnegie disdained speculation. Livermore (the real subject of Lefevre's book) reveled in it. Indeed, after studying the market for a long time, the book's protagonist begins visiting **bucket shops**, soon earning more through speculation than through office work. As he tells the reader: 'I gave up my position. My folks objected, but they couldn't say much when they saw what I was making. I was only a kid and office-boy wages were not very high. I did mighty well on my own hook' (Lefevre, 1923). From there, the young boy mirrors Horatio Alger's kid heroes in some respects, though Alger's emphasis on work ethic, prudence and thrift is all gone. Visiting bucket shops and placing bets, the narrator describes himself as a 'one-man business.' Indeed, this lone operation is at the center of the stock operator's work. As he tells the reader:

> Prices either were going the way I doped them out, without any help from friends or partners, or they were going the other way, and nobody

> could stop them out of kindness to me. I couldn't see where I needed to tell my business to anybody else. I've got friends, of course, but my business has always been the same – a one-man affair. That is why I have always played a lone hand.
>
> (Lefevre, 1923: 13)

Such lines were deeply individualistic expressions, and persisted as cornerstones of the world of high finance.

Lefevre's book was just one example of the mythologies about individualism that persisted in the twentieth century. One of the twentieth century's most successful Black businessmen was **Samuel B. Fuller**. Fuller's story largely followed that of the mythic self-made man. Much like other biographies that were shaped to fit this narrative, Fuller hitchhiked from Louisiana to Chicago and started working as a salesman for the Commonwealth Burial Association, eventually working his way up to manager. Soon, though, Fuller struck out on his own to found Fuller Products, a door-to-door sales cosmetics company, in 1935. Throughout his career, Fuller professed the same faith in the business system and capitalism that Carnegie and others had in the previous century. By the 1960s, Fuller Products had sales of $10 million a year. Not only was he the first Black businessman to join the otherwise white National Association of Manufacturers, Fuller also supported other Black entrepreneurs. Controversially, he downplayed systemic racism, insisting that Black Americans needed to engage more with the country's capitalist system. Such remarks were not received well in some quarters. With white supremacist groups already boycotting Fuller Products, sales declined.

Mythologies of heroic individualism persisted even during the postwar era, when economic life was dominated by very large, bureaucratic institutions. In the United States, though, perhaps the greatest popularizer of these ideas was the novelist and self-styled philosopher, **Ayn Rand**. Rand grew up in Russia, where her father, a small business owner, lost much of what he had during the Russian Revolution in 1917. This experience profoundly influenced Rand's political beliefs and her deep mistrust of government involvement in economic matters. Eventually, she emigrated to the United States where she attempted to launch a career in Hollywood. By the mid-1930s, though, she had moved to New York with her husband and had turned to writing novels. In addition to her writing and developing her own brand philosophy, which she called **Objectivism**, Rand also became involved in politics, even working on the presidential campaign for FDR's Republican challenger in the 1940 election, Wendell Wilkie.

While she was working on her fiction writing, Rand also began developing her philosophical ideas. In 1941, she wrote, though never published, a 'Manifesto of Individualism.' In this manifesto, Rand argued that individual rights and pursuits should trump any attempt to work toward the common good. In a sly reference to *The Communist Manifesto* that Karl Marx and Richard Engels had written nearly a century earlier, Rand ended her manifesto with a clear call: 'Individualists of the World, Unite!' What made Rand so influential, though, was how she used her fiction to showcase and dramatize these ideas. The first of her two famous novels was *The Fountainhead*, published in 1943. Though the novel's protagonist is an architect and not, strictly speaking, a businessman, the character embodied many of the principles Rand introduced in her manifesto. The book was popular and was soon made into a movie. However, her next novel, *Atlas Shrugged*, proved to be even more influential. Both of these novels were intended as a way for Rand to dramatize and promote her ideas.

In *Atlas Shrugged*, published in 1957, Rand tells the story of the world's greatest industrialists going on strike and disappearing to 'Galt's Gulch,' a hidden utopia where business executives, engineers, and artists are all free from government regulation and have organized their ideal society around a free market. The novel's plot follows Dagney Taggart and Hank Reardon, two strong-willed business executives, when they finally discover Galt's Gulch, which has been created by John Galt, an engineer who has built the world's greatest engine. The three characters eventually lead a counter-revolution against a government that had gone out of control with regulation. Despite the book's excessive length – John Galt's famous radio address near the end of the novel runs dozens of pages – *Atlas Shrugged* quickly found an enthusiastic audience, particularly among businessmen. The media mogul Ted Turner, for example, bought billboard advertisements featuring one of the book's most famous phrases 'Who is John Galt?' In California, *Atlas Shrugged* also found an audience among members of the counterculture who would later go on to help build the computer industry in Silicon Valley. Indeed, Rand's ideas would prove to be very influential to both businesspeople and politicians. However, Rand's most famous disciple was an economist, not a businessperson. While she was working on *Atlas Shrugged* in the 1950s, a group of young people gravitated toward her, including the future Chairman of the Federal Reserve, **Alan Greenspan**. Rand may have been particularly extreme and strident in her insistence on the primacy of the individual over any and all systems and institutions, but she was far from alone.

Similar notions of a lone individual operating against a large institution could also be found elsewhere in postwar popular culture. For instance, the 1960 movie *The Apartment*, which starred Jack Lemmon and Shirley McLaine, dramatized many of the concerns in Whyte and Riesman's books about corporate conformity. The movie told the story of C.C. Baxter, a young office worker who lends out his apartment to executives at his company, Consolidate Life Insurance, so that they can affairs. Throughout the movie, it is clear that the character is uncomfortable with the arrangement and knows better. Yet this other-directed behavior allows him to climb up the corporate ladder. His redemption only comes when he quits his job (motivated in part by his love for an elevator girl – played by McLaine). Throughout the movie, his neighbor, an older doctor, tells him to be a 'mensch.' In other words, be a man. Likewise, McLaine's character makes several comments suggesting Baxter isn't very masculine. In fact, his masculinity only seems secured when he tells his boss that he's decided to be a man. This through-line in the movie dramatized the tension between American gender identity, individualism, and capitalism at midcentury.

Other cultural artifacts, such as **Sloan Wilson**'s 1955 novel, *The Man in the Grey Flannel Suit*, took a more ambivalent approach to the idea of the organization man. In that novel, the protagonist struggles with the loss of identity and the strain on his marriage as he climbs the corporate ladder – even witnessing the sadness and loneliness that the head of his company experiences. In the end, the novel's hero learns to be satisfied with this middle-man existence. While clearly critical of office politics, the sense of contentment that the novel's protagonist, Tom Rath, ultimately feels at the end of the novel was precisely the sort of middle-ness that Whyte would critique in *The Organization Man* the following year. Still, the phrase 'the man in the grey flannel suit' became a cultural shorthand for the very problem Whyte was describing.

Ultimately, though, the conformist anxieties suggested by *The Apartment* and *The Man in the Grey Flannel Suit* still reflected a position of power. Even if books and movies challenged midcentury corporate life, they did little to examine the gendered ideas of work. Indeed, all of the women work at the fictional Consolidated Life Insurance in *The Apartment* are either secretaries or elevator girls. Likewise, the only Black actor to appear in the film is an elevator operator. Such details reflected the gender and racial disparities that had been baked into corporate life.

Mythologies of Entrepreneurs in the Neoliberal Era

Even as the power of large-scale American corporations appeared to decline in the 1970s, cultural understandings of individualism and its relationship to capitalism persisted. As finance took hold as an active presence in the American economy, new versions of the self-made man proliferated. Much like contrarian thinking and playing the market in the 1920s, popular understandings of **financialization** in the 1980s suggested a link between individualism and Wall Street. The rise of finance was so dramatic that it seemed to represent the future of American business, spawning a number of stories and business celebrities. As the stock market took off, newspapers were filled with stories about ordinary Americans doing well in the stock market.

Likewise, books like 1989's *Liar's Poker* told stories of self-made men from humble beginnings making fortunes in a world dominated by expensively educated investment bankers. Movies like *Wall Street* also contained elements of the self-made man. Though the film's villain, Gordon Gekko, became famous for his 'greed is good' speech, the movie also emphasized his impoverished beginnings. It is significant that Gekko's primary business rival is a British nobleman. What is more, Gekko takes the movie's protagonist, Bud Fox, under his wing because of Bud's own blue-collar background. Similar ideas of individualism in the world of high finance persisted long after the business celebrities and Wall Street scandals of the 1980s faded from view.

Even in the twenty-first century, after the 2008 financial crisis, the movie *The Big Short* told the story of the crash from the perspective of different contrarian thinkers – individuals going against the grain and against conventional wisdom. Years later, the 2021 Gamestop episode, which pitted individual investors in the stock market against larger firms and institutions in a protracted stock market battle over the price of the video game retailer, offered yet another instance of individualism and stories of self-made men. Significantly, in all of these instances, questions of race and gender remained conspicuously absent (even if these stories dealt with class head-on). Even in the twenty-first century, the self-made man was still assumed to be white and male.

In other areas of the economy, though, race did play a role in some narratives of the self-made man. Later in the twentieth century, for instance, some Black entrepreneurs blurred the line between business and entertainment. Most prominently, the talk show host Oprah Winfrey created a vast media empire, eventually including a magazine and cable television network. The basketball great Magic Johnson similarly used the wealth he accrued as an athlete to enter into a number of businesses. In both instances, business success became a central part of each person's public identity. However, it would be in popular music where the rhetoric of the self-made man would be so clearly discernible.

Hip hop artists such as Jay-Z and Sean Combs fashioned their public personas around the idea of the self-made man, highlighting their business acumen. In fact, Jay-Z's company, Rock-A-Fella, slyly referenced the Gilded Age era of the self-made man and Robber Barons. Despite these examples, though, the self-made man has been a narrative surrounded by racial and gender barriers. Popular representations of the self-made man and individualism have most often helped mythologize white entrepreneurs while obscuring the ways in which such men (usually) have benefited from the contributions of others.

Mythologies of individualism also permeated cultural understandings of the Internet in the 1990s. Though such technologies had been developed as part of the defense establishment, marshaling all the resources of the federal government, when dazzling new web companies began to emerge with increasing frequency, the face of this new entrepreneur was often a young white man with little patience for tradition or bureaucracy. It was a pattern that began with the founders of Microsoft's **Bill Gates** and Apple's Steve Jobs. Though Gates enjoyed a privileged upbringing, it was his decision to leave Harvard before finishing college in order to start his own company that became the most famous part of his public persona. Likewise, Jobs crafted his image (and Apple's) around a sense of defying larger corporations. Apple's advertising campaigns in the 1980s and 1990s also unabashedly celebrated individualism. The company's advertisements encouraging potential customers to "think different" was just the most overt example of this theme.

The individualistic tropes that Gates and Jobs established early in their careers had a lasting influence on presentation and style in Silicon Valley. Much like Gates, Facebook's Mark Zuckerberg dropped out of college to build his company (a story which was also romanticized on film). Taking a cue from Apple, the infamous energy company Enron's ad campaign titled 'ask why,' in which the company declared this was the cry of the 'nonconformist.' Some of these ads also featured a number of famous individualistic thinkers. In some ways, of course, there is deep irony in large multinational corporations (such as Apple) grabbing onto the lone figure of the self-made man. Yet this very irony is a testament to just how persistent such myths of individualism factor into cultural understandings of capitalism.

The myth of the self-made man and heroic entrepreneur turned out to be especially well-suited to the tech age. Midcentury technology companies like IBM seemed to be the epitome of the giant bureaucracies that squashed individuality. The company even had an employee chorus and songbook exhorting the listener to 'Hail the IBM.' Such a stiff corporate culture, which mirrored some of the basic stereotypes of postwar work life, also turned out to be the perfect foil for upstart businesses in Silicon Valley. Soon-to-be wealthy businessmen, such as Bill Gates and Steve Jobs had compelling, if embellished, backstories, such as dropping out of college to risk starting a business in a garage. It was, in many ways, the same story that had been told time and time again, though it now had a number of late twentieth-century updates. However, as the historian Juliet Walker points out, technological and business achievement at companies like Apple and IBM would have been impossible without the foundational work of Philip Emeagwali (Walker, 2003).

Likewise, Silicon Valley attempts at social commentary could also be profoundly individualistic. The Facebook executive **Sheryl Sandberg** published a book titled *Lean In* which she likened to a feminist manifesto. In the book, Sandberg argued that one of the primary ways in which working women should fight for more gender equality in the workplace was to be more personally assertive and ambitious. While Sandberg acknowledged institutional barriers, her solution was grounded in long-standing ideas of individualism. In the introduction to her book, Sandberg wrote that 'women are hindered by barriers that exist within' themselves. Women, she argued, needed to be more self-confident and professionally ambitious. For Sandberg, such individual, personal transformation was a necessary prerequisite to a broader sense of justice. Sandberg wrote that these 'internal obstacles' were what women should focus on because they were 'under our own control' (Sandberg, 2013: 9). The solution to greater gender equality in the workplace, she argued, was to be found in American individualism. However, much like other supposed tales of self-making and rugged individualism, Sandberg had benefited from her membership in elite networks that provided her with opportunities not available to many other women.

Even at the start of the twenty-first century, and in an age of globalization, the perennial American mythology of the individual and self-made man was thriving. One has to look no further than the newspaper columnist and popular writer Thomas Friedman to find an example. In the late 1990s and throughout the first years of the twenty-first century, Friedman was arguably the most popular and influential writer about globalization. His books were best-sellers and he coined a number of terms and phrases that influenced everyday discourse and understandings of globalization. Significantly, Friedman was enthusiastic about globalization, seeing it as a way to connect lots of different people from around the world, providing many with opportunities that they did not have before the fall of the Berlin Wall. Friedman's ideas about globalization may have seemed forward looking, but in many ways, they fell back on some of the oldest mythologies and tropes when it came to individualism. In the late 1990s, Friedman wrote about 'superempowered' individuals who could shape world events. In his 2005 best-seller, *The World Is Flat*, Friedman described the global economy as empowering individuals around the world. He imagined a talented, poor young man in India, for example, who could now compete with American children for the first time. He wrote that 'when the world is flat,' any talented young person with 'access to Google and a cheap wireless laptop can join in the innovation fray' (Friedman, 2005). In essence, Friedman was offering his readers a globalized version of the self-made man. The context may have seemed different from Franklin's time, but the basic commitment to an optimistic focus on the individual was still there. Friedman's critics (and there were many) were often quick to point out that his worldview was fundamentally an elite one. In his books, the writer would often describe having an epiphany about the global economy after interviewing a successful entrepreneur or executive from a country such as India. However, it was in these episodes that Friedman would offer readers an updated, globalized story that, in the end, did not stray too far from the sort of mythology that men like Andrew Carnegie had built for themselves in an earlier historical moment.

It is, of course, significant that these same narratives, characters, and ideas appear again and again across centuries. Such repetitions attest to the power and appeal of these stories. Moreover, these narratives have real-world effects, shaping our understanding of events and people. They provide a basis from which Americans have valued and judged success. Yet as powerful and appealing as these stories are, they silence as many people as they celebrate. The phrase 'self-made man' is inherently misleading, pointing away from the networks, systems, and other factors that aided in that one person's success. The stories can also form the basis for a specific type of politics that eschews broader systemic change. The very existence of the self-made man, up from poverty, this argument goes, suggests that American capitalism as it exists is a just and democratic system that does not require reform. This mythology of individualism at the heart of American capitalism, in other words, can produce very real consequences.

5 Collectives

The persistence of individualism as an ideal in so many aspects of American capitalism reveals just how central that idea is in order for modern capitalism to work. Moreover, the centrality of this idea suggests that American capitalism is more than just an economic system, but one that depends on cultural concepts that cut through and inform political and business decisions, and structure everyday life. In other words, there is a great deal at stake in the idea of individualism. Yet as powerful as that idea is, there is also a tremendous amount of power in subordinating this idea of individualism when circumstances call for it. To put it another way, whenever groups of people temporarily set aside their sense of individualism to push for a shared interest, it can have enormous weight.

The figure of the individual has been a central organizing figure in philosophical and political-economic thought, systems of governance and production, organizations and institutions, and, finally, the popular imagination. However, as capitalism has become ever more complex and large in scope, individuals – in their various economic roles and workers and consumers – have often advanced their own interests by banding together and acting as a collective force. Conversely, corporations recognized tremendous advantages in preserving cultural and psychological attachments to individualism. Two of the most prominent economic identities any one individual occupies are those of a worker and a consumer, and both of these identities and activities have been sites of contests between individualist ideology and collective action.

Unions during the Gilded Age

The idea that individual workers should try to advance their collective interests is nothing new. Long before the founding of the nation, workers around the world and in different trades have often come together in the form of 'guilds.' Unions in the United States began to appear alongside the larger Gilded Age corporations that were dramatically remaking

DOI: 10.4324/9781003090526-6

working life. As these corporations became better organized operations, they encroached on the autonomy of individual workers.

These new corporations required masses of new workers to operate steel mills and factories. By and large, many of these new workers were recent arrivals in the United States from parts of Europe that were different from earlier arrivals. As historians such as Alan Trachtenberg have argued, these different national origins meant that a sense of 'Americanness' might be entirely out of reach. Consequently, the relationships these workers had to the ideals of individualism and the narrative of the self-made man were more complicated than they were for someone like Andrew Carnegie, who had emigrated from Scotland (Trachtenberg, 1982). While here, they faced tremendous discrimination. Life for some of these workers could be miserable. Working conditions were often dangerous and unpleasant – and the wages were not nearly enough to compensate for this work. Individualism as it was experienced in this new context was in many ways synonymous with precarity. The 'tramp' – a term for workers who followed industrial work across the country – for instance, became a new figure in the popular imagination. It was deeply ironic that these tramps would sometimes make their trips by hopping on railroads – the very sort of businesses that had played a hand in remaking working life. As at least one historian has argued, for many Americans, tramps and 'tramping' signified a type of individualism that was threatening (Photinos, 2007).

In other words, working life was an unstable situation. Throughout the late nineteenth century, workers repeatedly clashed with their employers and the government. Worker uprisings such as the Great Railroad Strike of 1877 and the Haymarket Riot in 1886 were vivid and violent demonstrations of the era's turmoil. In these clashes, questions of individual freedom and autonomy lurked just beneath the surface. One particular episode pitted the Gilded Age's most famous 'self-made man,' Andrew Carnegie, against many of his workers. The discord began in 1892, when members of the Amalgamated Association of Iron and Steel Workers at Carnegie's operation in Homestead, Pennsylvania, objected to wage cuts. **Henry Frick**, one of Carnegie Steel's managers, responded with a lockout in an attempt to dismantle the union altogether. The standoff quickly turned violent, with Frick calling in **Pinkertons** to help break up the strike.

Similar conflicts even spelled doom for the 'White City' that was a part of the Columbian Exposition, where Turner was declaring the closing of the frontier. In this instance, workers for the Pullman Car Company, who were living in a **company town** objected to simultaneous rent increases and wage cuts. In the ensuing conflict, both Pullman and the White City burned to the ground. However, these spasms of violence were just one manifestation of growing collective action among workers.

Paradoxically, it was by banding together that workers were able to exercise a degree of control over their individual lives within capitalism's rapidly shifting power dynamics. Indeed, worker collectives and unions such as the Knights of Labor and the American Federation of Labor appeared right alongside the Gilded Age's new corporations. Oftentimes, labor unions immediately raised questions of power, identity, and individualism. At times, they could even involve contests over what it even meant to be an American. Though terms such as 'solidarity' became associated with unions, labor rhetoric could be full of appeals to a sense of individual independence, if not the exact same sort of individualism that business owners might use to justify their wealth.

Confrontations pitted industrialists who had glommed onto the idea of the self-made man against workers attempting to forge a sense of independent identity in an economy that increasingly included wage labor. This new type of work was, of course, a significant change from a world of work defined by free labor.

Given how important the idea of individualism has been in mainstream American culture, it should not be surprising that laborers did not simply accept these new working arrangements. In fact, the idea of **wage slavery** reveals the ways in which both racial logic and individualistic ideas shaped how workers made sense of this new economic landscape. During the Gilded Age, even as workers banded together to form unions, they did so under the logic of free labor ideology and a commitment to a producerist ideal that ran all the way back to older ideas of republicanism. Even when **Eugene Debs** declared himself to be a socialist, his explanation hinged on the idea that he was supporting a system that justly rewarded workers for their labor. In some ways, all of these ideas and conflicts drew on understandings that connected property, labor, and value in much the same way that John Locke had articulated in the seventeenth century.

Other labor advocates also drew on the rhetoric of masculinity and its connection to production. Such labor organizations may have been arguing for mutual and collective benefit, but these men had not abandoned an attachment to individualism. As some historians have noted, the persistence of such ideas in the final decades of the nineteenth century demonstrates an economy and society in the middle of tremendous change. Cultural understandings had not yet caught up to an increasingly industrial economy. The language of individualism – still detectable in the rhetoric of people like Debs – reveals a core tension in American capitalism and culture. In other ways, though, the era's conflicts pitted labor unions like the Knights of Labor against individualistic self-made men.

Labor after the Wagner Act

In the twentieth century, the struggle over labor unions continued. The Great Steel Strike in 1919, in which over 360,000 workers took part – and which was violently suppressed – was just one example. To be sure, the major labor unions in the United States could have a range of different ideologies. Some, such as the International Workers of the World (or **Wobblies**) were more radical in their political orientation. However, the New Deal ushered in a dramatic change in fortune for labor unions. The Wagner Act established the right for workers to bargain collectively and the newly created National Labor Relations Board constituted a mechanism for the federal government to help resolve disputes. Previously, worker strikes could turn violent and the federal government had sometimes acted on behalf of business owners. Now, both a law and federal institutions offered protected avenues for workers to bargain collectively and form unions. It was a turning point for labor in the United States.

The first test of this new power came in 1936 in Flint, Michigan. During the 1930s the efforts of unionized labor focused less on wages and much more on issues such as modes of work that might be considered dehumanizing. For instance, in what became known as 'Sit-down Strikes', workers pushed back against the pace of their labor in the factory and occupied the buildings. In this way, union struggles could represent a push for a greater degree of individual autonomy in the workplace.

Earlier in the same year, the legendary comedian Charlie Chaplin released *Modern Times*, a film that was set in a factory. A classic of physical comedy, the first scenes of the movie find Chaplin, as his character 'the Tramp,' working an assembly line. As he goes throughout his day, the Tramp must adjust his rhythm to match the inhuman, machine pace of the assembly line. As the factory bosses speed up the line, the poor character can only move faster and faster, tightening nuts and bolts as they come down the line. At one point, Chaplin steps away from the line, but his body still jerks with the movement of the work. If the character dares to rest, a screen turns on with the manager sternly ordering him back to work. At one point, the poor man is pulled away from this routine that his boss can test a machine that automatically feeds employees, freeing their hands to keep working. With such efficiency, the workers won't even need breaks. Little machine arms force-feed Chaplin food and then roughly and robotically wipe his mouth with a napkin. The whole scene is played to great comic effect, but Chaplin was in many ways commenting on the fate of the individual in the face of an increasingly efficient and mechanized workplace. For manufacturing corporations, the joke simply wasn't funny. The whole episode was worrisome enough that GM had **Jam Handy** produce an industrial film, *Master Hands*, that presented the factory industrial worker as dignified – a figure to be celebrated.

The dehumanizing nature of modern factory life was one reason for the Sit-down Strike that lasted for six weeks. In an interview years later, one striker remembered how dehumanizing the work could seem. 'You might call yourself a man if you was on the street,' he remarked, 'but as soon as you went through the door and punched your card, you was nothing more or less than a robot' (Terkel, 1970: 127). Although workers chafed at the impersonal nature of working life at GM, the first big test of labor's new clout was undoubtedly a collective action. Ultimately, it was successful, with GM workers winning both pay increases and union recognition. Indeed, much like other parts of economic life, the Sit-down Strike's success was due in part to the efforts of entire families. Even if women were not working the factories, they were offering support in other ways. As one striker told the famed oral historian Studs Terkel, the striking workers had a 'ladies' auxiliary' that would 'visit the homes of the guys' to help out with 'any shortage of coal or food' (Terkel, 1970: 129). The Sit-down Strike was an early test of the new labor laws that were a part of the New Deal and gave labor a big boost. It, along with other developments, meant a big public relations problem for GM.

GM's response to the turmoil of the Sit-down Strike also emphasized collectivity over individualism. In 1937 GM again turned to Jam Handy, who created the industrial film, *From Dawn to Sunset*. Directed at GM's own employees, scene after scene depicted the company's workers all leaving for work at the same time all around the country. The depiction of life in the factory was uniformly pleasant. A job at a GM plant meant steady paychecks (indeed, much of the film emphasizes getting paid and buying a range of items for the home) and binding the country together in one great community (Marchand, 1998). Of course, in this idealized portrayal, the GM workers and their families depicted in these films were almost always white. As to be expected, GM's film was intended to present an overwhelmingly positive picture, but it was also one that notably did not leave room for the individual. Rather, the film emphasized middle-class stability. The workers may have all led nearly identical lives – leaving for work at the same time to fill one small role in an assembly line – but the work and paychecks that came from being a part of this undifferentiated mass translated into comfortable home lives.

Unions in the Cold War

General Motors was hardly the only company to try to combat the new power of unions through culture and symbols. Elizabeth and Kenneth Fones-Wolf have documented how in the late 1940s and 1950s, for instance, some businesses made use of pageants and other public events to engender a sense of patriotism that connected national values to ideas of economic individualism (Fones-Wolf, 2003). Organizations like the National Association of Manufacturers and local chapters of the Chamber of Commerce also supported these efforts. At the height of the Cold War, such displays had symbolic weight and they often did not leave much room for unions. Some business owners worked hard to align a sense of individualism and freedom with a business environment that would advance their own interests. The pageants that were held in these early days of the Cold War were attempts to conflate patriotism and American history with business values that did not include any sense of the collectivity that unions seemed to represent. Managers and businesses also used the rhetoric of individualism when directly confronting union drives. This same hostility toward unions sometimes spilled over into popular culture. Famously, the classic film *On the Waterfront* offered a plot that directly pitted the individual protagonist against a corrupt union.

However, these business interests did not necessarily have a monopoly on strategically using patriotic rhetoric. In fact, unions also found such rhetoric to be useful. Union drives often involved ideas of democracy and freedom. Unions like the United Steelworkers Association, for instance, used this rhetoric to offer the union as a contrast to what they described as authoritarian businesses. Similarly, both labor unions and business interests could invoke notions of 'slavery' to advance their particular goals. The way unions were organized also reflected an attempt to achieve some semblance of democratic practices in the workplace. Indeed, through mechanisms such as the grievance process, twentieth-century unions were pushing for a sense of **industrial democracy**.

However, the benefits of these unions were hardly distributed in an equal manner. Racial hostility and exclusion often characterized midcentury unions. Moreover, union rhetoric could often be given over to affirming the same sort of masculinity that was central to earlier notions of rugged individualism. The labor historian Nelson Lichtenstein writes that during the New Deal, union supporters in government and elsewhere placed 'the restoration of male dignity and livelihood at the center of concern' (Lichtenstein, 2002: 88).

In sum, labor unions, despite their flaws, represented a new power dynamic that individuals had to navigate. This was the precise reason why businesses and their political allies targeted unions in an effort to weaken their influence. Though such struggles had been taking place since the New Deal, one of the most dramatic turns in this struggle arrived when Ronald Reagan fired striking air traffic controllers in 1981. In general, union power and membership waned at the end of the twentieth century. Indeed, with neoliberal ideology and its emphasis on individualism taking center stage, some business commentators described unions as relics of an earlier era. What's more, that decline was one symptom of the broader economic instability that characterized the American economy at the end of the century.

Consumers

Much in the same way that labor unions reveal a tension between individualism and collective action, American consumers have also had to navigate this tension between individual agency and collective power. To purchase something is more than a simple economic transaction. Rather, consumerism is a complex topic when it comes to culture and identity. The sheer abundance of consumer goods provides multiple ways of fashioning one's identity, including unexpected and even subversive uses of those consumer goods. Yet at the same time, consumer capitalism might be deemed an oppressive system. If people are at least in part defined by their purchasing choices, then in very real ways corporations have an outsized role in dictating a large portion of someone's identity. Indeed, it's not just money; a lot gets exchanged in a market. Meaning and identity also get passed back and forth in what is supposed to be an economic process. And in that movement, meaning as well as identity – 'culture,' in a word – is transformed. The presence of culture in market exchange significantly raises the stakes when it comes to consuming. Consumer capitalism both opens up possibilities for individual expression and forecloses them.

Yet as important as these questions are, there are other equally significant issues at stake when it comes to consumerism. Just like workers, consumers are enmeshed in a web of power relations. Indeed, the very act of consumption sets all sorts of different processes in motion. For example, before the Civil War, American consumers (whether they realized it or not) benefited from the increasing efficiency of production on Southern slave plantations. In fact, because consumers are so important to the overall functioning of the U.S. economy, Americans have often wielded enormous power by collectively acting.

Though early American political economy depended on households to be self-sufficient, using the land to help sustain the family, consumer activity has long been a part of economic life in North America. For example, even in the era of the Early Republic, women operated as consumers (even if the category did not exist as we would understand today). A wife would haggle over prices. Women, Jeanne Boydston reports, even took part in food riots that might break out when a merchant's prices were deemed unjust (Boydston, 1996). As these examples suggest, there have long been ways in which individuals have exercised power through their role as consumers.

The power dynamics involved in consumer capitalism, though, are perhaps most visible in the late nineteenth century, especially after the Civil War. Of course, people consumed things before the 1860s, but the scope of production and consumption was vastly different from what it would become. It was really industrialization that made modern consumers. The historian Regina Lee Blaszczyk argues that industrialization and the mass production of consumer goods amounted to a 'democratization of things' (Blaszczyk, 2000). More than just making goods affordable, consumerism was a new economic role that provided a certain amount of agency and power for many Americans. Businesses had to develop 'feedback loops' as a way to understand what these consumers wanted. What's more, this new type of consumerism meant that these objects and products became some of the very materials that allowed Americans (and American women in particular) to craft their own sense of individual identity.

The rise of consumerism in the United States both upended and reinforced gender dynamics. For example, department stores, new spaces of consumption, provided some of the terrains on which issues of identity, class, and power were negotiated. Emerging in the 1890s, these stores represented a fundamentally new experience for the women who shopped there. Of course, the experience of shopping was not quite the same as possessing more tangible forms of democratic rights. Still, department stores at the end of the Gilded Age did offer a democratized experience. The stores themselves were palaces of opulence and luxury. Often huge, and filled with ornate details, late nineteenth-century department stores like Marshall Fields in Chicago and Wannamaker in Philadelphia rivaled great hotels and ballrooms. The displays behind glass offered a dreamworld of splendor. Shoppers would have been dazzled by the sheer abundance of new products wrapped up in branded and inviting packaging. The explosion of color, glass, and light amounted to what the historian William Leach described an 'aesthetic of desire' (Leach, 1993). In fact, the theatrical window displays all encouraged an orientation toward luxury and desire.

However, what is most significant about these palaces of consumption was the way that they could blur class distinctions. Leach points out that these spaces offered a mingling of 'desire' and 'refusal.' Indeed, these were spaces that present products that would have been unaffordable to some of these shoppers. Still, the spaces themselves allowed shoppers from different classes to mingle in the same spaces.

The relationship between capitalism and the individual changed in significant ways in the twentieth century. In particular, as mass production became increasingly efficient and possible, so did mass consumption. While this might seem to be a straightforward proposition, the emergence of mass consumption changed the experiences of Americans in all sorts of ways. In one of the most fundamental ways, mass consumerism raised interesting questions about democracy. The rise of the automobile offers one particularly salient example. Before the early twentieth century, automobiles were luxury, hobbiest items. However, it was Henry Ford who truly perfected the mass production process. With his factories' enormous scale (at places such as River Rouge) and the continuous assembly line, the Ford Motor Company was able to produce its Model T on a grand scale. As the process became more and more efficient, Ford drove down the retail price of the car as well. In this way, we might say that the Ford Model T 'democratized' the automobile, since it provided a product to many that had previously been unavailable. However, this sort of democratization only applied to that one, specific car.

It was another big car manufacturer, General Motors (GM), that would provide consumers with a range of choices when it came to cars. General Motors came together when the stock operator **Billy Durant** haphazardly purchased a number of different car makers before the Du Pont family gained control. In the 1920s, under the management of Alfred Sloan, GM organized these different car brands into different price categories – 'a car for every purse and purpose' – as the saying went. Wealthy consumers might prefer a Cadillac, while the Chevrolet Touring was meant to compete directly with the Model T. Along with annual model and body changes, GM offered consumers variety and style. Access or abundance – these were the two forms of consumer democracy that these two car companies offered Americans. It was also a choice that reverberated throughout the twentieth century.

Henry Ford abhorred the idea of a consumer's individuality. Catering to the whims and shifting tastes of individual people would have wreaked havoc on the company's highly efficient continuous assembly line. Even Ford's major competitor, General Motors, basically recognized this idea. As Alfred Sloan commented, GM's management was initially opposed to the annual model change because of how complicated it would be. Yet at the same time, Sloan and others understood the policy as meeting consumer demands. These two different approaches to the car business illustrate the complex ways in which consumer capitalism and individualism can intersect. Ford's business model expanded access to that quintessentially individualistic form of travel – the car – for a much broader group of Americans. Conversely, GM's 'car for every purse and purpose' offered car buyers enormous choices and the ability to fashion individual identity through their purchase in a way that Ford's exceedingly standardized Model T simply could not. GM's strategy was just one way in which the explosive growth of consumer products in the twentieth century afforded Americans the opportunity to forge a sense of identity.

Consumerism and Identity

For instance, beauty products that catered to the needs of specific consumers could have an enormous amount of political and cultural import when it came to identity. The case of **Madam CJ Walker** in the early twentieth century offers a particularly interesting example. Walker used beauty products to build a business, facing a number of challenges. First, at a time when standards of female beauty were implicitly coded as white, Walker intended to market beauty products specifically for Black women. Walker was not simply offering a beauty product. Instead, she was providing her customers with a degree of agency over their identities through the act of consumption. Additionally, Walker did have access to traditional methods of distribution. Simply put, white-owned retailers were not about to put products from a Black-owned company – especially one run by a woman – on their shelves. To get around this obstacle, Walker's saleswomen went door to door, often traveling in unfriendly terrain, during a time when lynching was widespread.

Similarly, the ways in which businesses communicated with American consumers also turned on questions of individualism and individual identity. The appeals that businesses made to consumers were very often as individuals. The advertisements that appeared in print, radio, and on television often promised to enrich the personal life of the potential buyer. In the twentieth century, advertising quickly became bound up with questions of individuality. At times, advertisers tried to suppress any notion of individuality. At other times, though, advertisers offered up their products as avenues to individuality.

Advertising grew up alongside an increasing sense of modernity in the first decades of the twentieth century. As the historian Roland Marchand argued in his classic study on the subject, this fast-paced, disorienting new world presented an opportunity for companies to sell their products (Marchand, 1985). During the 1920s, for instance, advertisers used their text-heavy advertisements as ways to position their products and companies as helpful guides for navigating this new and modern world. Along the way, through a prose style called 'scare copy,' the advertisements stoked modern fears. Bad breath might prevent business success for men. Without a specific beauty product, a wife might be less attractive to her husband. The solution to these problems, of course, was to use a branded product, like Listerine or Palmolive. Along the way, these advertisers also communicated unambiguous messages about gender roles.

Such advertisements were not a celebration of American individualism. Rather, they offered products as a way for people to fit in better with a wider society. Later in the twentieth century, though, advertisers moved in the opposite direction and pitched their products as avenues of individual expression. In the 1960s, advertisers for companies such as 7-Up devised campaigns that deliberately catered to a youthful counterculture – the same group of young Americans who explicitly rejected a sense of postwar conformity. In the 1980s, and in tandem with its overall corporate ethos, Apple Computers perfected the advertisement as a manifesto of individualism. The company's famous 1984 ad for the Macintosh computer featured a woman dressed in color who smashes a giant television screen broadcasting a dictatorial face dispensing propaganda to a mass of gray, nearly identical figures. The television spot was, of course, a nod to George Orwell's classic novel. But it was also a rhetorical slap in the face to IBM. In the 1990s, the company also launched the 'Think Different' advertising campaign, which featured a number of famous iconoclasts.

Consumer capitalism has also played a role in fostering and supporting all sorts of different communities in the United States. For example, in the middle of the twentieth century, the marketing of products like bodybuilding magazines to gay consumers helped grow and sustain a shared sense of gay identity and community. While many of us would point to the 1969 Stonewall riots as the start of the gay liberation movement, as the historian David Johnson argues, it was gay consumer culture that first created the conditions for the more overtly political moment (a moment, it is worth noting, that started off in a commercial space). In this case, gay men became one of the primary audiences for physique magazines in the 1950s and 1960s (Johnson, 2010). During these years, some entrepreneurial magazine publishers specifically catered to gay buyers. In other words, they had discovered a consumer market. The significance here was more than just the magazine. As Johnson notes, the magazines helped consumers form an '**imagined community**.' In other words, the gay men who bought these magazines began to picture themselves as connected to like-minded consumers in different parts of the country. It was through this act of consumption that these men could more fully develop their individual identities. Yet the full impact of this development was more than just cultural – as significant as that was. As authorities moved to crack down on these magazines, that group of consumers was primed for political action. These entrepreneurial magazine publishers began running editorials pushing back against censorship. In fact, even later, as some of these publishers went to court, the outcome of the trial, at least in part, hinged on the rights of consumers. Consumerism, then, has played a big role in helping to foster and sustain gay culture.

As this experience suggests, there was a lot at stake in being able to participate in American consumer society. For instance, as the historian Brenna Wynn Greer has argued, during the height of the Cold War in the middle of the twentieth century, American ideology explicitly linked consumerism and citizenship (Greer, 2019). Indeed, during the famous 'Kitchen Sink Debate' in 1959 between then-vice president Richard Nixon and Soviet premier Nikita Krushev, the back and forth about which nation's economic system was better hinged on which system offered the most to consumers.

For Black Americans, the stakes were even higher. After all, these were the same years as the civil rights movement, when Black Americans were working towards a fuller sense of American citizenship. As a part of this, representations of Black Americans acting as middle-class consumers carried a great deal of weight. The advertising campaigns that the African American public relations executive **Moss Kendrix** created for the Coca-Cola company in the 1950s offer a particularly telling example of this dynamic. Up until the 1950s, the Atlanta-based soda company did not advertise to Black consumers. Yet after Pepsi-Cola launched their own advertising campaign aimed at Black consumers, Coca-Cola relied on Kendrix. The resulting advertising campaign featured Black models drinking the soda in the same settings that the company's other marketing campaigns that featured white models did. In some ways, it was not all that exceptional or innovative. What is more, such advertisements contained no trace of the sort of individualism that would be celebrated in other facets of American society. The marketing campaign presented an idealized image of pleasant middle-class conformity. However, in the context of the Cold War and the civil rights struggle, an image of Black consumers had a lot of political import. In an era in which Black Americans were engaged in a struggle for political representation, the end of segregation, and access to the sort of rights and privileges routinely afforded white families, being perceived as consumers on par with the unstated, but clearly imagined, white consumers, meant that it was more than just a bottle of Coke.

However, such attempts to wed marketing campaigns to an emerging sense of identity could also fall flat. As the historian Neil Foley demonstrates, in the 1970s and 1980s, businesses began to cater to the suddenly sizable 'Hispanic market' (Foley, 2014). A range of consumer companies such as McDonalds directed marketing efforts squarely at Latinos. However, some of these companies, such as Frito-Lay, came under fire for marketing campaigns that some advocacy groups decried as racist. As all of these examples illustrate, consumer capitalism has played an important role in the evolution of American individualism. Indeed, the act of consumption has given some Americans a sense of agency and control over fashioning their own identity.

To be sure, though, consumer society was not without its critics. These complaints against consumerism and what it does to the individual have become a persistent theme in American literature. **Theodore Dreiser**'s Gilded Age novel, *Sister Carrie*, offered a very clear and pointed criticism of Gilded Age consumption. Likewise, the nineteenth-century economist **Thornstein Veblen** blasted what he termed **conspicuous consumption**. In the twentieth century, a number of different figures have challenged and critiqued consumerism. These critics warned about the threat to individualism throughout the twentieth century. In the early, heady days of the postwar era, for instance, **Vance Packard** argued that Americans were victims of sophisticated ways of manipulating tastes and desires in his book, *The Hidden Persuaders* (Doc. 16). Such complaints did not fade in subsequent years. In the 1990s and early 2000s, writers such as Naomi Klein and Thomas Frank described the ways in which corporations had effectively capitalized on identity politics, rendering people's sense of self nothing more than a commodity.

Consumer Activism in the Early Twentieth Century

As these struggles over representation, individuality, and identity suggest, consumption was a deeply political act. In fact, consumption has carried significant political weight for Americans who are not white. Mirroring experiences in other aspects of economic life, Black consumers also found themselves excluded from fully participating in the economy. In some cases, businesses simply did not welcome Black consumer dollars. For example, a Black consumer might not have been able to buy a new Cadillac, even when he or she had the ability to pay cash. Even amid the economic boom of the postwar era, the American Dream was systematically denied to Black Americans. For instance, practices such as 'blockbusting' and 'redlining' meant that homeownership remained out of reach for many Black families.

However, the nature of consumerism meant that power could flow in both directions. Some white businesses might have balked at accepting Black dollars, but money was still money and throughout the twentieth century, Black Americans effectively used the power of the consumer's wallet toward a political end. Such efforts were particularly notable in the 1930s. Through organized strategies and slogans such as 'Don't Buy Where You Can't Work,' Black consumers placed pressure on white businesses to hire Black employees. In the middle of the twentieth century, 'Double-Duty Dollar' drives framed consumer spending as an inherently political act. Black women often took the lead in marshaling this consumer power. Working through 'Housewives Leaves,' these women even collected information on white-owned stores that were not hiring Black workers.

In short, even a seemingly everyday individual activity like shopping has vast implications for capitalism's functioning and individual identity. To act as a consumer is not to simply maintain a household or keep up with the latest fashion. Our personal buying choices are also deeply connected to these larger systems.

Consumer-Worker Coalitions

Though the history of unions and consumerism involved questions and contests over the nature of identity and individualism, both roles provided workers and consumers unique opportunities for momentarily exercising economic power to advance their own interests. Repeatedly during the twentieth and twenty-first centuries, individual Americans were often able to exercise power often by subsuming their own sense of individualism into a larger collective of workers or consumers. Indeed, as the economy became more and more complex, organized groups such as unions and organized consumer actions, such as boycotts, altered – even if only briefly – capitalism's power dynamics.

There were also instances when groups of workers and consumers could work together. One notable example was the Delano Grape Strike, which began in 1965. The strike started in Delano, California, with unionized Filipino workers after their wages were cut, but it was the arrival of **Cesar Chavez** and the National Farm Workers Association that truly galvanized the action. Through dramatic actions, such as leading a 300-mile trek to Sacramento (the state's capitol) and his own hunger strike, Chavez and other strikers were able to garner both media attention and support. Crucially, the strike was particularly effective when Chavez and others were able to bring consumers into the struggle. After the creation of the United Farm Workers union, the strikers and organizers made direct appeals to consumers.

Before long, the Delano Grape Strike was a matter not just of union actions but also of consumer power. For instance, in 1973, Chavez and his supporters began a boycott of Gallo wines. T-shirts that exclaimed 'There's Blood on Those Grapes! Don't Buy Gallo Wine,' served to put pressure on companies from both the production and consumption side of the economy. It was a strategy that Chavez repeated again when calling attention to the dangers of specific pesticides in agriculture. Chavez understood that such environmental concerns had the potential to unite consumers and producers. In 1986, he again worked to unite these two groups around these issues in what has become known as the 'Wrath of the Grapes Boycott,' which he launched with a speech. In this speech, Chavez located common areas of immediate concern for both farm workers and consumers. Significantly, in doing so, he also articulated the strength of collective work, declaring: 'I see us as one family. We cannot turn our backs on each other and our future. We farm workers are closest to food production. We were the first to recognize the serious health hazards of agriculture pesticides to both consumers and ourselves' (Chavez, 1986). As always, in his rhetoric, Chavez cast the immediate issue of pesticide use in grand moral terms about mutual responsibility and a shared sense of humanity before detailing some of the specific dangers of the chemicals. Behind such moral appeals, though, was the awareness of the power that both consumers and laborers could wield by setting aside – even if only temporarily – American cultural celebrations of individualism.

Worker-consumer boycotts could indeed prove to be a potent weapon, especially when they were organized by different groups. As Allyson Brantley details, in the second part of the twentieth century, Mexican Americans led a strike and boycott against the Coors brewery (Brantley, 2021). At first, the complaint had to do with exclusionary hiring practices, though the trouble for the beer company would grow beyond this initial focus, involving many different groups and lasting, ultimately, for years. In the 1970s, gay rights groups and the National Organization of Women (NOW) also joined the boycott because of the brewery owners' staunch conservativism regarding a range of social issues. The Coors boycott offers a vivid demonstration of how power dynamics and geometries can shift rapidly under capitalism.

These combinations of different groups of consumers, workers, women, LGBTQ activists, and Latinos also reveal the ways in which American values of individualism have run up against hard limits amid capitalism's complexities. To be sure, the image of the rugged individual is one that immediately conjures a sense of agency and ability. However, the examples of the Delano Grape Strike and the Coors Boycott suggest that in many cases, agency and power can only be achieved through (at least temporarily) subsuming one's individualism into a broader collective in order for each individual to achieve their specific goals.

Collectivity in the Twenty-First Century

The **World Trade Organization** protests in 1999 offered the first sign of a growing sense of discontent with capitalism in the age of globalization. At this meeting, a number of different activists, from unions to environmental groups, converged on Seattle to protest what they saw as global capitalism's destructive and anti-democratic tendencies. While the protests did not involve the same degree of coordination between consumers and workers that the Delano Grape Strike and the Coors Boycott did, the WTO protests offered further evidence of the ways in which collective action could sometimes be more effective politically than the efforts of lone individuals.

A similar sense of discontent erupted in 2011 in Zuccotti Part, near Wall Street. The people who assembled there as **Occupy Wall Street** were animated by the 2008 crisis. The movement's structure was explicitly non-individualistic. Occupy Wall Street was intended to be leaderless, with decisions being reached through consensus. The camps, which popped up in other cities around the country, offered vivid and pessimistic critiques of the massive wealth inequalities that characterized the neoliberal era. To be sure, Occupy Wall Street was short-lived. Police ultimately cleared them out. However, the phrase 'We are the 99%' – as opposed to the planet's wealthiest one percent – stuck around. The Democratic politician Bernie Sanders invoked it in his ultimately unsuccessful presidential bids in 2016 and 2020. Still, it was a signal that a sense of collectivity and society – as opposed to individualism – had gained some measure of purchase in American political discourse.

The story of labor collectives such as unions and consumer groups suggests yet another layer to consider when it comes to the relationship between capitalism and individualism in the United States. Much like the ways in which systems and organizations have shaped the fortunes and options for individuals in American capitalism, the periodic collective power of individual Americans reveals the layers of complexity in American capitalism. Much as individuals have struggled to find their place in a capitalist system filled with large businesses, the experiences of worker unions and consumer movements suggest ways in which assumptions of power and agency can shift.

6 Assessment

The history of capitalism in the United States is, in the end, a story of the unsettled dynamic between ideal and reality. Moreover, American notions of individualism have played a consequential role in this back and forth. From a very early point, individualism has held a cherished place in American thought and culture. Given the nation's origins in the struggle for independence from England, this emphasis on personal liberty and freedom may indeed seem understandable. Since that time, this core sense of individual autonomy and freedom has appeared in many different guises. It is a value that in many ways cuts across political divides. No one party or politician has been able to lay complete and total claim to individualism as a value (though many have tried). Likewise, both business owners and laborers have at times grabbed onto the idea to justify their actions or to help them shape a sense of identity.

Beyond being an American value, individualism has proven to be a perfect complement for capitalism in the United States. Much as personal liberty was an early value in American politics and culture, the lone economic actor has long been a staple of economic thought. Little wonder, then, that individualism has been central to understandings of American capitalism. Yet individualism – as it appears in political rhetoric, economic treatises, works of fiction, and self-consciously crafted public images – has always represented an ideal, not a reality.

The lived experience of American capitalism is not the story of lone actors but, rather, of many different people's negotiations with a big and complex environment. Changing political winds, the growth of whole industries, new technologies, and global patterns of trade are just some of the broader factors that bear directly on individual success. These forces have both limited options and created opportunities for Americans. The parts of a person's identity have also played an important role in shaping one's fortunes. Black Americans and women, for instance, have not had access to the same freedom of movement that white men have always enjoyed. For people of

DOI: 10.4324/9781003090526-7

Asian and Latin American descent, questions of citizenship, and all the rights that citizenship confers, have also presented barriers.

And so, the history of American capitalism is one of the tension and attempts to reconcile myth and experience. Just as importantly, individualism is not simply a cultural belief but an idea that has actively shaped American capitalism. It is an idea that has motivated politicians, blocked union power, forestalled legislation, and made celebrities out of businesspeople. Ultimately, American capitalism and individualism have changed through this complex interplay. Neither the idea nor the system is stable. Both have morphed and evolved – sometimes gradually and sometimes suddenly – since the nation's founding. What this means, of course, is that the dynamic between capitalism and individualism that we experience today is not necessarily the one we will experience tomorrow. As the twenty-first century continues to unfold, the American experience will continue to be – at least in some way – the product of this unstable relationship.

Documents

Document 1: Adam Smith, *The Wealth of Nations*: Book I, Chapter II (1776)

Smith's work is undoubtedly one of the core intellectual foundations of capitalism. Early on in The Wealth of Nations, *Smith describes the division of labor, which would later become a fixture of American industry and factory work. Though it would, in this way, appear to frustrate a sense of individualism, in this passage, Smith connects the division of labor to individual agency and self-interest.*

This division of labour, from which so many advantages are derived, is not originally the effect of any human wisdom, which foresees and intends that general opulence to which it gives occasion. It is the necessary, though very slow and gradual, consequence of a certain propensity in human nature, which has in view no such extensive utility; the propensity to truck, barter, and exchange one thing for another.

[. . .] In almost every other race of animals, each individual, when it is grown up to maturity, is entirely independent, and in its natural state has occasion for the assistance of no other living creature. But man has almost constant occasion for the help of his brethren, and it is in vain for him to expect it from their benevolence only. He will be more likely to prevail if he can interest their self-love in his favour, and shew them that it is for their own advantage to do for him what he requires of them. Whoever offers to another a bargain of any kind, proposes to do this. Give me that which I want, and you shall have this which you want, is the meaning of every such offer; and it is in this manner that we obtain from one another the far greater part of those good offices which we stand in need of. It is not from the benevolence of the butcher, the brewer, or the baker that we expect our dinner, but from their regard to their own interest. We address ourselves, not to their humanity, but to their self-love, and never talk to them of our own necessities, but of their advantages. Nobody but a beggar chooses to depend chiefly upon the benevolence of his fellow-citizens. Even a beggar does not depend upon it entirely. The charity of well-disposed people, indeed, supplies him with the whole fund of his subsistence. But though this principle ultimately provides him with all the necessaries of life which he has occasion for, it neither does nor can provide him with them as he has occasion for them. The greater part of his occasional wants are supplied in the same manner as those of other people, by treaty, by barter, and by purchase. With the money which one man gives him he purchases food. The old clothes which another bestows upon him he exchanges for other clothes which suit him better, or for lodging, or for food, or for money, with which he can buy either food, clothes, or lodging, as he has occasion.

As it is by treaty, by barter, and by purchase, that we obtain from one another the greater part of those mutual good offices which we stand in need of, so it is this same trucking disposition which originally gives occasion to the division of labour. In a tribe of hunters or shepherds, a particular person makes bows and arrows, for example, with more readiness and dexterity than any other. He frequently exchanges them for cattle or for venison, with his companions; and he finds at last that he can, in this manner, get more cattle and venison, than if he himself went to the field to catch them. From a regard to his own interest, therefore, the making of bows and arrows grows to be his chief business, and he becomes a sort of armourer. Another excels in making the frames and covers of their little huts or moveable houses. He is accustomed to be of use in this way to his neighbours, who reward him in the same manner with cattle and with venison, till at last he finds it his interest to dedicate himself entirely to this employment, and to become a sort of house-carpenter. In the same manner a third becomes a smith or a brazier; a fourth, a tanner or dresser of hides or skins, the principal part of the clothing of savages. And thus the certainty of being able to exchange all that surplus part of the produce of his own labour, which is over and above his own consumption, for such parts of the produce of other men's labour as he may have occasion for, encourages every man to apply himself to a particular occupation, and to cultivate and bring to perfection whatever talent of genius he may possess for that particular species of business.

Source: www.gutenberg.org/files/38194/38194-h/38194-h.htm

Document 2: Thomas Jefferson, *Notes on the State of Virginia*, Query XIX (1785)

Jefferson was deeply suspicious of manufacturing, and instead envisioned a nation of yeoman farmers. In this passage, he articulates the reasoning behind his opposition to manufacturing in the United States.

The present state of manufactures, commerce, interior and exterior trade?

The political economists of Europe have established it as a principle that every state should endeavour to manufacture for itself: and this principle, like many others, we transfer to America, without calculating the difference of circumstance which should often produce a difference of result. In Europe the lands are either cultivated, or locked up against the cultivator. Manufacture must therefore be resorted to of necessity not of choice, to support the surplus of their people. But we have an immensity of land courting the industry of the husbandman. Is it best then that all our citizens should be employed in its improvement, or that one half should be called off from that to exercise manufactures and handicraft arts for the other? Those who labour in the earth are the chosen people of God, if ever he had a chosen people, whose breasts he has made his peculiar deposit for substantial and genuine virtue. It is the focus in which he keeps alive that sacred fire, which otherwise might escape from the face of the earth. Corruption of morals in the mass of cultivators is a phenomenon of which no age nor nation has furnished an example. It is the mark set on those, who not looking up to heaven, to their own soil and industry, as does the husbandman, for their subsistence, depend for it on the casualties and caprice of customers. Dependence begets subservience and venality, suffocates the germ of virtue, and prepares fit tools for the designs of ambition. This, the natural progress and consequence of the arts, has sometimes perhaps been retarded by accidental circumstances: but, generally speaking, the proportion which the aggregate of the other classes of citizens bears in any state to that of its husbandmen, is the proportion of its unsound to its healthy parts, and is a good-enough barometer whereby to measure its degree of corruption. While we have land to labour then, let us never wish to see our citizens occupied at a work-bench, or twirling a distaff. Carpenters, masons, smiths, are wanting in husbandry: but, for the general operations of manufacture, let our work-shops remain in Europe. It is better to carry provisions and materials to workmen there, than bring them to the provisions and materials, and with them their manners and principles. The loss by the transportation of commodities across the Atlantic will be made up in happiness and permanence of government. The mobs of great cities add just so much to the support of pure government, as sores do to the strength of the human body. It is the manners and spirit of a people which preserve a republic in vigour. A degeneracy in these is a canker which soon eats to the heart of its laws and constitution.

Source: https://web.archive.org/web/20080914030942/http://etext.lib.virginia.edu/toc/modeng/public/JefVirg.html

Document 3: Benjamin Franklin, Selection from *Poor Richard Improved* 1758

Franklin was a prolific writer. In this book, Franklin (writing under various guises) expounded on the idea of character and economy. In this selection, Franklin espouses the role of individual responsibility when it comes to financial and economic matters.

Friends, says he, and Neighbours, the Taxes are indeed very heavy, and if those laid on by the Government were the only Ones we had to pay, we might more easily discharge them; but we have many others, and much more grievous to some of us. We are taxed twice as much by our *Idleness*, three times as much by our *Pride*, and four times as much by our *Folly*, and from these Taxes the Commissioners cannot ease or deliver us by allowing an Abatement. However let us hearken to good Advice, and something may be done for us; *God helps them that help themselves*, as Poor Richard says, in his Almanack of 1733.

[. . .]

So what signifies *wishing* and *hoping* for better Times. We may make these Times better if we bestir ourselves. *Industry need not wish*, as Poor

Richard says, and *He that lives upon Hope will die fasting. There are no Gains, without Pains*; then *Help Hands, for I have no Lands*, or if I have, they are smartly taxed. And, as Poor Richard likewise observes, *He that hath a Trade hath an Estate*, and *He that hath a Calling hath an Office of Profit and Honour*; but then the *Trade* must be worked at, and the *Calling* well followed, or neither the *Estate*, nor the *Office*, will enable us to pay our Taxes. If we are industrious we shall never starve; for, as Poor Richard says, *At the working Man's House Hunger looks in, but dares not enter*. Nor will the Bailiff nor the Constable enter, for *Industry pays Debts, while Despair encreaseth them*, says Poor Richard. What though you have found no Treasure, nor has any rich Relation left you a Legacy, *Diligence is the Mother of Good luck*, as Poor Richard says, and *God gives all Things to Industry*. Then *plough deep, while Sluggards sleep, and you shall have Corn to sell and to keep*, says Poor Dick. Work while it is called To-day, for you know not how much you may be hindered To-morrow, which makes Poor Richard say, *One To-day is worth two Tomorrows*; and farther, *Have you somewhat to do To-morrow, do it To-day*. If you were a Servant, would you not be ashamed that a good Master should catch you idle? Are you then your own Master, *be ashamed to catch yourself idle*, as Poor Dick says.

Source: https://founders.archives.gov/documents/Franklin/01-07-02-0146

Document 4: Alexis de Tocqueville: *Democracy in America*, Book I, Chapter XIII: Government Of The Democracy In America – Part II (1835)

In this passage, Tocqueville discusses the importance of business and commerce in the United States.

Independently of the laws, all these causes concur to exercise a very powerful influence upon the conduct of the finances of the State. If the Americans never spend the money of the people in galas, it is not only because the imposition of taxes is under the control of the people, but because the people takes no delight in public rejoicings. If they repudiate all ornament from their architecture, and set no store on any but the more practical and homely advantages, it is not only because they live under democratic institutions, but because they are a commercial nation. The habits of private life are continued in public; and we ought carefully to distinguish that economy which depends upon their institutions from that which is the natural result of their manners and customs.

Source: https://gutenberg.org/ebooks/815

Document 5: Alexis de Tocqueville: *Democracy in America*, Book II, Section 2, Chapter 2 (1840)

Tocqueville is often credited with coining the term 'individualism.' In this passage, he explains the term and discusses some of its implications.

I have shown how it is that in ages of equality every man seeks for his opinions within himself: I am now about to show how it is that, in the same ages, all his feelings are turned towards himself alone. Individualism a is a novel expression, to which a novel idea has given birth. Our fathers were only acquainted with egotism. Egotism is a passionate and exaggerated love of self, which leads a man to connect everything with his own person, and to prefer himself to everything in the world. Individualism is a mature and calm feeling, which disposes each member of the community to sever himself from the mass of his fellow-creatures; and to draw apart with his family and his friends; so that, after he has thus formed a little circle of his own, he willingly leaves society at large to itself. Egotism originates in blind instinct: individualism proceeds from erroneous judgment more than from depraved feelings; it originates as much in the deficiencies of the mind as in the perversity of the heart. Egotism blights the germ of all virtue; individualism, at first, only saps the virtues of public life; but, in the long run, it attacks and destroys all others, and is at length absorbed in downright egotism. Egotism is a vice as old as the world, which does not belong to one form of society more than to another: individualism is of democratic origin, and it threatens to spread in the same ratio as the equality of conditions.

Amongst aristocratic nations, as families remain for centuries in the same condition, often on the same spot, all generations become as it were contemporaneous. A man almost always knows his forefathers, and respects them: he thinks he already sees his remote descendants, and he loves them. He willingly imposes duties on himself towards the former and the latter; and he will frequently sacrifice his personal gratifications to those who went before and to those who will come after him. Aristocratic institutions have, moreover, the effect of closely binding every man to several of his fellow-citizens. As the classes of an aristocratic people are strongly marked and permanent, each of them is regarded by its own members as a sort of lesser country, more tangible and more cherished than the country at large. As in aristocratic communities all the citizens occupy fixed positions, one above the other, the result is that each of them always sees a man above himself whose patronage is necessary to him, and below himself another man whose co-operation he may claim. Men living in aristocratic ages are therefore almost always closely attached to something placed out of their own sphere, and they are often disposed to forget themselves. It is true that in those ages the notion of human fellowship is faint, and that men seldom think of sacrificing themselves for mankind; but they often sacrifice themselves for other men. In democratic ages, on the contrary, when the duties of each individual to the race are much more clear, devoted service to any one man becomes more rare; the bond of human affection is extended, but it is relaxed.

Amongst democratic nations new families are constantly springing up, others are constantly falling away, and all that remain change their condition; the woof of time is every instant broken, and the track of generations effaced. Those who went before are soon forgotten; of those who will come after no one has any idea: the interest of man is confined to those in close propinquity to himself. As each class approximates to other classes, and intermingles with them, its members become indifferent and as strangers to one another. Aristocracy had made a chain of all the members of the community, from the peasant to the king: democracy breaks that chain, and severs every link of it. As social conditions become more equal, the number of persons increases who, although they are neither rich enough nor powerful enough to exercise any great influence over their fellow-creatures, have nevertheless acquired or retained sufficient education and fortune to satisfy their own wants. They owe nothing to any man, they expect nothing from any man; they acquire the habit of always considering themselves as standing alone, and they are apt to imagine that their whole destiny is in their own hands. Thus not only does democracy make every man forget his ancestors, but it hides his descendants, and separates his contemporaries from him; it throws him back forever upon himself alone, and threatens in the end to confine him entirely within the solitude of his own heart.

Source: https://gutenberg.org/ebooks/816

Document 6: Ralph Waldo Emerson: 'Self-Reliance,' 1841

Emerson's essay has proven to be one of the earliest and clearest articulations of individualism in the United States.

The populace think that your rejection of popular standards is a rejection of all standard, and mere antinomianism; and the bold sensualist will use the name of philosophy to gild his crimes. But the law of consciousness abides. There are two confessionals, in one or the other of which we must be shriven. You may fulfil your round of duties by clearing yourself in the *direct*, or in the *reflex* way. Consider whether you have satisfied your relations to father, mother, cousin, neighbour, town, cat, and dog; whether any of these can upbraid you. But I may also neglect this reflex standard, and absolve me to myself. I have my own stern claims and perfect circle. It denies the name of duty to many offices that are called duties. But if I can discharge its debts, it enables me to dispense with the popular code. If any one imagines that this law is lax, let him keep its commandment one day.

And truly it demands something godlike in him who has cast off the common motives of humanity, and has ventured to trust himself for a taskmaster. High be his heart, faithful his will, clear his sight, that he may in good earnest be doctrine, society, law, to himself, that a simple purpose may be to him as strong as iron necessity is to others!

If any man considers the present aspects of what is called by distinction society, he will see the need of these ethics. The sinew and heart of man seem to be drawn out, and we are become timorous, desponding whimperers. We are afraid of truth, afraid of fortune, afraid of death, and afraid of each other. Our age yields no great and perfect persons. We want men and women who shall renovate life and our social state, but we see that most natures are insolvent, cannot satisfy their own wants, have an ambition out of all proportion to their practical force, and do lean and beg day and night continually. Our housekeeping is mendicant, our arts, our occupations, our marriages, our religion, we have not chosen, but society has chosen for us. We are parlour soldiers. We shun the rugged battle of fate, where strength is born.

If our young men miscarry in their first enterprises, they lose all heart. If the young merchant fails, men say he is ruined. If the finest genius studies at one of our colleges, and is not installed in an office within one year afterwards in the cities or suburbs of Boston or New York, it seems to his friends and to himself that he is right in being disheartened, and in complaining the rest of his life. A sturdy lad from New Hampshire or Vermont, who in turn tries all the professions, who *teams it, farms it, peddles*, keeps a school, preaches, edits a newspaper, goes to Congress, buys a township, and so forth, in successive years, and always, like a cat, falls on his feet, is worth a hundred of these city dolls. He walks abreast with his days, and feels no shame in not 'studying a profession,' for he does not postpone his life, but lives already. He has not one chance, but a hundred chances.

[. . .]

It is easy to see that a greater self-reliance must work a revolution in all the offices and relations of men; in their religion; in their education; in their pursuits; their modes of living; their association; in their property; in their speculative views.

Source: www.gutenberg.org/files/2944/2944-h/2944-h.htm

Document 7: Homestead Act (May 20, 1862)

The Homestead Act mobilized the value of individualism as a way to encourage settler-colonialism in the western United States.

CHAP. LXXV. – *An Act to Secure Homesteads to Actual Settlers on the Public Domain*

Be it enacted by the Senate and House of Representatives of the United States of America in Congress assembled, That any person who is the head of a family, or who has arrived at the age of twenty-one years, and is a citizen of the United States, or who shall have filed his declaration of intention to become such, as required by the naturalization laws of the United States, and who has never borne arms against the United States Government or given aid and comfort to its enemies, shall, from and after the first January, eighteen hundred and sixty-three, be entitled to enter one quarter section or a less quantity of unappropriated public lands, upon which said person may have filed a preemption claim, or which may, at the time the application is made, be subject to preemption at one dollar and twenty-five cents, or less, per acre; or eighty acres or less of such unappropriated lands, at two dollars and fifty cents per acre, to be located in a body, in conformity to the legal subdivisions of the public lands, and after the same shall have been surveyed: Provided, That any person owning and residing on land may, under the provisions of this act, enter other land lying contiguous to his or her said land, which shall not, with the land so already owned and occupied, exceed in the aggregate one hundred and sixty acres.

SEC. 2. And be it further enacted, That the person applying for the benefit of this act shall, upon application to the register of the land office in which he or she is about to make such entry, make affidavit before the said register or receiver that he or she is the head of a family, or is twenty-one years or more of age, or shall have performed service in the army or navy of the United States, and that he has never borne arms against the Government of the United States or given aid and comfort to its enemies, and that such application is made for his or her exclusive use and benefit, and that said entry is made for the purpose of actual settlement and cultivation, and not either directly or indirectly for the use or benefit of any other person or persons whomsoever; and upon filing the said affidavit with the register or receiver, and on payment of ten dollars, he or she shall thereupon be permitted to enter the quantity of land specified:

Source: www.archives.gov/milestone-documents/homestead-act

Document 8: Horatio Alger, from *Ragged Dick* (1868)

In this passage from Horatio Alger's children's novel, Ragged Dick, *the main character, Dick, learns a lesson in individual initiative from his friend Frank's wealthy uncle. The novel was meant to instruct children in moral living and included lessons about hard work. The title character is essentially a self-made man in training.*

'Now,' said Frank, 'I think I'll go back to the Astor House. Uncle has probably got through his business and returned.'

'All right,' said Dick.

The two boys walked up to Broadway, just where the tall steeple of Trinity faces the street of bankers and brokers, and walked leisurely to the hotel. When they arrived at the Astor House, Dick said, 'Good-by, Frank.'

'Not yet,' said Frank; 'I want you to come in with me.'

Dick followed his young patron up the steps. Frank went to the reading-room, where, as he had thought probable, he found his uncle already arrived, and reading a copy of 'The Evening Post,' which he had just purchased outside.

'Well, boys," he said, looking up, 'have you had a pleasant jaunt?'

'Yes, sir,' said Frank. 'Dick's a capital guide.'

'So this is Dick,' said Mr. Whitney, surveying him with a smile. 'Upon my word, I should hardly have known him. I must congratulate him on his improved appearance.'

'Frank's been very kind to me,' said Dick, who, rough street-boy as he was, had a heart easily touched by kindness, of which he had never experienced much. 'He's a tip-top fellow.'

'I believe he is a good boy,' said Mr. Whitney. 'I hope, my lad, you will prosper and rise in the world. You know in this free country poverty in early life is no bar to a man's advancement. I haven't risen very high myself,' he added, with a smile, 'but have met with moderate success in life; yet there was a time when I was as poor as you.'

'Were you, sir,' asked Dick, eagerly.

'Yes, my boy, I have known the time I have been obliged to go without my dinner because I didn't have enough money to pay for it.'

'How did you get up in the world,' asked Dick, anxiously.

'I entered a printing-office as an apprentice, and worked for some years. Then my eyes gave out and I was obliged to give that up. Not knowing what else to do, I went into the country, and worked on a farm. After a while I was lucky enough to invent a machine, which has brought me in a great deal of money. But there was one thing I got while I was in the printing-office which I value more than money.'

'What was that, sir?'

'A taste for reading and study. During my leisure hours I improved myself by study, and acquired a large part of the knowledge which I now possess. Indeed, it was one of my books that first put me on the track of the invention, which I afterwards made. So you see, my lad, that my studious habits paid me in money, as well as in another way.'

'I'm awful ignorant,' said Dick, soberly.

'But you are young, and, I judge, a smart boy. If you try to learn, you can, and if you ever expect to do anything in the world, you must know something of books.'

'I will,' said Dick, resolutely. 'I aint always goin' to black boots for a livin'.'

'All labor is respectable, my lad, and you have no cause to be ashamed of any honest business; yet when you can get something to do that promises better for your future prospects, I advise you to do so. Till then earn your living in the way you are accustomed to, avoid extravagance, and save up a little money if you can.'

'Thank you for your advice,' said our hero. 'There aint many that takes an interest in Ragged Dick.'

'So that's your name,' said Mr. Whitney. 'If I judge you rightly, it won't be long before you change it. Save your money, my lad, buy books, and determine to be somebody, and you may yet fill an honorable position.'

'I'll try,' said Dick. 'Good-night, sir.'

Source: www.gutenberg.org/files/5348/5348-h/5348-h.htm

Document 9: Booker T. Washington: *Up from Slavery* (1901)

In his book, Washington draws heavily from the narrative of the self-made man. In this chapter, Washington describes how he raised money for the Tuskegee Institute, an endeavor which brought him into contact with other iconic individualists, including Andrew Carnegie.

[. . .] Time and time again I have been asked, by people who are trying to secure money for philanthropic purposes, what rule or rules I followed to secure the interest and help of people who were able to contribute money to worthy objects. As far as the science of what is called begging can be reduced to rules, I would say that I have had but two rules. First, always to do my whole duty regarding making our work known to individuals and organizations; and, second, not to worry about the results. This second rule has been the hardest for me to live up to. When bills are on the eve of falling due, with not a dollar in hand with which to meet them, it is pretty difficult to learn not to worry, although I think I am learning more and more each year that all worry simply consumes, and to no purpose, just so much physical and mental strength that might otherwise be given to effective work. After considerable experience in coming into contact with wealthy and noted men, I have observed that those who have accomplished the greatest results are those who "keep under the body"; are those who never grow excited or lose self-control, but are always calm, self-possessed, patient, and polite. I think that President William McKinley is the best example of a man of this class that I have ever seen.

[. . .]

My experience in getting money for Tuskegee has taught me to have no patience with those people who are always condemning the rich because they are rich, and because they do not give more to objects of charity. In the first place, those who are guilty of such sweeping criticisms do not know how many people would be made poor, and how much suffering would result, if wealthy people were to part all at once with any large proportion of their wealth in a way to disorganize and cripple great business enterprises. Then very few persons have any idea of the large number of applications for help that rich people are constantly being flooded with. I know wealthy people who receive as much as twenty calls a day for help. More than once when I have gone into the offices of rich men, I have found half a dozen persons waiting to see them, and all come for the same purpose, that of securing money. And all these calls in person, to say nothing of the applications received through the mails. Very few people have any idea of the amount of money given away by persons who never permit their names to be known. I have often heard persons condemned for not giving away money, who, to my own knowledge, were giving away thousands of dollars every year so quietly that the world knew nothing about it.

[. . .]

Although it has been my privilege to be the medium through which a good many hundred thousand dollars have been received for the work at Tuskegee, I have always avoided what the world calls 'begging.' I often tell people that I have never 'begged' any money, and that I am not a 'beggar.' My experience and observation have convinced me that persistent asking outright for money from the rich does not, as a rule, secure help. I have usually proceeded on the principle that persons who possess sense enough to earn money have sense enough to know how to give it away, and that the mere making known of the facts regarding Tuskegee, and especially the facts regarding the work of the graduates, has been more effective than outright begging. I think that the presentation of facts, on a high, dignified plane, is all the begging that most rich people care for.

While the work of going from door to door and from office to office is hard, disagreeable, and costly in bodily strength, yet it has some compensations. Such work gives one a rare opportunity to study human nature. It also has its compensations in giving one an opportunity to meet some of the best people in the world – to be more correct, I think I should say the best people in the world. When one takes a broad survey of the country, he will find that the most useful and influential people in it are those who take the deepest interest in institutions that exist for the purpose of making the world better.

[. . .]

A short time ago we received twenty thousand dollars from Mr. Andrew Carnegie, to be used for the purpose of erecting a new library building. Our first library and reading-room were in a corner of a shanty, and the whole thing occupied a space about five by twelve feet. It required ten years of work before I was able to secure Mr. Carnegie's interest and help. The first time I saw him, ten years ago, he seemed to take but little interest in our school, but I was determined to show him that we were worthy of his help. After ten years of hard work I wrote him a letter reading as follows:

[. . .]

The next mail brought back the following reply: "I will be very glad to pay the bills for the library building as they are incurred, to the extent of twenty thousand dollars, and I am glad of this opportunity to show the interest I have in your noble work."

Source: https://gutenberg.org/files/2376/2376-h/2376-h.htm

Document 10: William Graham Sumner: 'The Concentration of Wealth: Its Economic Justification,' (1902)

Sumner was a vocal proponent of a particularly strident brand of individualism and social Darwinism. In this essay, he explains how specific individuals will come to dominate the industrial economy.

The concentration of wealth I understand to include the aggregation of wealth into large masses and its concentration under the control of a few. In this sense the concentration of wealth is indispensable to the successful execution of the tasks which devolve upon society in our time. Every task of society requires the employment of capital, and involves an economic problem in the form of the most expedient application of material means to ends. Two features most prominently distinguish the present age from all which have preceded it: first, the great scale on which all societal undertakings must be carried out; and second, the transcendent importance of competent management, that is, of the personal element in direction and control.

I speak of 'societal undertakings' because it is important to notice that the prevalent modes and forms are not confined to industrial undertakings, but are universal in all the institutions and devices which have for their purpose the satisfaction of any wants of society. A modern church is a congeries of institutions which seeks to nourish good things and repress evil ones; it has buildings, apparatus, a store of supplies, a staff of employees, and a treasury. A modern church (parish) will soon be as complex a system of institutions as a mediaeval monastery was. Contrast such an establishment with the corresponding one of fifty years ago. A university now needs an immense 'concentration of wealth' for its outfit and work. It is as restricted in its work as the corresponding institution of fifty years ago was, although it may command twenty times as much capital and revenue. Furthermore, when we see that all these and other societal institutions pay far higher salaries to executive officers than to workers, we must recognize the fact that the element of personal executive ability is in command of the market, and that means that it is the element which decides success. To a correct understanding of our subject it is essential to recognize the concentration of wealth and control as a universal societal phenomenon, not merely as a matter of industrial power, or social sentiment, or political policy.

Stated in the concisest terms, the phenomenon is that of a more perfect integration of all societal functions. The concentration of power (wealth), more dominant control, intenser discipline, and stricter methods are but modes of securing more perfect integration. When we perceive this we see that the concentration of wealth is but one feature of a grand step in societal evolution.

Some may admit that the concentration of wealth is indispensable, but may desire to distinguish between joint-stock aggregations on the one side and individual fortunes on the other. This distinction is a product of the current social prejudice and is not valid. The predominance of the individual and personal element in control is seen in the tendency of all joint-stock enterprises to come under the control of very few persons. Every age is befooled by the notions which are in fashion in it. Our age is befooled by 'democracy'; we hear arguments about the industrial organization which are deductions from democratic dogmas or which appeal to prejudice by using analogies drawn from democracy to affect sentiment about industrial relations. Industry may be republican; it never can be democratic, so long as men differ in productive power and in industrial virtue. In our time joint-stock companies, which are in form republican, are drifting over into oligarchies or monarchies because one or a few get greater efficiency of control and greater vigor of administration. They direct the enterprise in a way which produces more, or more economically. This is the purpose for which the organization exists and success in it outweighs everything else. We see the competent men refuse to join in the enterprise, unless they can control it, and we see the stockholders willingly put their property into the hands of those who are, as they think, competent to manage it successfully. The strongest and most effective organizations for industrial purposes which are formed nowadays are those of a few great capitalists, who have great personal confidence in each ether and who can bring together adequate means for whatever they desire to do. Some such nucleus of individuals controls all the great joint-stock companies.

Source: William Graham Sumner, *Social Darwinism: Selected Essays of William Graham Sumner* (Englewood Cliffs, N.J.: Prentice-Hall, 1963).

Document 11: Herbert Hoover, Campaign Speech, October 22, 1928: Principles and Ideals of the United States Government

In this speech, Hoover used the phrase 'rugged individualism,' linking the idea to his overall economic philosophy, which left little room for government. Such ideas would lose purchase with the onset of the Great Depression.

In my acceptance speech I endeavored to outline the spirit and ideals by which I would be guided in carrying that platform into administration. Tonight, I will not deal with the multitude of issues which have been already well canvassed. I intend rather to discuss some of those more fundamental principles and ideals upon which I believe the Government of the United States should be conducted.

[. . .]

It detracts nothing from the character and energy of the American people, it minimizes in no degree the quality of their accomplishments to say that the policies of the Republican Party have played a large part in recuperation from the war and the building of the magnificent progress which shows upon every hand today. I say with emphasis that without the wise policies which the Republican Party has brought into action during this period, no such progress would have been possible.

[. . .]

It is not my purpose to enter upon a detailed recital of the great constructive measures of the past seven and a half years by which this has been brought about. It is sufficient to remind you of the restoration of employment to the millions who walked your streets in idleness; to remind you of the creation of the budget system; the reduction of six billions of national debt which gave the powerful impulse of that vast sum returned to industry and commerce; the four sequent reductions of taxes and thereby the lift to the living of every family; the enactment of adequate protective tariff and immigration laws which have safeguarded our workers and farmers from floods of goods and labor from foreign countries; the creation of credit facilities and many other aids to agriculture; the building up of foreign trade; the care of veterans; the development of aviation, of radio, of our inland waterways, of our highways; the expansion of scientific research, of welfare activities, the making of safer highways, safer mines, better homes; the spread of outdoor recreation; the improvement in public health and the care of children; and a score of other progressive actions.

Nor do I need to remind you that Government today deals with an economic and social system vastly more intricate and delicately adjusted than ever before. That system now must be kept in perfect tune if we would maintain uninterrupted employment and the high standards of living of our people. The Government has come to touch this delicate web at a thousand points. Yearly the relations of Government to national prosperity become more and more intimate. Only through keen vision and helpful cooperation by the Government has stability in business and stability in employment been maintained during this past seven and a half years. There always are some localities, some industries and some individuals who do not share the prevailing prosperity. The task of government is to lessen these inequalities. Never has there been a period when the Federal Government has given such aid and impulse to the progress of our people, not alone to economic progress but to the development of those agencies which make for moral and spiritual progress.

But in addition to this great record of contributions of the Republican Party to progress, there has been a further fundamental contribution – a contribution underlying and sustaining all the others – and that is the resistance of the Republican Party to every attempt to inject the Government into business in competition with its citizens.

After the war, when the Republican Party assumed administration of the country, we were faced with the problem of determination of the very nature of our national life. During 150 years we have builded up a form of self-government and a social system which is peculiarly our own. It differs essentially from all others in the world. It is the American System. It is just as definite and positive a political and social system as has ever been developed on earth. It is founded upon a particular conception of self-government; in which decentralized local responsibility is the very base. Further than this, it is founded upon the conception that only through ordered liberty, freedom and equal opportunity to the individual will his initiative and enterprise spur on the march of progress. And in our insistence upon equality of opportunity has our system advanced beyond all the world.

During the war we necessarily turned to the Government to solve every difficult economic problem. The Government having absorbed every energy of our people for war, there was no other solution. For the preservation of the State, the Federal Government became a centralized despotism which undertook unprecedented responsibilities, assumed autocratic powers, and took over the business of citizens. To a large degree we regimented our whole people temporarily into a socialistic state. However justified in time of war, if continued in peace time it would destroy not only our American System but with it our progress and freedom as well.

When the war closed, the most vital of all issues both in our own country and throughout the world was whether Governments should continue their wartime ownership and operation of many instrumentalities of production and distribution. We were challenged with a peace-time choice between the American System of rugged individualism and a European philosophy of diametrically opposed doctrines – doctrines of paternalism and state socialism. The acceptance of these ideas would have meant the destruction of self-government through centralization of government. It would have meant the undermining of the individual initiative and enterprise through which our people have grown to unparalleled greatness.

The Republican Party from the beginning resolutely turned its face away from these ideas and these war practices. A Republican Congress cooperated with the Democratic administration to demobilize many of our war activities. At that time the two parties were accord upon that point. When the Republican Party came into full power, it went at once resolutely back to our fundamental conception of the state and the rights and responsibilities of the individual. Thereby it restored confidence and hope in the American people, it freed and stimulated enterprise, it restored the Government to its position as an umpire instead of a player in the economic game. For these reasons the American people have gone forward in progress while the rest of the world has halted, and some countries have even gone backwards. If anyone will study the causes of retarded recuperation in Europe, he will find much of it due to the stifling of private initiative on one hand, and overloading of the Government with business on the other.

There has been revived in this campaign, however, a series of proposals which, if adopted, would be a long step toward the abandonment of our American System and a surrender to the destructive operation of governmental conduct of commercial business. Because the country is faced with difficulty and doubt over certain national problems – that is, prohibition, farm relief and electrical power – our opponents propose that we must thrust government a long way into the businesses which give rise to these problems. In effect, they abandon the tenets of their own party and turn to state socialism as a solution for the difficulties presented by all three. It is proposed that we shall change from prohibition to the state purchase and sale of liquor. If their agricultural relief program means anything, it means that the Government shall directly or indirectly buy and sell and fix prices of agricultural products. And we are to go into the hydroelectric-power business. In other words, we are confronted with a huge program of government in business.

There is, therefore, submitted to the American people a question of fundamental principle. That is: shall we depart from the principles of our American political and economic system, upon which we have advanced beyond all the rest of the world, in order to adopt methods based on principles destructive of its very foundations? And I wish to emphasize the seriousness of these proposals. I wish to make my position clear; for this goes to the very roots of American life and progress.

I should like to state to you the effect that this projection of government in business would have upon our system of self-government and our economic system. That effect would reach to the daily life of every man and woman. It would impair the very basis of liberty and freedom not only for those left outside the fold of expanded bureaucracy but for those embraced within it.

Let us first see the effect upon self-government. When the Federal Government undertakes to go into commercial business, it must at once set up the organization and administration of that business, and it immediately finds itself in a labyrinth, every alley of which leads to the destruction of self-government.

Commercial business requires a concentration of responsibility. Self-government requires decentralization and many checks and balances to safeguard liberty. Our Government to succeed in business would need become in effect a despotism. There at once begins the destruction of self-government.

The first problem of the government about to adventure in commercial business is to determine a method of administration. It must secure leadership and direction. Shall this leadership be chosen by political agencies or shall we make it elective? The hard practical fact is that leadership in business must come through the sheer rise in ability and character. That rise can only take place in the free atmosphere of competition. Competition is closed by bureaucracy. Political agencies are feeble channels through which to select able leaders to conduct commercial business.

Government, in order to avoid the possible incompetence, corruption and tyranny of too great authority in individuals entrusted with commercial business, inevitably turns to boards and commissions. To make sure that there are checks and balances, each member of such boards and commissions must have equal authority. Each has his separate responsibility to the public, and at once we have the conflict of ideas and the lack of decision which would ruin any commercial business. It has contributed greatly to the demoralization of our shipping business. Moreover, these commissions must be representative of different sections and different political parties, so that at once we have an entire blight upon coordinated action within their ranks which destroys any possibility of effective administration.

Moreover, our legislative bodies cannot in fact delegate their full authority to commissions or to individuals for the conduct of matters vital to the American people; for if we would preserve government by the people we must preserve the authority of our legislators in the activities of our government.

Thus every time the Federal Government goes into a commercial business, 531 Senators and Congressmen become the actual board of directors of that business. Every time a state government goes into business, one or two hundred state senators and legislators become the actual directors of that business. Even if they were supermen and if there were no politics in the United States, no body of such numbers could competently direct commercial activities; for that requires initiative, instant decision. and action. It took Congress six years of constant discussion to even decide what the method of administration of Muscle Shoals should be.

When the Federal Government undertakes to go into business, the state governments are at once deprived of control and taxation of that business; when a state government undertakes to go into business, it at once deprives the municipalities of taxation and control of that business. Municipalities, being local and close to the people, can, at times, succeed in business where Federal and State Governments must fail.

We have trouble enough with log rolling in legislative bodies today. It originates naturally from desires of citizens to advance their particular section or to secure some necessary service. It would be multiplied a thousandfold were the Federal and state governments in these businesses.

The effect upon our economic progress would be even worse. Business progressiveness is dependent on competition. New methods and new ideas are the outgrowth of the spirit of adventure, of individual initiative and of individual enterprise. Without adventure there is no progress. No government administration can rightly take chances with taxpayers' money.

There is no better example of the practical incompetence of government to conduct business than the history of our railways. During the war, the government found it necessary to operate the railways. That operation continued until after the war. In the year before being freed from Government operation, they were not able to meet the demands for transportation. Eight years later we find them under private enterprise transporting 15 per cent more goods and meeting every demand for service. Rates have been reduced by 15 per cent and net earnings increased from less than 1 per cent on their valuation to about 5 per cent. Wages of employees have improved by 13 per cent. The wages of railway employees are today 121 per cent above pre-war, while the wages of Government employees are today only 65 per cent above pre-war. That should be a sufficient commentary upon the efficiency of Government operation.

[. . .]

The Government in commercial business does not tolerate amongst its customers the freedom of competitive reprisals to which private business is subject. Bureaucracy does not tolerate the spirit of independence; it spreads the spirit of submission into our daily life and penetrates the temper of our people not with the habit of powerful resistance to wrong but with the habit of timid acceptance of irresistible might.

Bureaucracy is ever desirous of spreading its influence and its power. You cannot extend the mastery of the government over the daily working life of a people without at the same time making it the master of the people's souls and thoughts. Every expansion of government in business means that government in order to protect itself from the political consequences of its errors and wrongs is driven irresistibly without peace to greater and greater control of the nations' press and platform. Free speech does not live many hours after free industry and free commerce die.

It is a false liberalism that interprets itself into the Government operation of commercial business. Every step of bureaucratizing of the business of our country poisons the very roots of liberalism – that is, political equality, free speech, free assembly, free press, and equality of opportunity. It is the road not to more liberty, but to less liberty. Liberalism should be found not striving to spread bureaucracy but striving to set bounds to it. True liberalism seeks all legitimate freedom first in the confident belief that without such freedom the pursuit of all other blessings and benefits is vain. That belief is the foundation of all American progress, political as well as economic.

Liberalism is a force truly of the spirit, a force proceeding from the deep realization that economic freedom cannot be sacrificed if political freedom is to be preserved, Even if governmental conduct of business could give us more efficiency instead of less efficiency, the fundamental objection to it would remain unaltered and unabated. It would destroy political equality. It would increase rather than decrease abuse and corruption. It would stifle initiative and invention. It would undermine the development of leadership. It would cramp and cripple the mental and spiritual energies of our people. It would extinguish equality and opportunity. It would dry up the spirit of liberty and progress. For these reasons primarily it must be resisted. For a hundred and fifty years liberalism has found its true spirit in the American System, not in the European systems.

I do not wish to be misunderstood in this statement. I am defining a general policy. It does not mean that our government is to part with one iota of its national resources without complete protection to the public interest. I have already stated that where the government is engaged in public works for purposes of flood control, of navigation, of irrigation, of scientific research or national defense, or in pioneering a new art, it will at times necessarily produce power or commodities as a by-product. But they must be a by-product of the major purpose, not the major purpose itself.

Nor do I wish to be misinterpreted as believing that the United States is free-for-all and devil-take-the-hind-most. The very essence of equality of opportunity and of American individualism is that there shall be no domination by any group or combination in this Republic, whether it be business or political. On the contrary, it demands economic justice as well as political and social justice. It is no system of **laissez faire**.

I feel deeply on this subject because during the war I had some practical experience with governmental operation and control. I have witnessed not only at home but abroad the many failures of government in business. I have seen its tyrannies, its injustices, its destructions of self-government, its undermining of the very instincts which carry our people forward to progress. I have witnessed the lack of advance, the lowered standards of living, the depressed spirits of people working under such a system. My objection is based not upon theory or upon a failure to recognize wrong or abuse, but I know the adoption of such methods would strike at the very roots of American life and would destroy the very basis of American progress.

Our people have the right to know whether we can continue to solve our great problems without abandonment of our American System. I know we can. We have demonstrated that our system is responsive enough to meet any new and intricate development in our economic and business life. We have demonstrated that we can meet any economic problem and still maintain our democracy as master in its own house and that we can at the same time preserve equality of opportunity and individual freedom.

[. . .]

To me the foundation of American life rests upon the home and the family. I read into these great economic forces, these intricate and delicate relations of the Government with business and with our political and social life, but one supreme end – that we reinforce the ties that bind together the millions of our families, that we strengthen the security, the happiness and the independence of every home.

My conception of America is a land where men and women may walk in ordered freedom in the independent conduct of their occupations; where they may enjoy the advantages of wealth, not concentrated in the hands of the few but spread through the lives of all, where they build and safeguard their homes, and give to their children the fullest advantages and opportunities of American life; where every man shall be respected in the faith that his conscience and his heart direct him to follow; where a contented and happy people, secure in their liberties, free from poverty and fear, shall have the leisure and impulse to seek a fuller life.

Source: https://millercenter.org/the-presidency/presidential-speeches/october-22-1928-principles-and-ideals-united-states-government

Document 12: Franklin Delano Roosevelt, Speech before the Democratic National Convention, 1936

Roosevelt campaigned for reelection after many of his New Deal reforms had already been passed or initiated. It earned him the disdain of those opposed to what they saw as an offensive government intrusion into business and economic matters. In this famous address, Roosevelt addressed his detractors. In this selection, Roosevelt reframed the nation's founding to warn that concentrated wealth represented a threat to individualism. He ultimately won reelection in a landslide.

That very word *freedom*, in itself and of necessity, suggests freedom from some restraining power. In 1776 we sought freedom from the tyranny of a political autocracy – from the eighteenth-century royalists who held special privileges from the crown. It was to perpetuate their privilege that they governed without the consent of the governed; that they denied the right of free assembly and free speech; that they restricted the worship of God; that they put the average man's property and the average man's life in pawn to the mercenaries of dynastic power; that they regimented the people.

And so it was to win freedom from the tyranny of political autocracy that the American Revolution was fought. That victory gave the business of governing into the hands of the average man, who won the right with his neighbors to make and order his own destiny through his own government. Political tyranny was wiped out at Philadelphia on July 4, 1776.

Since that struggle, however, man's inventive genius released new forces in our land which reordered the lives of our people. The age of machinery, of railroads; of steam and electricity; the telegraph and the radio; mass production, mass distribution – all of these combined to bring forward a new civilization and with it a new problem for those who sought to remain free.

For out of this modern civilization economic royalists carved new dynasties. New kingdoms were built upon concentration of control over material things. Through new uses of corporations, banks and securities, new machinery of industry and agriculture, of labor and capital – all undreamed of by the Fathers – the whole structure of modern life was impressed into this royal service.

There was no place among this royalty for our many thousands of small-businessmen and merchants who sought to make a worthy use of the American System of initiative and profit. They were no more free than the worker or the farmer. Even honest and progressive-minded men of wealth, aware of their obligation to their generation, could never know just where they fitted into this dynastic scheme of things.

It was natural and perhaps human that the privileged princes of these new economic dynasties, thirsting for power, reached out for control over government itself. They created a new despotism and wrapped it in the robes of legal sanction. In its service new mercenaries sought to regiment the people, their labor, and their property. And as a result the average man once more confronts the problem that faced the Minute Man.

The hours men and women worked, the wages they received, the conditions of their labor – these had passed beyond the control of the people, and were imposed by this new industrial dictatorship. The savings of the average family, the capital of the small-businessmen, the investments set aside for old age – other people's money – these were tools which the new economic royalty used to dig itself in.

Those who tilled the soil no longer reaped the rewards which were their right. The small measure of their gains was decreed by men in distant cities.

Throughout the nation, opportunity was limited by monopoly. Individual initiative was crushed in the cogs of a great machine. The field open for free business was more and more restricted. Private enterprise, indeed, became too private. It became privileged enterprise, not free enterprise.

An old English judge once said: 'Necessitous men are not free men.' Liberty requires opportunity to make a living – a living decent according to the standard of the time, a living which gives man not only enough to live by, but something to live for.

For too many of us the political equality we once had won was meaningless in the face of economic inequality. A small group had concentrated into their own hands an almost complete control over other people's property, other people's money, other people's labor – other people's lives. For too many of us life was no longer free; liberty no longer real; men could no longer follow the pursuit of happiness.

Against economic tyranny such as this, the American citizen could appeal only to the organized power of government. The collapse of 1929 showed up the despotism for what it was. The election of 1932 was the people's mandate to end it. Under that mandate it is being ended.

The royalists of the economic order have conceded that political freedom was the business of the government, but they have maintained that economic slavery was nobody's business. They granted that the government could protect the citizen in his right to vote, but they denied that the government could do anything to protect the citizen in his right to work and his right to live.

Today we stand committed to the proposition that freedom is no half-and-half affair. If the average citizen is guaranteed equal opportunity in the polling place, he must have equal opportunity in the market place.

These economic royalists complain that we seek to overthrow the institutions of America. What they really complain of is that we seek to take away their power. Our allegiance to American institutions requires the overthrow of this kind of power. In vain they seek to hide behind the flag and the Constitution. In their blindness they forget what the flag and the Constitution stand for. Now, as always, they stand for democracy, not tyranny; for freedom, not subjection; and against a dictatorship by mob rule and the over-privileged alike.

Source: https://millercenter.org/the-presidency/presidential-speeches/june-27-1936-democratic-national-convention

Document 13: Peter Drucker: Selection from *The Concept of the Corporation*: 1946 (p. 141)

Though he was known as a management theorist, Drucker also had a clear philosophical bent. In the books that he wrote in the middle of the twentieth century, he contemplated how people could achieve a sense of personal meaning amid large industrial and bureaucratic organizations, such as corporations.

The demand for status and function as an individual means that in the modern industrial society the citizen must obtain both standing in his society and individual satisfaction through his membership in the plant, that is, through being an employee. Individual dignity and fulfillment in an industrial society can only be given in and through work. Hence the painful futility of all the brave attempts to give the modern citizen individual fulfillment in 'cultural,' 'recreational,' or 'leisure-hours' activities. The first demand thus is that our citizens are citizens because they are engaged in industry. This is the problem with which Social Security has tried to grapple. For you are not a citizen if your status in society depends on forces over which you have absolutely no control such as the business cycle. Equally important is that the individual must be able to realize through his work in industry that satisfaction which comes from one's own meaningfulness for society and which expresses the basic conviction of the uniqueness of the person. The industrial society must give its members that sense the importance which cannot be produced by propaganda or by other psychological means, but can only come from the reality of having importance. This is not a demand for 'industrial democracy' if by that is meant a structure of industry in which everybody is equal in rank, income or function. On the contrary it is basically a hierarchical concept in which positions of widely divergent rank, power and income are each seen as equally important to the success of the whole because of the subordination of one man under another.

Source: Peter Drucker, *The Concept of the Corporation* (New York, NY: The John Day Company, 1946).

Document 14: Haft-Hartley Act (1947)

The Taft-Hartley Act dealt a huge blow to union power, in part through its 'right to work' provisions, which had the potential to drain unions of income sources. As the text of the law reveals, the Taft-Hartley Act is

infused with a preoccupation on individualism, and a disdain for the sort of collective power that unions represented.

Section 1. (a) This Act may be cited as the 'Labor Management Relations Act, 1947'.

(b) Industrial strife which interferes with the normal flow of commerce and with the full production of articles and commodities for commerce, can be avoided or substantially minimized if employers, employees, and labor organizations each recognize under law one another's legitimate rights in their relations with each other, and above all recognize under law that neither party has any right in its relations with any other to engage in acts or practices with jeopardize the public health, safety, or interest.

It is the purpose and policy of this Act, in other to promote the full flow of commerce to prescribe the legitimate rights of both employees and employers in their relations affecting commerce, to provide orderly and peaceful procedures for preventing the interference by either with the legitimate rights of the other, to protect the rights of individual employees in their relations with labor organizations whose activities affect commerce, to define and proscribe practices on the part of labor and management which affect commerce and are inimical to the general welfare, and to protect the rights of the public in connection with labor disputes affecting commerce.

[. . .]

Sec. 502. Nothing in this Act shall be construed to require an individual employee to render labor or service without his consent, nor shall anything in this Act be construed to make the quitting of his labor by an individual employee an illegal act; nor shall any court issue any process to compel the performance by an individual employee of such labor or service, without his consent; nor shall the quitting of labor by an employee or employees in good faith because of abnormally dangerous conditions for work at the place of employment of such employee or employees be deemed a strike under this Act.

Source: www.govinfo.gov/content/pkg/COMPS-8190/pdf/COMPS-8190.pdf

Document 15: William Whyte: Selection from *The Organization Man*: 1956

In the introduction to his book, Whyte made it clear that he was ultimately concerned about the fate of individualism in a country that seemed increasingly dominated by large organizations, especially corporations.

I speak of individualism within organization life. This is not the only kind, and someday it may be that the mystics and philosophers more distant from it may prove the crucial figures. But they are affected too by the center of society, and they can be of no help unless they grasp the nature of the mainstream. Intellectual scoldings based on an impossibly lofty ideal may be of some service in upbraiding organization man with his failures, but they can give him no guidance. The organization man may agree that industrialism has destroyed the moral fabric of society and that we need to return to the agrarian virtues, or that business needs to be broken up into a series of smaller organizations, or that it's government that needs to be broken up, and so on. But he will go his way with his own dilemmas left untouched.

I am going to argue that he should fight the organization. But not self-destructively. He may tell the boss to go to hell, but he is going to have another boss, and, unlike the heroes of popular fiction, he cannot find surcease by leaving the arena to be a husbandman. If he chafes at the pressures of his particular organization, either he must succumb, resist them, try to change them, or move to yet another organization.

Every decision he faces on the problem of the individual versus authority is something of a dilemma. It is not a case of whether he should fight against black tyranny or blaze a new trail against patent stupidity. That would be easy – intellectually, at least. The real issue is far more subtle. For it is not the evils of organization life that puzzle him, but its very beneficence. He is imprisoned in brotherhood. Because his area of maneuver seems so small and because the trapping so mundane, his fight lacks the heroic cast, but it is for all this as tough a fight as ever his predecessors had to fight.

Source: William Whyte, *The Organization Man* (New York, NY: Simon and Schuster, 1956).

Document 16: Vance Packard: Selection from *The Hidden Persuaders* (1957)

In this passage from The Hidden Persuaders, *Packard illustrates how automobile companies marketed their products in a way that takes advantage of a consumer's desire to express their own unique personality and sense of individuality.*

The automobile has become far more than a mere means of conveyance. In the words of Pierre Martineau, 'The automobile tells who we are and what we think we want to be . . . It is a portable symbol or our personality and our position . . . the clearest way we have telling people our exact position. [In buying a car] you are saying in a sense, "I am looking for the car that expressed who I am." '

Buick, in fact, has suggested this in its ad when it offers this promise to the public: 'It makes you feel like the man you are.'

One of the most remarkable documents I came across in my investigation was a pamphlet called 'Automobiles, What They Mean to Americans.' It reports on a study made for *The Chicago Tribune* by Social Research, Inc. The major merchandising journals have discussed its findings in great detail. Their study was conducted by a team of social scientists who used a variety of probing techniques on 352 car owners in the Chicago area.

The investigators found that only a minority of the population, mostly men in the lower class, have any real interest in the technical aspect of cars. And the major finding that stands out in the survey is that automobiles are heavily laden with social meanings and are highly esteemed because they 'provide avenues for the expression . . . of the character, temperament and self -concept of the owner and the driver . . . The buying process is an interaction between the personality of the car and the personality of the individual.'

Source: Vance Packard, *The Hidden Persuaders* (New York, NY: D. McKay Co, 1957).

Document 17: Milton Friedman: Selection from *Capitalism and Freedom* (1962)

Apart from his work as an academic economist, throughout his career, Friedman was provided the opportunity to expound on and promote the basic ideals of neoliberalism. In this selection from his 1962, Capitalism and Freedom, Friedman draws a direct line between individual freedom and an unregulated marketplace.

As liberals, we take freedom of the individual, or perhaps the family, as our ultimate goal in judging social arrangements. Freedom as a value in this sense has to do with the interrelations among people; it has no meaning whatsoever to a Robinson Crusoe on an isolated island (without his Man Friday). Robinson Crusoe on his island is subject to 'constraint,' he has limited 'power,' and he has only a limited number of alternatives, but there is no problem of freedom in the sense that is relevant to our discussion. Similarly, in a society freedom has nothing to say about what an individual does with his freedom; it is not an all-embracing ethic. Indeed, a major aim of the liberal is to leave the ethical problem for the individual to wrestle with. The 'really' important ethical problems are those that face an individual in a free society – what he should do with his freedom. There are thus two sets of values that liberals will emphasize – the values that are relevant to relations among people, which is the context in which he assigns first priority to freedom; and the values that are relevant to the individual in the exercise of his freedom, which is the realm of individual ethics and philosophy.

[. . .]

The basic problem of social organization is how to co-ordinate the economic activities of large numbers of people. Even in relatively backward societies, extensive division of labor and specialization of function is required to make effective use of available resources. In advanced societies, the scale on which co-ordination is needed, to take full advantage of the opportunities offered by modern science and technology, is enormously greater. Literally millions of people are involved in providing one another with their daily bread, let alone with their yearly automobiles. The challenge to the believer in liberty is to reconcile this widespread interdependence with individual freedom.

Fundamentally, there are only two ways of co-ordinating the economic activities of millions. One is central to direction involving the use of coercion – the technique of the army and of the modern totalitarian state. The other is voluntary co-operation of individuals – the technique of the marketplace.

Source: Milton Friedman, *Capitalism and Freedom* (Chicago: University of Chicago Press, 1962).

Document 18: Ronald Reagan: Remarks to State Chairpersons of the National White House Conference on Small Business (August 15, 1986)

In the late twentieth century, Reagan was one of the most vocal and persuasive champions of capitalist individualism embodied by the term, 'entrepreneur.' This is one of many speeches in which he expounds on these ideas.

It's wonderful to be having this White House Conference on Small Business again after almost 6 years. Things certainly have changed in the meantime. Back then, government's view of the economy could be summed up in a few short phrases: If it moves, tax it. If it keeps moving, regulate it. And if it stops moving, subsidize it. Well, with your help, I think we've turned all that around. We cut taxes. We squashed inflation. We brought interest rates down, threw out needless regulations, setting the economy on a growth path that has created somewhere in the neighborhood of 11 million new jobs in under 4 years. Now, most people know that history. What isn't widely enough recognized, however, is the leading role of entrepreneurs and small businesses in our ongoing expansion.

According to the Small Business Administration, small businesses account for nearly half of all the innovations and over 70 percent of all those new jobs – you heard right, over 70 percent. That increase in these last few years was by what we call small business. And incidentally, a figure that is astounding today – when we still keep being concerned with an unemployment rate – is that 61.2 percent of what is known as the potential job market is employed. And that is the highest percentage in all our history, because that figure is 61.2 percent of all the human beings, male and female, from ages 16 up. And there never has been that great a percentage employed before.

But it's individuals and small firms who are on the cutting edge of growth and technological development. It's entrepreneurs with a new idea or a different approach, visionaries with an impossible dream and the determination to make it happen – these are the people who are propelling our economy forward. And the best way to keep up the momentum is to give them the freedom they need by cutting tax rates – and then cutting them again. If you thought our 1981 tax rates were good, wait till you feel the added horsepower that tax reform injects into our economy. We're slashing the top individual and corporate tax rates and wiping out unfair tax breaks at the same time. We're going to get America's investments out from under the tax shelters and back into the productive economy where they belong.

[. . .]

The next stage is to convince our trading partners to follow suit, to take the path of high real growth. Maybe then we could get the world economy moving faster and stronger, and it wouldn't just be us out there in front all alone, trying to pull the rest of the world behind us. The Europeans call our economic performance – to my face they've called it the American miracle. In fact, it is thousands of individual miracles of faith, hard work, and imagination – thousands of entrepreneurs and small business people like you. I've often thought that America's entrepreneurs, like the men and women here at this conference, would make the best ambassadors of progress. You'd not only be convincing proponents of low tax rates and stable monetary policies, deregulation, you'd show the world that economic growth doesn't come from government spending or planning, but from the heart and soul of entrepreneurs – men and women who are willing to take risks, who brave failure to seek success on the frontiers of enterprise.

Source: www.reaganlibrary.gov/archives/speech/remarks-state-chairpersons-national-white-house-conference-small-business

Document 19: Bill Clinton: State of the Union Address, 1996

In this address to Congress, Clinton declared the end of big government in the United States. Such rhetoric would have once been unthinkable for a Democratic president. However, after the ***Reagan revolution****, such neoliberal ideas had moved to the center of political discourse.*

We live in an age of possibility. A hundred years ago we moved from farm to factory. Now we move to an age of technology, information, and global competition. These changes have opened vast new opportunities for our people, but they have also presented them with stiff challenges. While more Americans are living better, too many of our fellow citizens are working harder just to keep up, and they are rightly concerned about the security of their families.

We must answer here three fundamental questions: First, how do we make the American Dream of opportunity for all a reality for all Americans who are willing to work for it? Second, how do we preserve our old and enduring values as we move into the future? And, third, how do we meet these challenges together, as one America?

We know big government does not have all the answers. We know there's not a program for every problem. We have worked to give the American people a smaller, less bureaucratic government in Washington. And we have to give the American people one that lives within its means.

The era of big government is over. But we cannot go back to the time when our citizens were left to fend for themselves. Instead, we must go forward as one America, one nation working together to meet the challenges we face together. Self-reliance and teamwork are not opposing virtues; we must have both.

I believe our new, smaller government must work in an old-fashioned American way, together with all of our citizens through state and local governments, in the workplace, in religious, charitable and civic associations. Our goal must be to enable all our people to make the most of their own lives – with stronger families, more educational opportunity, economic security, safer streets, a cleaner environment in a safer world.

To improve the state of our Union, we must ask more of ourselves, we must expect more of each other, and we must face our challenges together.

Here, in this place, our responsibility begins with balancing the budget in a way that is fair to all Americans. There is now broad bipartisan agreement that permanent deficit spending must come to an end.

Source: https://clintonwhitehouse4.archives.gov/WH/New/other/sotu.html

Document 20: Barack Obama, Remarks by the President at a Campaign Event in Roanoke, Virginia (July 13, 2012)

While on the running for reelection, President Obama spoke at a campaign rally and made some remarks about how government helps individuals succeed. His opponent pounced on these remarks, suggesting (inaccurately) that Obama had little regard for individual success and initiative.

But you know what, I'm not going to see us gut the investments that grow our economy to give tax breaks to me or Mr. Romney or folks who don't need them. So I'm going to reduce the deficit in a balanced way. We've already made a trillion dollars' worth of cuts. We can make another trillion or trillion-two, and what we then do is ask for the wealthy to pay a little bit more. And, by the way, we've tried that before – a guy named Bill Clinton did it. We created 23 million new jobs, turned a deficit into a surplus, and rich people did just fine. We created a lot of millionaires.

There are a lot of wealthy, successful Americans who agree with me – because they want to give something back. They know they didn't – look, if you've been successful, you didn't get there on your own. You didn't get there on your own. I'm always struck by people who think, well, it must be because I was just so smart. There are a lot of smart people out there. It must be because I worked harder than everybody else. Let me tell you something – there are a whole bunch of hardworking people out there.

If you were successful, somebody along the line gave you some help. There was a great teacher somewhere in your life. Somebody helped to create this unbelievable American System that we have that allowed you to thrive. Somebody invested in roads and bridges. If you've got a business – you didn't build that. Somebody else made that happen. The Internet didn't get invented on its own. Government research created the Internet so that all the companies could make money off the Internet.

The point is, is that when we succeed, we succeed because of our individual initiative, but also because we do things together. There are some things, just like fighting fires, we don't do on our own. I mean, imagine if everybody had their own fire service. That would be a hard way to organize fighting fires.

So we say to ourselves, ever since the founding of this country, you know what, there are some things we do better together. That's how we funded the GI Bill. That's how we created the middle class. That's how we built the Golden Gate Bridge or the Hoover Dam. That's how we invented the Internet. That's how we sent a man to the moon. We rise or fall together as one nation and as one people, and that's the reason I'm running for President – because I still believe in that idea. You're not on your own, we're in this together.

Source: https://obamawhitehouse.archives.gov/the-press-office/2012/07/13/remarks-president-campaign-event-roanoke-virginia

Glossary

Entrepreneurial firm: A small business that is operated and managed by the owners. This form of business organization was common in the first half of the nineteenth century.

Joint-stock company: A precursor to the limited liability corporation, this form of business organization pooled the finances of different investors. This type of business form had the advantage of spreading the risk among the investors.

Red scare: A public panic over the potential infiltration and spread of communism in the United States. The first scare emerged during the 1920s, while a second one appeared in the 1950s, when the Cold War dominated political thought.

Occupy Wall Street: A protest movement that began in New York City in 2011 in the wake of the 2008 financial crisis. Though the protesters had many grievances, wealth inequality and the power of the financial services industry were chief among them. The movement was deeply influenced by an anarchist and collectivist ethos. The movement did not have a formal hierarchical structure and all decisions were made by process of reaching a consensus.

World Trade Organization: A international organization established in 1995 after a round of the General Agreement on Tariffs and Trade. The World Trade Organization helps set the rules for global trade.

Imagined community: A term coined by Benedict Anderson that describes the avenues, such as stories and symbols, that encourage people to think of themselves as citizens of a particular nation who share a set of values and experiences with other citizens of that nation.

Conspicuous consumption: The practice of purchasing and consuming goods as a way to demonstrate one's wealth.

Industrial democracy: The ethos and practice of shared decision-making inside a firm. It is often associated with unions in the middle of the twentieth century.

Wage slavery: The idea that working for wages as an employee constitutes a form of unfreedom. The phrase has been invoked as a critique of industrial capitalism, but in the antebellum South, slaveholders and Southern politicians drew on the idea to suggest that slave plantations were more humane than factories in the North.

Wobblies: The popular name of the Industrial Workers of the World, a radical labor organization that was active in the early twentieth century.

Company town: An artifact of early iterations of ***welfare capitalism***, these were entire towns built by a company for its workers. Pullman, Illinois, established by the Pullman Car Company, was one example. Pullman was ultimately destroyed by a violent clash between the company and its workers, exposing the limits of this practice.

Welfare capitalism: A set of corporate practices in which a company assumes a certain amount of responsibility for the well-being of its workers. In the United States, early versions of this were often deeply paternalistic, assuming a certain amount of control over the lives of employees.

Pinkertons: Members of the Pinkerton Detective Agency, which grew in importance in the late nineteenth century. During the Gilded Age, corporations, such as Carnegie Steel, employed the Pinkertons as a private army to help break labor strikes.

Objectivism: Philosophy devised by the fiction writer Ayn Rand that insists on objective truth and triumphs the rights of the individual.

Contrarian thinking: A type of thinking that many stock traders strive toward which emphasizes rejecting, or at least deeply questioning, the standard view of the market or, more broadly, business conditions. Contrarian thinkers seek out investment and trading opportunities that other investors and stock market participants do not see.

Columbian Exposition: World's Fair held in Chicago from 1893 to 1894.

Naturalism: A literary movement and style dating to the late nineteenth century which was informed by new scientific understanding, especially new theories of evolution. In contrast to writers from earlier literary periods, American naturalists depicted both nature and society as amoral, rather than inherently benevolent. Significantly, naturalist authors such as Theodore Dreiser and Frank Norris were primarily concerned with different aspects of capitalism.

Multinational corporation: A business that operates in more than one country.

Entrepreneur: Someone who starts a business.

New Left: A movement that emerged in the 1960s that emphasized cultural and social issues over the economic issues that the Old Left focused on.

International Monetary Fund: Fund established as part of the Bretton Woods system at the end of World War II to help stabilize the global economy and provide assistance to countries in economic turmoil.

Annual model change: A strategy that was first devised by General Motors in the 1920s. Through this policy, the company introduced new versions of its different car lines on a regular, standardized schedule. The practice helped General Motors satisfy customers' desires for new products, but along a set timeline that allowed the company to rationalize and carefully plan both production and marketing. The annual model change has become a standard practice in the automobile industry.

World Bank: The informal name for the International Bank for Reconstruction and Development, which was established as part of the Bretton Woods Agreements in 1944. The bank finances development projects around the world.

Plessy v. Ferguson: The 1896 Supreme Court decision declared segregation laws did not violate the Constitutional rights of Black Americans.

Trade associations: Organizations devoted to the affairs of a specific industry. These organizations began to appear in the early twentieth century and engage in a range of activities that included political lobbying and developing industry standards.

The National Association of Manufacturers: Much like the U.S. Chamber of Commerce, this organization is a national lobbying organization that engages in political advocacy for American businesses. It is notable for its conservative politics.

Jim Crow laws: A set of laws in the United States that enforced racial subjugation of Black Americans in myriad ways.

Dust Bowl: The name given to an area in the Great Plains in the south and southwest that experienced persistent droughts followed by dust storms during the 1930s.

Executive Order 8802: A 1941 Order that prohibited employment discrimination by Federal agencies signed by FDR in response to A. Philip Randolph's threat of a protest.

Muckrakers: Investigative journalists who were active during the Progressive Era, many of whom focused on the problems with big businesses.

Bank War: Refers to the political debate and conflict over the Second Bank of the United States.

Money Trust: The name that Progressive reformers in the early twentieth century gave to the tangled web of leadership positions that bankers such as J.P. Morgan used to control the economy. Brandeis and others suggested that through 'interlocking directorates' – the same people having seats on the board of directors at different companies – a group of financial elites was stifling American business and smaller, independent producers.

Chain store menace: A term that independent shop owners used to describe what they saw as the threat that large chain stores posed to smaller businesses. Oftentimes, their complaints about chain stores included racist and nativist sensibilities.

Division of labor: A key principle in economics that was also a centerpiece of Adam Smith's *Wealth of Nations*. The principle of dividing labor among many different people has proven to be extremely efficient.

Laissez faire: A philosophy of government that holds that the economic activity should be allowed to proceed without interference or management from the state. Advocates of this principle oppose measures such as tariffs.

Separate spheres: An ideology that developed in the nineteenth century that defined different roles for men and women. Men were charged with success in public life, whether that be in politics or business. Women were given dominion over domestic spaces and were responsible for securing morality.

Liberalism: A philosophical system that prioritizes the rights of the individual and limits the government's powers over that individual that can be traced back to European philosophers, chiefly John Locke. Liberalism emphasized the natural rights of individuals, which has a number of different implications, such as a right to property and limits to the power of political leaders. Liberalism has informed both political and economic thinking in the United States. Though contemporary political parties identify as either 'liberal' or 'conservative,' both belong to this older tradition.

Mercantilism: A loose system of economic thought that preceded capitalism. Mercantilists emphasized the interests of the state and the need for a nation to export more than it imports.

Progressive Era: The period of time that began in the last decade of the nineteenth century and lasted until the 1920s. The period was characterized by a strong reform impulse that touched on many different areas of American life. Some of the most prominent figures of this era, such as Ida Tarbell and Theodore Roosevelt, focused their efforts on limiting the power of big businesses and monopolies.

Social Darwinsim: In the late nineteenth century, ***Herbert Spencer*** developed a theory of society that was based on Charles Darwin's theories of evolution, particularly the notion of the 'survival of the fittest.' Beyond Spencer, William Graham Sumner was an adherent. Wealthy business magnates in the Gilded Age often drew on this idea to justify their wealth.

Artisan Republicanism: The Revolutionary-era belief in the ideal worker as an independent producer and that such work was fundamentally good for the health of the Republic.

Reagan Revolution: The dramatic rise of conservative politics in the 1980s that touched on many different aspects of American life, including economic and business regulation, as well as cultural and social issues.

American System: The term for the approach to the economy devised championed by Henry Clay. This approach relied on tariffs to help the U.S. economy become self-sufficient.

Endorsement: The practice of vouching for the credit-worthiness of an individual businessperson.

Emotional labor: A type of work that requires both the performance of emotions and manipulating or otherwise catering to one's emotions.

U.S. Chamber of Commerce: This trade organization was established in the 1920s with the help of U.S. president Herbert Hoover. The Chamber advocates for business interests and has numerous smaller, local chapters. The organization has often entered policy debates and advocated for free enterprise principles.

Yeoman farmer: The idealized image of an individual farmer (often the head of a household) who owns the land he tills and is self-sufficient. Americans such as Thomas Jefferson romanticized this type.

Neoliberalism: A political and economic philosophy that emphasizes individual choice over collective solutions. Beginning in the 1970s, this philosophy moved to the center of policy-making in both the United States and the United Kingdom.

Sharecropping: A system for agricultural labor that appeared after the Civil War. Sharecroppers were caught in a state of perpetual indebtedness to landlords. In effect, these sharecroppers paid rent to landlords in the form of a portion of the harvest. The contractual terms of such arrangements favored landlords. Many of the first sharecroppers had been enslaved prior to emancipation.

Bucket shops: Parlors or shops that allowed people to place bets on the movement of stocks. It was an early way in which individual Americans would become involved in the stock market.

Power geometries: A term coined by the geographer Doreen Massey that describes one's power in relation to others and to places.

Intersectionality: The interactions and relationships between different components of a person's identity, such as race, class, and gender. **Intersectionality** implies that one aspect of a person's identity, such as race or ethnicity, cannot be considered without these other components.

Racial capitalism: A concept that suggests that racial and racist thought was present in capitalism when it first emerged in Europe. This idea implies that capitalism operates through ideologies and understandings of race and that, ultimately, capitalist processes cannot be understood without a consideration of race.

Deregulation: The process of removing rules that govern some aspect of economic activity. Advocates of deregulation have typically insisted that excessive rules and restrictions on business inhibit the full potential of American business.

Financialization: As the role of financial services practices and institutions played a more visible and active role in the U.S. economy, they also influenced the operations and organizations of other industries and institutions.

Fordism: The dominant form of production for much of the twentieth century that involved large-scale mass production. It was named after the automobile maker Henry Ford, who operated gigantic factories and perfected and mechanized the division of labor.

Post-Fordism: The style of production that emerged in the late 1960s or early 1970s that took advantage of global networks. In this system, different parts of the production process take places in different parts of the world.

New Deal: A set of government programs and actions meant to provide economic stability and recovery during the Great Depression.

Wagner Act: A 1935 law that provided a boost to labor in the United States giving workers the right to organize in order to bargain for their collective interests. Business leaders and politicians opposed to the Wagner Act often invoked the spirit of individualism when arguing against the law.

Taft-Hartley Act: 1947 law that significantly curtailed the power of labor unions. The right-to-work provisions dealt a significant blow to the ability of unions to raise money.

Mont Pelerin Society: A group that primarily consisted of European economists and philosophers who believed that the ideals of classical liberalism were in retreat around the world and needed to be defended. The group, which included Ludwig von Mises and Friedrich von Hayek, identified as 'neoliberals' and played a significant role in influencing policy and economic though in the United States and England.

Foundation for Economic Education: An organization dedicated to promoting free market ideals.

Redlining: A practice of classifying certain neighborhoods as unstable and ineligible for home loans. This classification system was created by the Home Owners Loan Corporation during the New Deal and effectively shut out many Black Americans from obtaining mortgages.

Inflation: The economic phenomenon of rising prices. The causes of inflation can be numerous and the effect can be harmful because it reduces consumers' purchasing power.

Oil embargo: From 1973 to 1974, OPEC (Organization of Petroleum Exporting Countries) imposed an embargo on oil in response to U.S. support of Israel during its war with Egypt. The embargo badly exacerbated an already existing problem with inflation.

Graham-Leach-Bliley Act: A 1999 law intended to modernize the regulation of the financial services industry in the United States. Crucially, the law removed New Deal-era provisions separating commercial and investment banking, which, in part, set the stage for the 2008 financial crisis.

Stagflation: During the 1970s, the U.S. economy suffered from both price and wage inflation and stagnant economic growth.

New Economic Policy: A controversial set of policies, including price and wage controls, that the Nixon Administration introduced to fight inflation in the early 1970s.

Atari Democrats: Informal name of Democratic politicians who, beginning in the 1980s, focused on high-tech jobs and industries.

Regulatory capture: The process whereby industry interests are able to dictate the terms under which they are regulated.

Four freedoms: A set of ideals that FDR articulated for U.S. entry into World War II. These included Freedom from Want, Freedom from Fear, Freedom of Expression, and Freedom of Worship.

Economies of scale: The benefits of decreasing production costs that can accompany mass production.

Vertical integration: A type of business strategy and organization where a firm attempts to gain control of the entire production process, from extracting raw materials to making finished product. Along with horizontal integration, it is one of two ways that a company might attempt to establish a monopoly.

Preferential shipping rates: In the nineteenth century, railroads would often give favorable rates to long-distance shipments. Though in some ways this made sense from an economic perspective, small companies complained that this practice gave larger businesses too much of a competitive advantage.

Horizontal integration: A type of business strategy and organization where a firm attempts to gain control of one part of the production process or an industry. Along with vertical integration, it is one of two ways that a company might attempt to establish a monopoly.

Neurasthenia: This was a diagnosis in the late nineteenth century that was comprised of different and vague symptoms, such as fatigue. It was believed that this ailment was the result of people losing their 'nervous energy.' Most often, the men who were diagnosed with this disease were a part of the new workforce contending with the new large corporations.

Piecework: A form of compensation whereby a worker is paid for the number of individual pieces produced, instead of a time-base wage. The piecework system was an early part of Frederick Taylor's 'scientific management.'

Continuous assembly line: This process was developed primarily by Henry Ford in the early twentieth century. In this arrangement, goods are produced by moving down an assembly line as individual workers completed discreet tasks. This production method builds substantially off the much older principle of the division of labor.

Whitecapping: The racist practice of forcing Black businesses from operating in a specific town, often through the threat of violence.

Family wage: The idea that a male worker should be paid a wage that is large enough to support an entire family. While in some ways the family wage was emblematic of a patriarchal society, the eventual decline of the family wage imposed a substantial burden on American families. In effect, by the end of the twentieth century, many middle- and working-class families required two incomes to maintain the financial security formerly provided by a single income.

Charismatic capitalism: A business or business practice that is largely dependent on the personality and public image of its leader. Examples include Apple's Steve Jobs or Madam CJ Walker.

Objectivism: A philosophy developed by the fiction writer Ayn Rand that extols individual achievement and self-interest.

Right-to-work laws: A provision allowed by the Taft-Hartley Act that allows states to outlaw closed shops, meaning that workers do not have to join a union in order to work somewhere. Such laws undercut the financial power of unions in the second half of the twentieth century.

Regulatory capture: The idea that industries have acquired undue influence over the regulatory agencies intended to oversee their businesses.

NAFTA: The controversial North American Free Trade Agreement signed by President Clinton in 1993. The agreement linked Mexico, the United States, and Canada in a way that facilitated easier trade across borders.

Rollback neoliberalism: The form of neoliberal policies in the 1970s and 1980s that emphasized austerity politics and removal of government welfare services.

Ownership society: The idea promoted by President George W. Bush in the early twenty-first century that Americans would achieve financial security by owning assets such as homes and investments in the stock market. Bush argued that this principle would become increasingly important as the global economy became more dynamic and sometimes unstable.

Globalization: The increased interconnectivity and cross-border flow of goods and services that emerged as a result of developments in communication and transportation technologies. The effects of globalization in the final decades of the twentieth century were vast. Cultural exchange quickened and could often result in hybrid forms. The production process for a single good could now involve different places around the world.

Managerial revolution: Term coined by the historian Alfred Chandler which described the appearance of professional managers working inside corporations towards the end of the nineteenth century. Crucially, these managers were not owners in these businesses and emphasized long-term stability over profits.

Further Reading

Because individualism is such a central idea in American cultural thought, primary documents can be rife with traces of this concept. In fact, close reading a number of different documents can yield insights about the connection between capitalism and individualism in the United States. Owing to the ubiquity of the concept, a number of authors – ranging from politicians to fiction writers – have directly addressed this topic. In fact, the place of individualism in a widely expanding capitalist system is an idea that has been worked over and developed by writers, politicians, business leaders, and others over the course of centuries.

Primary Documents

There are a number of widely available primary documents where questions of individualism and capitalism come to the fore. Many of these primary texts are widely available. Some of these ideas can be found in the works left behind by leaders of the American Revolution. Benjamin Franklin's books, such as *The Autobiography of Benjamin Franklin* and *Poor Richard's Almanack*, are among the earliest examples of a 'self-made man' story that has since appeared repeatedly in a number of different guises. Similarly, Thomas Jefferson's *Notes of the State of Virginia* offers some ideas about his vision of the yeoman farmer, a figure that shares much in common with the self-made man and connects the idea of individualism to a specific type of political economy. Documents from the nineteenth century also take up the question of the self-made man. Alexis du Tocqueville's *Democracy in America* specifically addresses the question of individualism amid the market revolution. *The Autobiography of Andrew Carnegie* and the essay 'The Gospel of Wealth' offer clear examples of how wealthy capitalists have framed their own biographies as narratives of individual initiative. In fact, Carnegie's biography is just one early example of what is a much wider trend. Any number of subsequent corporate biographies also place these issues at the core. The twentieth and twenty-first centuries also produced numerous primary documents that address some aspect of capitalism and individualism. For instance, politicians from all corners have been unable to resist the rhetorical pull of individualism. On balance, though, Republican politicians have been the trope's most enthusiastic users because individualism more closely aligns with American political conservatism. Students will find remarks by Ronald Reagan, Herbert Hoover, and Theodore Roosevelt to be full of references to individualism. In order to study the recent past, students will find materials connected to Silicon Valley to be relevant. Profiles of figures such as Bill Gates and Steve Jobs can be replete with individualistic thinking. Other relevant primary documents are not as readily available online, but still useful.

Much in the same way that a range of different primary documents involve the connection between capitalism and individualism, a number of historical studies can be useful in addressing this subject. However, adequately addressing the subject requires consulting different areas of historical scholarship that focus on some aspect of either American capitalism or American culture. The relationship between individualism and capitalism in the United States is a broad topic, and numerous scholars in different subfields within history have written in ways that touch directly on this question. Many of the books on this list are not wholly or directly concerned with the question of individualism within capitalism. However, each of the works listed here devote at least some space to questions of individuality and its connection to some aspect of capitalism. Some of the works listed do not fit so neatly into the different historical periods. In these cases, the scope of the work spills over into either the earlier or later period.

Though the new history of capitalism is a relatively recent field that has emerged, historians have been writing about different aspects of capitalism for years. Most directly, business history, labor history, and consumer studies are all long established fields that can provide good starting points for a consideration of capitalism and individualism in the United States. Recent overviews of the history of capitalism can be particularly helpful in this regard. Jonathan Levy's *Ages of American Capitalism* (Cambridge: Harvard University Press, 2021) and Benjamin Waterhouse's *The Land of Enterprise* (New York: Simon and Schuster, 2017) both provide broad and comprehensive overviews of the history of capitalism in the United States. Other broad histories of capitalism have focused on tracing flow of commodities around the world. Sven Beckert's *Empire of Cotton* (New York: Vintage, 2014) is by far the most significant work in this regard. Joseph Pratt and Louis Galambos's *Rise of the Corporate Commonwealth* (New York: Basic, 1988) provides a good introduction to American political economy and the regulatory state, particularly in the twentieth century. In addition to these single-author works, a number of edited collections, such as *Constructing Corporate America* (Oxford: Oxford University Press,

2004), *Capitalism's Hidden Worlds* (Philadelphia: University of Pennsylvania Press, 2020), *Capital Gains* (Philadelphia: University of Pennsylvania Press, 2016), and *Histories of Racial Capitalism* (New York: Columbia University Press, 2021), all contain relevant essays. Peer-reviewed journals such as *Enterprise and Society*, *Business History*, and *Capitalism: A Journal of History and Economics* all publish articles that may be relevant to the topic. Other studies are more narrowly focused on a specific topic or historical period that address some aspect of capitalism and individualism. Of course, there is a vast wealth of literature on every different period in U.S. history and, in some cases, a great deal of business history is focused on certain periods. However, not all of these works are directly relevant to questions of individualism and capitalism.

From the Colonial Era to the Civil War

Among the vast array of historical studies of early American history, a number of different books have either directly or indirectly addressed individualism and aspects of capitalism. Laurel Thatcher Ulirch's *A Midwife's Tale* (New York: Vintage, 1991) charts the world of women's participation in household economies in the colonial and early national period. William Cronon's *Changes in the Land* (New York: Hill and Wang, 1983) maps out differing ideas of land and property between European colonists and indigenous Americans. Thomas Doerflinger's *A Vigorous Spirit of Enterprise* (Chapel Hill: University of North Carolina Press, 1986) looks at Philadelphia merchants around the time of Revolutionary War. Michael O'Conner's *A Commercial Republic* (Lawrence: University of Kansas Press, 2014) details long-standing debates about U.S. political economy and includes a discussion of Hamilton and Jefferson's contrasting ideas. Edmund Morgan's *American Slavery, American Freedom* (New York: Norton, 1975) charts how slavery was an important reference point for figures such as Thomas Jefferson. Similarly, Winthrop Jordan's *White Over Black* (Chapel Hill: University of North Carolina Press, 1968) is an early piece of essential scholarship on slavery.

Without question, slavery constituted the central economic, political, and cultural issue in the antebellum period. There is a vast scholarly literature on the history of slavery in the United States. Works such as Peter Kolchin's *American Slavery* (New York: Hill and Wang, 2003) and Eugene Genovese's *Roll Jordan Roll* (New York: Vintage, 1976) have been foundational in the scholarship on American slavery. In the past ten years, historians of capitalism have drawn direct connections between slavery and capitalism in the United States. Ed Baptist's *The Half Has Never Been Told* (New York: Basic, 2014) and Walter Johnson's *River of Dark Dreams* (Cambridge: Harvard University Press, 2013) are the most comprehensive account of American slavery from the perspective of the history of capitalism. Johnson's earlier work on slavery, *Soul by Soul: Life Inside the Antebellum Trade Market* (Cambridge: Harvard University Press, 1999) is also relevant to the connections between slavery and capitalism. Caitlin Rosenthal's *Accounting for Slavery* (Cambridge: Harvard University Press, 2018) also draws a tight connection between slavery and capitalist development. In her book *Unfree Markets* (New York: Columbia University Press, 2021), Justene Hill Edwards has focused on the ways in which enslaved people engaged in wage work. In addition to these single-author volumes, *Slavery's Capitalism* (Philadelphia: University of Pennsylvania Press, 2016) is a useful edited collection that includes many of these arguments.

In addition to these studies of American slavery, other historians have considered the burgeoning world of capitalism and the Market Revolution in the first half of the nineteenth century. Edward Balleisen's *Navigating Failure* (Chapel Hill: University of North Carolina Press, 2001) provides a good introduction to how independent businessmen experienced the Market Revolution. Jonathan Kasson's *Civilizing the Machine* (New York: Grossman, 1976) contains an early and substantial account of the Lowell Mills. William Cronon's *Nature's Metropolis* (New York: Norton, 1991) provides a good overview of the ways in which the commercial activity became more efficient and standardized in the nineteenth century. Walter Licht's *Industrializing America* (Baltimore: Johns Hopkins University Press, 1995) also covers business during the nineteenth century.

Eric Foner's *Free Soil, Free Labor, Free Men* (Oxford: Oxford University Press, 1970) is essential reading for understanding free labor ideology and its connection to individualism before the Civil War. Jonathan Levy's *Freaks of Fortune* (Cambridge: Harvard University Press, 2012) charts how concepts of individual risk developed over the course of the nineteenth century. David Roediger's *The Wages of Whiteness* (New York: Verso, 1991) and Eric Lott's *Love and Theft* (Oxford: Oxford University Press, 1993) both explore the connections between race and working class culture in the nineteenth century.

The Gilded Age and Progressive Era

The Gilded Age is a particularly important period in the development of American business, witnessing the appearance of large corporations and labor unions. Consequently, there is a wide-ranging literature on this period of American capitalism, many of which have implications for individuality. To a large degree, the literature on large-scale corporations begins with the work of Alfred Chandler, whose books established the foundation for much of the subsequent research. However, his book *The Visible Hand* (Cambridge: Bellknap Press of Harvard, 1977) has proven to be one of the most influential accounts of big business in the second half of the nineteenth century. Other studies have examined different aspects of capitalism and the United States during the Gilded Age.

Alan Trachtenberg's *The Incorporation of America* (New York: Hill and Wang, 1982) offers a good account cultural change in response to economic change in the late nineteenth century. Peter Knight's *Picturing the Market* (Baltimore: Johns Hopkins University Press, 2017) includes a consideration how Americans conflated individuals with both markets and companies in the Gilded Age. Other histories of business in the United States have focused on specific industries and professions. Richard White's *Railroaded* (New York: Norton, 2011) focuses on railroads in the late nineteenth century. William Leach's *Land of Desire* (New York: Pantheon, 1993) examines consumer culture and department stores during this era. Leon Fink's *Workingman's Democracy* (Urbana and Chicago: University of Illinois Press, 1985) and *The Long Gilded Age* (Philadelphia: University of Pennsylvania Press, 2015) specifically address labor history during these years. Daniel Nelson's *Frederick W. Taylor and the Rise of Scientific Management* (Madison: University of Wisconsin Press, 1980) will also be of interest. Barbara Young Welke's *Recasting American Liberty* (New York: Cambridge University Press, 2001) treats the law and individual liberty during the Gilded Age and Progressive Eras.

Roger Ransom and Richard Sutch's *One Kind of Freedom* (New York: Cambridge University Press, 1977) is an excellent starting point for studying **sharecropping** after the Civil War. Juliet Walker's *The History of Black Business in America* (New York: MacMillan, 1998) is also essential reading for understanding the connection between race and capitalism in the United States.

Some investigations of the Progressive Era in the early twentieth century have also addressed some questions of individuality, identity, and capitalism. Julia Ott's *When Wall Street Met Main Street* (Cambridge: Harvard University Press, 2011) considers the role of women in promoting individual investing in the early twentieth century. Paul Rego's *American Ideal: Theodore Roosevelt's Search for American Individualism* (Lanham: Lexington, 2009) considers how Roosevelt consciously promoted such ideas. More broadly, works such as Warren Susman's *Culture as History* (New York: Pantheon, 1984) address issues of character and personality and the implications for individuality amid the transition between centuries.

The Twentieth Century before 1950

The first half of the twentieth century introduced a number of different developments that had implications for the connection between capitalism and individualism. The rise of mass production and the accompanying mass consumption and mass culture all contributed to a new sense of identity for

Americans. Students interested in capitalism and individualism during this period can consult a number of different areas of historical scholarship.

Significantly, there are a number of studies of the advertising business that are especially relevant. Roland Marchand's *Advertising the American Dream* (Berkley: University of California Press, 1986) remains a touchstone for advertising histories in the first half of the twentieth century. His companion book, *Creating the Corporate Soul* (Berkley: University of California Press, 1998). is a similarly excellent study. Richard Tedlow's *New and Improved* (New York: Basic, 1990) and Nancy Koehn's *Brand New* (Boston: Harvard Business School Press, 2001) are also worthwhile treatments of mass marketing in the twentieth century.

There are also many treatments of different political developments in the twentieth century. Most important, Lawrence Glickman's *Free Enterprise* (New Haven: Yale University Press, 2019) offers a cultural and political history of that term and its implications for individuality. Nelson Lichtenstein's *State of the Union* (Princeton: Princeton University Press, 2002) offers an indispensable history of labor unions during the twentieth century. Lizabeth Cohen's *Making a New Deal* (Cambridge: Cambridge University Press, 1990) offers a discussion of labor and work during the 1930s. Meg Jacobs's *Pocketbook Politics* (Princeton: Princeton University Press, 2005) explores the role that consumers (and women in particular) have exercised at different points in time. Kathy Peiss's *Hope in a Jar* (New York: Metropolitan, 1998) offers a consideration of beauty culture in the United States that includes discussions of different female entrepreneurs in the cosmetics industry.

Postwar America

Some historians have focused on changing ideologies and philosophies about individuality and political economy after World War II. Though neoliberalism would not take center stage as a political and economic ideology until later in the twentieth century, Angus Burgin's *The Great Persuasion* (Cambridge: Harvard University Press, 2012) and Quinn Slobodian's *Globalists* (Cambridge: Harvard University Press, 2018) both provide accounts of the intellectual roots of these ideas. Jennifer Burns's biography of Ayn Rand, *Goddess of the Market* (Oxford: Oxford University Press, 2009) situates the writer's life in a broader historical and cultural context. Kimberly Philips-Fein's *Invisible Hands* (New York: Norton, 2010) provides an excellent account of how corporations in the middle of the twentieth century developed conservative and antiunion politics.

Business historians have also addressed further developments of the large-scale corporation. Christopher McKenna's *The World's Newest Profession* (New York: Cambridge University Press, 2006) deals explicitly with management consulting as a profession. Pamela Laird's *Pull* (Cambridge:

Harvard University Press, 2006) offers a clear account of the challenges that both women and Black Americans faced in the firm. Louis Hyman's *Temp* (New York: Viking, 2018) explores how the assumed stability in white-collar work has slowly changed. Because consumerism is such a central feature of the twentieth century, Lizbeth Cohen's *A Consumers' Republic* (New York: Knopf, 2003) and Regina Lee Blaszczyk's sweeping volume, *Imagining Consumers* (Baltimore: Johns Hopkins University Press, 1999), are both important studies.

Other studies have considered different aspects of postwar advertising and marketing. Brenna Wynn Greer's *Represented* (Philadelphia: University of Pennsylvania Press, 2019) specifically considers how Black businessmen in the twentieth century used commercial representation. Thomas Frank's *The Conquest of Cool* (Chicago: University of Chicago Press, 1997) details the ways in which advertisers in the 1960s and 1970s crafted marketing strategies around a nascent counterculture. David Johnson's *Buying Gay* (New York: Columbia University Press, 2019) explores consumer capitalism and its connection to gay culture in the United States. In addition to these single-author books, edited volumes such as *American Capitalism* (Philadelphia: University of Pennsylvania Press, 2006) and *What's Good for Business* (Oxford: Oxford University Press, 2012) both feature contributions that are relevant to the relationship between capitalism and individualism.

The Neoliberal Era

Scholars have paid a lot of attention to neoliberalism as both an era and policy regime around the world. A focus on neoliberalism is so pervasive that works about more specific historical events, people, or companies also raise important questions about the idea. However, scholars from across different fields have produced books directly focused on neoliberalism itself. David Harvey's *A Brief History of Neoliberalism* (Oxford: Oxford University Press, 2006) still offers an excellent primer on the subject. Daniel Rodgers's *Age of Fracture* (Cambridge: Bellknap Press of Harvard, 2011) also provides an excellent historical overview of how neoliberal thought and policy developed in the 1970s and 1980s. Thomas Piketty's *Capital in the 21st Century* (Cambridge: Bellknap Press of Harvard, 2014) and *Capital and Ideology* (Cambridge: Bellknap Press of Harvard, 202) both provide a sense of the scale of personal wealth in the neoliberal era. Benjamin Waterhouse's *Lobbying America* (Princeton: Princeton University Press, 2014) traces the growth and influence of business lobbying groups.

Other books and articles have addressed specific industries and businesses that thrived during the neoliberal era. Bethany Moreton's *To Serve God and WalMart* (Cambridge: Harvard University Press, 2010) takes up the specific case of women in the service economy. Additionally, "Make

Payroll, Not War: Business Culture and Youth Culture," Moreton's contribution to the edited collection, *Rightward Bound* (Cambridge: Harvard University Press, 2008), explains how entrepreneurialism became entrenched as a cultural value during the 1970s. Allison Elias's *The Rise of Corporate Feminism: Women in the American Office, 1960–1990* (New York: Columbia University Press, 2022) offers a discussion of issues surrounding white collar women in the postwar era. The anthropologist Karen Ho's *Liquidated* (2009) provides both a historical overview of investment banking in the late twentieth century along with an ethnographic investigation of Wall Street firms.

Silicon Valley has received a good deal of attention in the scholarly literature when it comes to capitalism and individualism. Margaret O'Mara's *The Code* (New York: Penguin, 2019) provides a comprehensive history of Silicon Valley. Fred Turner's *From Counterculture to Cyberculture* (Chicago: University of Chicago Press, 2008) also examines an individualistic ethos in the computer industry. Eric Guthey's article 'New Economy Romanticism, Narratives of Corporate Personhood, and the Antimanagerial Impulse' in *Constructing Corporate America: History, Politics, Culture* (2004) directly addresses individualism in Silicon Valley.

This list is hardly exhaustive. There are many more scholarly works that students will find useful exploring the connection between individualism and capitalism in the United States. Likewise, there are a number of excellent studies that address different historical moments in American history.

References

Alger, H. (1868) *Ragged Dick, or, Street Life in New York with the Boot-Blacks*. Available at: www.gutenberg.org/files/5348/5348-h/5348-h.htm (Downloaded 20 May 2022).

Balleisen, E. (2001) *Navigating Failure: Bankruptcy and Commercial Society in Antebellum America*. Chapel Hill, NC: University of North Carolina Press.

Balogh, B. (2015) *The Associational State: American Governance in the Twentieth Century*. Philadelphia, PA: University of Pennsylvania Press.

Baptist, E. (2014) *The Half Has Never Been Told: Slavery and the Making of American Capitalism*. New York, NY: Basic Books.

Baptist, E. (2016) 'Toward a Political Economy of Slave Labor: Hands, Whipping-Machines, and Modern Power', in S. Beckert and S. Rockman (eds), *Slavery's Capitalism: A New History of American Economic Development*. Philadelphia, PA: University of Pennsylvania Press, pp. 31–61.

Baxter, M. (1995) *Henry Clay and the American System*. Lexington, KY: University of Kentucky Press.

Beckert, S. (2014) *Empire of Cotton: A Global History*. New York, NY: Vintage Books.

Berry, D. (2016) '"Broad Is de Road day Leads ter Death": Human Capital and Enslaved Mortality', in S. Beckert and S. Rockman (eds), *Slavery's Capitalism: A New History of American Economic Development*. Philadelphia, PA: University of Pennsylvania Press, pp. 146–162.

Blaszczyk, R. (2000) *Imagining Consumers: Design and Innovation from Wedgwood to Corning*. Baltimore, MD: Johns Hopkins University Press.

Bogan, V. and Darity, W. (2008) 'Culture and Entrepreneurship? African American and Immigrant Self-Employment in the United States', *The Journal of Socio-Economics*, 37(5), pp. 1999–2019.

Boydston, J. (1996) 'The Woman Who Wasn't There: Women's Market Labor and the Transition to Capitalism in the United States', *Journal of the Early Republic*, 16(2), pp. 183–206.

Brandeis, L. (1914) *Other People's Money, and How the Bankers Use It*. New York: NY: Frederick A. Stokes Company. Available at: www.gutenberg.org/files/57819/57819-h/57819-h.htm (Downloaded 24 May 2022).

Brantley, A. (2021) *Brewing a Boycott: How a Grassroots Coalition Fought Coors and Remade American Consumer Activism*. Chapel Hill, NC: University of North Carolina Press.

Burns, J. (2009) *Goddess of the Market: Ayn Rand and the American Right*. Oxford: Oxford University Press.

Carnegie, A. (1885) 'The Road to Business Success', in J. Wall (ed), *The Andrew Carnegie Reader*. Pittsburgh, PA: The University of Pittsburgh Press, pp. 42–50.

Chandler Jr., A. (1977) *The Visible Hand: The Managerial Revolution in American Business*. Cambridge, MA: Harvard University Press.

Chavez, C. (1986) *Wrath of Grapes Boycott Speech*. Available at: https://learn.nrm.org/media/1242/cesar-chavez-wrath-of-grapes-speech.pdf (Downloaded 22 May 2022).

Cohen, L. (1990) *Making a New Deal: Industrial Workers in Chicago, 1919–1939*. Cambridge: Cambridge University Press.

Cook, E. (2020) 'Lifting the Veil of Money: What Economic Indicators Hide', in K. Lipartito and L. Jacobson (eds), *Capitalism's Hidden Worlds*. Philadelphia, PA: University of Pennsylvania Press, pp. 25–43.

Cronon, W. (1991) *Nature's Metropolis: Chicago and the Great West*. New York, NY: W.W. Norton.

Davies, A.R. and Frink, B.D. (2014) 'The Origins of the Ideal Worker: The Separation of Work and Home in the United States from the Market Revolution to 1950', *Work and Occupations*, 41(1), pp. 18–39.

Drucker, P. (1942) *The Future of Industrial Man: A Conservative Approach*. New York, NY: The John Day Company.

Drucker, P. (1946) *The Concept of the Corporation*. New York, NY: The John Day Company.

Elias, A. (2015) 'Learning to Lead: Women and Success in Corporate America', *BEH Online*, 13. Available at: https://thebhc.org/file-download/download/public/2191 (Downloaded 20 May 2022).

Elias, A. (2018) '"Outside the Pyramid": Clerical Work, Corporate Affirmative Action, and Working Women's Barriers to Upward Mobility', *Journal of Policy History*, 30(2), pp. 301–333.

Emerson, R.W. (1841) *Self Reliance*. Available at: www.gutenberg.org/files/2944/2944-h/2944-h.htm (Downloaded 22 May 2022).

Foley, N. (2014) *Mexicans in the Making of America*. Cambridge, MA: Harvard University Press.

Foner, E. (1970) *Free Soil, Free Labor, Free Men: The Ideology of the Republican Party Before the Civil War*. Oxford: Oxford University Press.

Fones-Wolf, E. and Fones-Wolf, K. (2003) 'Cold War Americanism: Business, Pageantry, and Antiunionism in Weirton, West Virginia', *The Business History Review*, 77(1), pp. 61–91.

Franklin, B. (1784) *Information to Those Who Would Remove to America*. Available at: https://founders.archives.gov/documents/Franklin/01-41-02-0391 (Downloaded 22 May 2022).

Friedman, M. (1962) *Capitalism and Freedom*. Chicago, IL: University of Chicago Press.

Friedman, M. (n.d.) 'Interview on freedom and free markets.' Available at: https://www.pbs.org/wgbh/commandingheights/press_site/people/friedman_intv.html (Downloaded 16 October 2022).

Friedman, T. (2005) 'It's a Flat World, After All', *The New York Times Magazine*, 3 April. Available at: www.nytimes.com/2005/04/03/magazine/its-a-flat-world-after-all.html (Downloaded 20 May 2022).

Garrett-Scott, S. (2009) 'A Historiography of African American Business', *BEH Online*, 7. Available at: https://thebhc.org/sites/default/files/garrett-scott.pdf (Downloaded 22 May 2022).

Gilman, N. (2006) 'The Prophet of Post-Fordism: Peter Drucker and the Legitimation of the Corporation', in N. Lichtenstein (ed), *American Capitalism: Social Thought and Political Economy in the Twentieth Century*. Philadelphia, PA: University of Pennsylvania Press, pp. 109–134.

Glenn, E.N. (2002) *Unequal Freedom: How Race and Gender Shaped American Citizenship and Labor*. Cambridge, MA: Harvard University Press.

Glickman, L. (2019) *Free Enterprise: An American History*. New Haven, CT: Yale University Press.

Greer, B.W. (2019) *Represented: The Black Imagemakers Who Reimagined African American Citizenship*. Philadelphia, PA: University of Pennsylvania Press.

Hamilton, A. (1791) *Report on the Subject of Manufactures*. Available at: https://founders.archives.gov/documents/Hamilton/01-10-02-0001-0007 (Downloaded 20 May 2022).

Hancock, B. (2018) 'Marcus Garvey's the Black Star Line: Hopes, Dreams, and the S.S. Yarmouth', *Journal of Caribbean History*, 52(1), pp. 68–104.

Hoover, H. (1928) *Principles and Ideas of the United States Government*. Available at: https://millercenter.org/the-presidency/presidential-speeches/october-22-1928-principles-and-ideals-united-states-government (Downloaded 8 June 2022).

Hosmer, B.C. (1999) *American Indians in the Marketplace: Persistence and Innovation among the Menominees and Metlakatlans, 1870–1920*. Lawrence, KS: University Press of Kansas.

Hyman, L. (2018) *Temp: How American Work, American Business, and the American Dream Became Temporary*. New York, NY: Viking.

Jefferson, T. (1785) *Notes on the State of Virginia*. Available at: https://web.archive.org/web/20080914030942/http://etext.lib.virginia.edu/toc/modeng/public/JefVirg.html (Downloaded 8 June 2022).

Johnson, D. (2010) 'Physique Pioneers: The Politics of 1960s Gay Consumer Culture', *Journal of Social History*, 43(4), pp. 867–892.

Kasson, J.F. (1976) *Civilizing the Machine: Technology and Republican Values in America, 1776–1900*. New York, NY: Grossman Publishers.

Knight, P. (2016) *Reading the Market: Genres of Financial Capitalism in Gilded Age America*. Baltimore, MA: Johns Hopkins University Press.

Koepp, S. (1987/2009) 'Riding the Wild Bull', in M. Lewis (ed), *Panic!: The Story of Modern Financial Insanity*. New York, NY: W.W. Norton, pp. 14–19.

Laird, P. (2005) *Pull: Networking and Success Since Benjamin Franklin*. Cambridge, MA: Harvard University Press.

Leach, W. (1993) *Land of Desire: Merchants, Power, and the Rise of a New American Culture*. New York, NY: Pantheon Books.

Lefevre, E. (1923) *Reminiscences of a Stock Operator*. Available at: www.gutenberg.org/files/60979/60979-h/60979-h.htm (Downloaded 20 May 2022).

Levy, J. (2012) *Freaks of Fortune: The Emerging World of Capitalism and Risk in America*. Cambridge, MA: Harvard University Press.

Levy, J. (2021) *Ages of American Capitalism: A History of the United States*. New York, NY: Random House.

Lichtenstein, N. (2002) *State of the Union: A Century of American Labor*. Princeton, NJ: Princeton University Press.

Locke, J. (1690) *Second Treatise on Government*. Available at: www.gutenberg.org/files/7370/7370-h/7370-h.htm (Downloaded 20 May 2022).

MacLardy, W. (1937) *To Thos. J. Watson, President, I.B.M.* Available at: https://cdn.arstechnica.net/wp-content/uploads/2014/08/songs-of-the-ibm.pdf (Downloaded 24 May 2022).

Marchand, R. (1985) *Advertising the American Dream: Making Way for Modernity, 1920–1940*. Berkeley, CA: University of California Press.

Marchand, R. (1998) *Creating the Corporate Soul: The Rise of Public Relations and Corporate Imagery in American Big Business*. Berkeley, CA: University of California Press.

Massey, D. (1994) *Space, Place, and Gender*. Minneapolis, MN: University of Minnesota Press.

McCampbell, J.B. (1999) 'Taking Stock in Black America', *Time Magazine*, Rochester.

Moreton, B. (2008) 'Make Payroll, Not War', in B. Schulman and J. Zelizer (eds), *Rightward Bound: Making America Conservative in the 1970s*. Cambridge, MA: Harvard University Press, pp. 52–70.

Moreton, B. (2009) *To Serve God and Wal-Mart: The Making of Christian Free Enterprise*. Cambridge, MA: Harvard University Press.

O'Conner, M. (2014) *A Commercial Republic: America's Enduring Debate Over Democratic Capitalism*. Lawrence, KS: University of Kansas Press.

Olmstead, A.L. and Rhode, P.W. (2008) 'Biological Innovation and Productivity Growth in the Antebellum Cotton Economy', *The Journal of Economic History*, 68(4), pp. 1123–1171.

O'Mara, M. (2019) *The Code: Silicon Valley and the Remaking of America*. New York, NY: Penguin Press.

Packard, V. (1957) *The Hidden Persuaders*. New York, NY: D. McKay Co.

Photinos, C. (2007) 'The Figure of the Tramp in Gilded Age Success Narratives', *Journal of Popular Culture*, 40(6), pp. 994–1018.

Piketty, T. (2014) *Capital in the Twenty-First Century*. Cambridge, MA: Harvard University Press.

Potter, D. (1954) *People of Plenty: Economic Abundance and the American Character*. Chicago: University of Chicago Press.

Reagan, R. (1981) *Inaugural Address*. Available at: www.reaganfoundation.org/media/128614/inaguration.pdf (Downloaded 20 May 2022).

Recken, S. (1993) 'Fitting-In: The Redefinition of Success in the 1930s', *Journal of Popular Culture*, 27(3), pp. 205–222.

Regaldo, P. (2021) '"They Speak Our Language . . . Business": Latinx Businesspeople and the Pursuit of Wealth in New York City', in D. Jenkins and J. Leroy (eds), *Histories of Racial Capitalism*. New York, NY: Columbia University Press, pp. 231–250.

Rego, P. (2008) *American Ideal: Theodore Roosevelt's Search for American Individualism*. Lanham, MD: Lexington Books.

Rockman, S. (2014) 'What Makes the History of Capitalism Newsworthy?', *Journal of the Early Republic*, 34(3), pp. 439–466.

Roediger, D. (1991) *The Wages of Whiteness: Race and the Making of the American Working Class*. New York, NY: Verso.

Romney, M. (2012) *Mitt Romney on Obama Voters*. Available at: www.youtube.com/watch?v=MU9V6eOFO38 (Downloaded 23 May 2022).

Roosevelt, F.D. (1936) *June 27, 1936: Democratic National Convention*. Available at: https://millercenter.org/the-presidency/presidential-speeches/june-27-1936-democratic-national-convention (Downloaded 8 June 2022).

Rosenthal, C. (2016) 'Slavery's Scientific Management: Masters and Managers', in S. Beckert and S. Rockman (eds), *Slavery's Capitalism: A New History of American Economic Development*. Philadelphia, PA: University of Pennsylvania Press, pp. 62–86.

Rothman, J. (2016) 'The Contours of Cotton Capitalism: Speculation, Slavery, and Economic Panic in Mississippi, 1832–1841', in S. Beckert and S. Rockman (eds), *Slavery's Capitalism: A New History of American Economic Development*. Philadelphia, PA: University of Pennsylvania Press, pp. 122–145.

Sandberg, S. (2013) *Lean in: Women, Work, and the Will to Lead*. New York, NY: Alfred A. Knopf.

Schumpeter, J. (1942) *Capitalism, Socialism, and Democracy*. London: Harper & Brothers.

Smith, A. (1776) *The Wealth of Nations*. Available at: www.gutenberg.org/files/38194/38194-h/38194-h.htm (Downloaded 20 May 2022).

Sumner, W.G. (1963) *Social Darwinism: Selected Essays of William Graham Sumner*. Englewood Cliffs, NJ: Prentice-Hall.

Tarbell, I. (1904) *History of the Standard Oil Corporation*. Available at: www.gutenberg.org/files/60692/60692-h/60692-h.htm (Downloaded 20 May 2002).

Terkel, S. (1970) *Hard Times: An Oral History of the Great Depression*. New York, NY: Pantheon Books.

Thatcher, M. (1987) 'Interview by Douglas Keay', *Woman's Day*, 23 September. Available at: www.margaretthatcher.org/document/106689 (Downloaded 20 May 2022).

Tocqueville, A. (1835) *Democracy in America: Volume 1*. Available at: www.gutenberg.org/files/815/815-h/815-h.htm (Downloaded 20 May 2022).

Trachtenberg, A. (1982) *The Incorporation of America: Culture and Society in the Gilded Age*. New York, NY: Hill and Wang.

Trustees of Dartmouth Coll. v. Woodward, 17 U.S. 4 Wheat. 518 518 (1819).

Turner, F. (1893) *The Significance of the Frontier in American History*. Available at: http://nationalhumanitiescenter.org/pds/gilded/empire/text1/turner.pdf (Downloaded 20 May 2022).

Twain, M. (1884) *The Adventures of Huckleberry Finn*. Available at: www.gutenberg.org/files/76/76-h/76-h.htm (Downloaded 20 May 2022).

Villa, D. (2005) 'Hegel, Tocqueville, and "Individualism"', *The Review of Politics*, 67(4), pp. 659–686.

Walker, J.E.K. (2003) 'War, Women, Song: The Tectonics of Black Business and Entrepreneurship, 1939–2001', *The Review of Black Political Economy*, 31(3), pp. 65–116.

Washington, B.T. (1895) *Speech to the Atlanta Cotton States and International Exposition*. Available at: http://americanradioworks.publicradio.org/features/blackspeech/btwashington.html (Downloaded 20 May 2022).

Washington, B.T. (1901) *Up From Slavery: An Autobiography*. Available at: https://gutenberg.org/files/2376/2376-h/2376-h.htm (Downloaded 8 June 2022).

Waterhouse, B. (2017) *The Land of Enterprise: A Business History of the United States*. New York, NY: Simon & Schuster.

Weber, M. (1930) *The Protestant Ethic and the Spirit of Capitalism*. Translated by T. Parsons. New York, NY: Charles Scribner's Sons.

White, R. (2011) *Railroaded: The Transcontinentals and the Making of Modern America*. New York, NY: W.W. Norton & Co.

Whyte, W. (1956) *The Organization Man*. New York, NY: Simon and Schuster.

Wilson, M. (2016) *Destructive Creation: American Business and the Winning of World War II*. Philadelphia, PA: University of Pennsylvania Press.

Index

Entries in *italics* refer to figures.